ALEGAL

Alegal

Biopolitics and the Unintelligibility of Okinawan Life

Annmaria M. Shimabuku

FORDHAM UNIVERSITY PRESS

New York 2019

This book is freely available in an open access edition thanks to
TOME (Toward an Open Monograph Ecosystem)—a
collaboration of the Association of American Universities, the
Association of University Presses, and the Association of
Research Libraries—and the generous support of the New York
University Center for the Humanities. Learn more at the TOME
website, available at: openmonographs.org.

Through the generous funding of New York University,
this publication is available on an open access basis
from the publisher's website.

Fordham University Press gratefully acknowledges
financial assistance and support provided for the
publication of this book by the New York University
Center for the Humanities.

Visit us online at www.fordhampress.com.

Library of Congress Cataloging-in-Publication Data
available online at https://catalog.loc.gov.

Printed in the United States of America
21 20 19   5 4 3 2 1
First edition

To the Okinawan women in my life:
Mitsuko, Lucina, and Luella

CONTENTS

In 2000, around the time of the G8 summit in Okinawa, another important event was unfolding. Higa Malia,[1] a woman born to an Okinawan mother and U.S. military–affiliated father on Okinawa, was in the midst of a modest yet powerful social movement. After a group of mothers established the AmerAsian School in Okinawa in 1998 in partial response to racial discrimination their children experienced in public schools,[2] Higa inaugurated the Children of Peace Network in 1999 as the first network organized autonomously by such individuals.[3] The network was momentous because the powerful anti-base culture in Okinawa, often evoking tropes of local women violated or exploited by American soldiers, had overshadowed mixed-race individuals to the point where it was difficult to share a conversation about this identity among those who experienced it firsthand.[4]

Keenly aware of these dynamics, Higa focused on disassociating mixed-race identity from base politics and empowering individuals by helping them locate their long-lost fathers. However, a day before the G8 summit convened, she was taken aback by her young daughter's wish to join in peaceful protest by forming a human chain around Kadena Air Base. In response, she wrote:

> Personally, I wanted to oppose the bases and join hands with others, but I simply couldn't. By participating, many *hāfu*[5] will say, "Hey, Malia is opposing bases. If you go over there [to her network], you will be made to do the same thing. Opposing bases with an American face is embarrassing for Okinawans, so I don't want to do it." Feelings such as these keep me at bay. In other words, people in need of consultation will cease to confide in me, and no one will come to the network. Since my priorities lie with these more vulnerable individuals, I could not participate in the human chain around the bases. In spirit only.[6]

Higa identified an incommensurable gulf between public anti-base protest and the private lives of those who intimately embody the reality of

U.S. military bases in Okinawa. Concerned with alienating the very individuals she was interested in starting a collective conversation with, she held back from her own daughter's invitation to join the protest.

Shortly after the G8 summit, the network ceased to exist, and Higa moved to mainland Japan. She contributed a fourteen-segment series of short articles to the *Okinawa Times* newspaper over a decade later from July to December 2012[7] and then posted a long poem on her public Facebook page entitled "U.S. Military Base" on July 19, 2013, that garnered more likes and shares than her publications.[8] It was this poem, uninhibited by newspaper form, that hit a deeply entrenched cultural nerve. In it, she returned to the disconnect between mixed-race identity and the politics of U.S. military base protest. Only this time, she was not speaking as the representative of a social movement, but as an individual.

The question that drives this poem is, what happens when the insertion of the cold machinery of institutional violence (i.e., U.S. military bases) into the fecund soil of Okinawa produces a new life force that threatens to grow wildly into its cogs? Or, how will Higa, who was "born precisely because of [the existence of] the base" on Okinawan soil, whose life painfully trellised alongside its barbed wire fence, come to terms with this thing that names her poem, the "U.S. Military Base"?

The first part of the poem operates through a dialectic of mutual exclusion where she is either a product of institutional violence or a private individual completely separate from it. Each side—the Okinawan and the U.S. military—assumes one at the expense of negating the other, leaving Higa bankrupt of a way of articulating her own existence as simultaneously both.

From the Okinawan side, she problematizes the objectifying language she associates with anti-base sentiment.

> A child sent from the base, a child who got dumped by the base[9]
> Those words that describe *me*
> Could be heard even if I covered my ears
> Those words that look down on my mother or other mothers like
>   her as an *Amejo*[10]
> Flowed everywhere
> Saying that my mother and I were a shameless and humiliating nuisance

Here, she and her mother are made to stand in for the U.S. military. She is either a "child sent from the base," suggesting that is her original point of creation, or her mother is an *"Amejo,"* a woman of the Americans, suggesting that is where she belongs. With both being treated in this way as objects of substitution, Higa responds by speaking of a life of unintelligibility. Born and raised in Okinawa, as products of Okinawa's historical condition, by what sleight of hand do they suddenly become a stand-in for an institution from which they are both alienated? Is there any room in their existences to not be completely determined by the U.S. military? Could they be both victims of U.S. military violence and also women who had loved a G.I. at the same time? The sovereign power that is suggested here is not the cold machinery of the U.S. military base, i.e., its weapons of death and destruction, but the violence of substitution that works performatively through language to erase the irreducibility of her life force as she shudders in response to "Those words that describe *me*." In other words, sovereign power here functions through the censorship, exclusion, and exception of the possibility of a life irreducible to institutional violence, which ironically operates through the very claim of its total victimization to sovereign power.

This drives Higa to the other extreme of a hyperidentification with her father as a stand-in for the U.S. military base to which she feels compelled to return. But when her father never comes for her as a young child, she pursues him during the summer of her final year of school and writes of her visit with her American family.

> I couldn't get through to them well with my shy English
> I was made to realize that I was not one of the people from *over there*
> The family with whom I was connected by blood was nice to me
>   on the surface
> But I could not sense in them even a modicum of remorse toward me
> My father, of course, was not a U.S. military base
> He was nothing more than a completely ordinary man

Here, her American family cannot see how her life was impacted by the public institutional violence that her father partook in and reduces the business of her birth to a private family affair. She recognizes this as a privilege that neither she nor other Okinawans have. Hence, she is "not one of the people from *over there*" because they can monopolize a clean-cut distinction between the public and the private. The ability to carry on with the messiness of private life in America is a stark contrast to the unchanging reality of the U.S. military that awaits her when she lands back in Okinawa.

Even when her father visits her in Okinawa years later in her adulthood, he does not waver in this distinction. He expresses the civilian wish that "Okinawa goes back to being a quiet island," but nonetheless surrenders his opinion on politics to the state.

"I do not have any words on the question of the U.S. military presence
And this is not something that I should talk about
Since this is a decision for the state
I have not lost my pride as a soldier"

The irony here is that while her father claims to surrender his words to the
state, he can only do so by using words. His ability to act as a cog of state
machinery is predicated on his capacity for language, which as he shows
himself, takes on a life of its own to the potential dismay of the state. Yet
he censors this life. Not only can we get a glimpse of the potential dilemma of a conscientious objector who does not self-censor, but Higa registers her own "disappointment" in her father's statement. What is at stake
here is not so much whether he supports or opposes bases in Okinawa as
it is how he, too, exercises sovereign power by censoring, excluding, and
excepting discrepancies not only within himself, but also within the relationship with his daughter by deflecting them onto the higher power of
the state where they become neutralized. This is where he locates his "pride
as a soldier" years after military service.

Higa is trapped by two mutually exclusive positions: one that diminishes the possibility for her private life to be undetermined by institutional
violence, and one that diminishes the effects of institutional violence in
her private life. Similar to the symbol "∞," the two are like diametrically
opposed circles that touch at a point. What connects them at this point
is a logic that censors, excludes, and excepts the discrepancies internal to
each side. But instead of owning up to the consequences of this act—of
embracing a life that lives the contradictions of the here and now—it is
instead deferred to a higher sovereign power that distracts with promises toward a utopian future. In this way, the anti-base sentiment that
discriminates against Higa interprets any mark left by the U.S. military
base in Okinawa as a mark of its victimization that must be erased for
the sake of recuperating the homogeneity of an ethnic community that
awaits liberation in the future. The U.S. military culture that Higa
evokes interprets any mark of suffering it inflicts on others as a necessary sacrifice that must be made for the sake of protecting the integrity
of a democratic state. Discrepancies that arise in everyday life are deferred to faith in the purity of this sovereign power and neutralized for
the sake of internal coherence; in the absence of faith in this sovereign
power, they would deflect back into the inner space of the circles of the ∞
symbol and implode from within. Precisely because she is foreclosed
from accessing this transcendental notion of purity, Higa is left with no

way to ground her existence, and is driven to what some might call a "social death."

> "You shouldn't have been born"
> How could I go on living with my head up
> I did not know
> If I could even be here
> I wanted to erase myself
> I felt as if living itself were a shame

Yet Higa does the impossible and not only continues to live on, but continues to thrive in her thought. Fast forward to 2000 when her daughter wishes to join a peaceful protest around Kadena Air Base the day before the 2000 G8 summit. Her daughter exclaims:

> "If grandpa was on the other side of the fence I would say Hi
> I love grandpa but I hate bombs that kill people
> That's why I'll say bases aren't necessary
> Even if you can't go Mom, I still want to go!"

In this remarkable moment, Higa's daughter allows for the coexistence of the "grandpa" whom she loves as a private individual with the institutional violence of the state that she hates. In failing to decide on one over the other, she refuses to ground her expression in faith in a higher power and instead grounds it in her own life force from within, in the here and now. Whether she realizes it or not, she exposes sovereign power as not merely the capacity to annihilate (although Okinawans have certainly been targets of military death and destruction), but also as the imperative to direct this life force away from the contradictions of the here and now to an abstract promise toward the future.

Once Higa is able to grab hold of this inner life force, things start to change, and her life starts to *matter*. In turning away from the logic of the exception, she refuses to allow her life force to be pruned back to ensure the smooth operation of the machinery of the U.S. military base and instead allows for it to grow into the cogs so as to threaten its composition with transformation from within.

> Flowers will also bloom in the U.S. military base
> Those seeds always go over the barbed wire fence with ease
> They sprout on this side
> And soon
> They will bloom

Higa's poem does not end triumphantly with the assertion of mixed-race or female agency predicated on the recuperation of a self-determining will, but enigmatically with the nonhuman agency of morphing matter. These seeds are the living matter that is not guided by any higher principle other than a life force internal to it. Although "[t]hose seeds always go over the barbed wire fence with ease," they nonetheless haphazardly arrive there without premeditated direction. The U.S. military base is not something that is willfully taken down by a sovereign subject, but it is something that is disengaged by allowing a life force to change its composition from within.

Higa's poem comes out of thirteen years of painstaking meditation on the contradictions of a short-lived social movement. Although much has been said about what is arguably the most contentious issue in U.S.-Japan politics—the presence of U.S. military bases in Japanese territory—her poem gives us a glimpse into the more intimate realities of life on both sides of the fence in Okinawa. What it demands is not so much that we put a softer human face to the cold and impersonal calculations of international politics. Rather, it demands a fundamental reconsideration of the nature of sovereign power based on the logic of mutual exclusion on both sides of the fence.

In their imagining of the trans-Pacific, Naoki Sakai and Hyon Joo Yoo suggest what such a reconsideration might look like. They urge us to turn away from focusing on the absolute power of individual sovereign states and instead turn to developing a better analysis of the systematicity of a network of states that they term the "global sovereign state."[11] Furthermore, this systematicity is driven by a logic of nationalism that discursively produces power from the bottom up through its dispersal throughout the population. In this way, they, like Higa, focus on how these macropolitics are channeled through the intimate and identify the common assumption of the United States as an imperialist institution of "oppression or repression" that, in turn, fans a very sexualized "victim fantasy" integral to "anti-colonial nationalism."[12]

Higa's poem offers a powerful testament to the real-life implications of this anti-colonial nationalism for mixed-race individuals who can never become purely Japanese. But by identifying these limitations, she simultaneously stumbles upon the impossibility of Okinawa's position vis-à-vis the global sovereign state. That is, Japan's "victim fantasy" is a useful decoy that diverts attention from its role in securing Okinawa as a U.S. military fortress of the Asia Pacific. And hence, to what degree can Okinawans really partake in anti-colonial *Japanese* nationalism when Okinawans have never been treated as first-class nationals by Japan in the first place? Higa writes:

> No matter how imperviously the U.S. military acts toward the locals
> It is due to its diplomacy with Japan
> Now I am able to see clearly
> All that I have turned my eyes away from thus far

Okinawa is only intelligible vis-à-vis global sovereignty under representation of the Japanese state, yet the Japanese state fails to represent Okinawa, allowing the U.S. military to act "imperviously . . . toward the locals." Although Higa could only see Okinawa's discrimination of mixed-race subjects growing up as a child, through her long journey, she comes to realize how this discrimination is informed by Okinawa's precarious position vis-à-vis not only Japan, but Japan in collusion with the United States, in the formation of a global sovereign state.

The point here is not to argue whether or not Okinawans are really Japanese. Rather, it is to show how the unintelligibility of Okinawan life gets channeled into a national political platform whereupon it emerges as evidence of the violation of a pure victim or the actions of a compromised collaborator. Because the most direct and intimate point of contact between the U.S. military and Japanese state comes through sexual relationships between U.S. military personnel and local women, their lives, as well as the lives of their mixed-race children, are excessively politicized as one or the other. But all this does is sanction the qualification of the "political" in terms of an intelligibility before the law. As suggested by Sakai and Yoo, even the mobilization of the so-called pure victim in this "victim fantasy" tends to collaborate with "anti-colonial nationalism." What it neglects to consider is the politicality of the alegal, or that which is unintelligibile to the law itself. It is this life force that harbors the potential of a more fundamental insurgency as that which dares to live irrespective of its intelligibility to the law.

Higa's poem, as a piece that somehow failed to reach published form ready to be consumed by area studies knowledge producers, performs the difficult task of articulating a sovereign power that is experienced most viscerally in the intimate spaces of everyday life. It is the product of years of struggle to find the words to articulate a life unintelligible to the state in a way that circumvented the danger of being targeted by a censoring violence. It forces us to consider the nature of sovereign power, not as the wheeling and dealing of faceless organs of the state, but as the censorship, exclusion, and exception of a life force that has always already been there.

Higa quit waiting to become intelligible to the norms of the publishing industry in order to exercise her own life force, but by writing of this unintelligibility, she took it back for herself. And it spread like wildfire. It is this life force that this book names the "alegal," and it is this life force that this book attempts to unleash.

Throughout this book, all translations from Japanese are mine unless otherwise indicated. The titles of Japanese texts are automatically given in English translation with the original given in the citation. For example, the English title of the newspaper *Ryukyu Shimpo* is given in Japanese romanization as *Ryukyu shinpō* in the citation.

Japanese and Korean names are provided as family name first and given name last when their corresponding texts are written originally in Japanese, while the reverse order is followed for all others. In romanizing Japanese and Korean, I follow the Hepburn and McCune-Reischauer systems respectively. For romanizing Okinawan, I alternate between the Hepburn system and indigenous Okinawan variations, such as "Ifa Fuyū," depending on historical usage. Terms in Japanese, particularly place names that have an established usage in English (for example "Ryukyu" and "Tokyo"), are not modified with diacritics.

CIC	Counter Intelligence Corps
GARIOA	Government Aid and Relief in Occupied Areas
GRI	Government of the Ryukyu Islands
JCP	Japanese Communist Party
MP	Military Police
OFNCA	Okinawa Federation of Night Clubs Association
OPP	Okinawa People's Party
RAA	Recreation and Amusement Association
SCAP	Supreme Commander for the Allied Powers
USCAR	U.S. Civil Administration of the Ryukyus

Introduction

Alegal

Alegal. The simplest definition of this unusual term that will be developed throughout the pages of this book is as follows: that which is irreducible to a binary of legal versus illegal or extralegal. The "a" preceding "legal" is analogous to the "a" preceding "moral"; *a*legal is neither legal nor illegal/extralegal, just as *a*moral is neither moral nor immoral. The function of the "a," therefore, does not refer to what or where the law is not: Words already exist for that—namely, "illegal," meaning that which is *against* the law, such as a criminal act, or "extralegal,"[1] meaning that which is *outside* of the law, such as an area in which other states exercise extraterritoriality. Rather, what this enigmatic "a" gets down to is an incongruous relationship between the alegal and the law.

On the one hand, alegal is discontinuous with the law because it always exceeds its intelligibility. Alegal can exist in the absence of the law, but on the other hand, the law cannot exist without the alegal. This is because the law does not exist *a priori*; it is not a preestablished, positive, or natural entity that is set in stone from time immemorial. The law is something that must be made up, and it is in the process of this fabrication that the alegal comes into play: Sovereign power arises by calibrating the infinite possibility of the alegal into a finite binary of legal versus illegal/extralegal. In other words, when Carl Schmitt defined the sovereign as "he who decides on the exception,"[2] he elucidated the ability to censor, exclude, or *except* an infinite array of possibilities so as to produce a spatiality (i.e., a *nomos*) in which territories become legible in terms of their legal codification. That which is irreducible to the law—the alegal—is drawn into a binary of the legal versus the illegal/extralegal.

The crisis of alegality, of that which is impervious to the law and hence a constant threat to sovereign power, is actually an enabling possibility, or a condition for the possibility of the emergence of sovereign power. Simply put, without the alegal, the sovereign would have nothing to do and no way to prove itself. Anyone can make up a law, but only sovereign power can enforce it through some form of complicity with the people, or a dynamic process called the "force of law."[3] In sum, the law, and by extension sovereign power, cannot obtain without the theoretical marker of the "a" in "alegal" that refers to not a property, but a performative operation of the calibration-*cum*-containment of the infinite possibility of the alegal into a legal intelligibility.

This distinction between the law as an *a priori* given of a static entity and an *a posteriori* effect of a performative operation is crucial for telling the story of miscegenation between U.S. military personnel and local women in Okinawa. Okinawa, also known as the Ryukyu Islands, is an archipelago that lies south of Kyushu, Japan, and east of Taiwan. Although it is but a few speckles on the world map, its geopolitical significance is enormous. Within the context of the United States, many have heard of Okinawa either through the news or through firsthand knowledge of it in relation to the U.S. military. This is for good reason. The United States has the most powerful military in world history, and Okinawa arguably has the most intense concentration of U.S. military bases in the world.[4] Put in numbers, this means that 46,334 active duty members of the U.S. armed forces (military personnel), civilian components (foreign civilians who are employed by the U.S. armed forces), and dependents (family members of the U.S. armed forces)[5] roam these tiny tropical islands of approximately 1.4 million people.[6] And they have been doing so for over the past seventy years since the 1945 Battle of Okinawa. Although women are increasingly represented in the armed forces, they still only make up about 16 percent of the military today.[7] Rather, a predominantly male institution founded on a culture of hypermasculinity is put into contact with an island people who have historically been subject to a feminizing Orientalist gaze. As a result, stories about Okinawa in the United States often circulate around contentious sexual encounters between U.S. military personnel and local Okinawans. The widely reported rape of a twelve-year-old girl by three U.S. military personnel in 1995 was but one chapter in a never-ending story that founds the U.S.-Okinawan relationship.

The central concern of this book is how American-Okinawan sexual encounters and, by extension, miscegenation become problematically narrated through a certain grammar governing trans-Pacific discourse, that is, the grammar of international law. The term "miscegenation" originates in the context of adjudicating the legality of interracial sex between whites and blacks in the United States.[8] Within the context of this book, miscegenation is defined as any type of sexual encounter between U.S. military personnel or their affiliates and local Okinawans that could (although not inevitably) result in the birth of mixed-race offspring.[9] In line with scholarship on critical race and postcolonial theory, this book does not assume that miscegenation is simply the mixing of subjects based upon sexual, racial, and national difference. Quite the contrary, it is examined as the performative process through which these differences become established as an effect of the contested encounter. While the politics of sex and race are predominant in mixed-race studies in the United States, the politics of national difference are exaggerated in discourses surrounding American-Okinawan miscegenation precisely because of Okinawa's precarious position vis-à-vis international law.

For starters, many today are still unclear about Okinawa's geopolitical disposition. U.S. military personnel commonly refer to Okinawa as the "Rock" and have thought of it as a giant U.S. military base protruding out of the Pacific Ocean instead of a group of Japanese islands that happen to contain U.S. military bases. Flights from China or Taiwan to Okinawa, furthermore, will be listed in the Chinese characters "琉球," reflecting a historical understanding of the area as a state that paid tribute to imperial China before it was annexed by Japan and turned into "Okinawa Prefecture" in 1879. In prewar Japan, public establishments often hung signs stating "No Koreans or Ryukyuans Allowed," while in postwar Japan, many mainlanders have assumed Okinawans can speak English because of the densely concentrated U.S. military presence. This differential treatment oddly coexists along with the official textbook answer to Okinawa's geopolitical disposition that it is one of the forty-seven prefectures of the Japanese state.

Okinawa's geopolitical ambiguity becomes a central concern for miscegenation because every time the law is evoked to adjudicate a sexual transgression, the question of Okinawa's very relationship to the law is thrown open to inquiry. Yes, the U.S. military may have infringed upon the law, but the law of . . . what state? As this book will show, interlocutors across the Pacific have gone to great lengths to make Okinawa fit into the system of international law by arguing that the U.S. military infringes upon *Japanese* sovereignty in Okinawa. In this bilateral configuration, the irreducible third space of Okinawa is but a subset of Japan in its relation to the United States. However, the problem is that Okinawa has always existed in a semi-colonial relationship with Japan and has never enjoyed the full protection of Japanese sovereignty. In fact, as this book will show, the greatest irony of this claim lies in the history of Japan's attempt to protect the sexual and racial integrity of so-called pure Japanese women and, by extension, its political sovereignty by sacrificing Okinawa to the United States so it could serve as a military outpost for a purportedly "mono-ethnic" Japanese state. Hence, different from literature predicated on the bilateralism of international law whereupon an American empire of military bases violates the sovereignty of its military colony in Japan, this book instead examines how both actors in the United States and Japan collaboratively translate Okinawa's alegality into the grammar of international law. By positioning Okinawa in terms of the alegal, this book therefore refuses to allow sovereignty to seduce it into a legal discourse so it can be manhandled by its trans-Pacific keepers.

In this way, Okinawa's alegality is not positioned vis-à-vis only the United States, but vis-à-vis the United States, Japan, and the larger network of global sovereignty that they constitute together. As shown in the next section, the so-called Okinawan problem is not about its denial or recuperation of sovereignty. More than anything, it is about the exercise of a particular kind of legal discourse—whether coded as a state that violates sovereignty (United States) or a state whose sovereignty is violated (Japan)—that allows for Okinawa's alegality to be collaboratively managed according to the whims of American militarism and the Japanese political economy. The next section introduces how this trans-Pacific triangulation operates through the problem of miscegenation.

Triangulation

On March 25, 1952, Takada Nahoko, a member of the Japanese Socialist Party, delivered a passionate speech before the Japanese Diet. Referring to the so-called occupation baby—that is the offspring of U.S. soldiers and mainland Japanese women—she proclaimed, "the atomic bomb is not the only thing that can destroy a race."[10] The United States had dropped atomic bombs on Hiroshima and Nagasaki just six-and-a-half years earlier that decimated the civilian population in what many believed was an act of genocide. Takada evoked these still fresh wounds in order to portray a second genocide perpetrated not by bombs during the war, but by U.S. soldiers during the occupation accused of sexually contaminating a purportedly pure Japanese population and producing a generation of mixed-race children. Her use of this term "occupation baby" to allude to the lives yet to come was politically charged because, technically speaking, the Allied occupation of Japan was about to end a month later on April 28, 1952, when the San Francisco Peace Treaty was to go into effect. At the time of her speech, Japan was on the eve of its liberation as a sovereign state with a U.S. military presence that would go on to be operated under the auspices of the accompanying U.S.-Japan Security Treaty. By suggesting that Japan would continue to be occupied nonetheless, Takada argued that irrespective of the formalities of international law, the ongoing U.S. military base presence would be evidence of Japan's compromised sovereignty and that the threat it faced therein took multiple forms, including a sexual one. At that time, many Japanese leftists claimed that the Administrative Agreement (renewed as the Status of Forces Agreement in 1960) referred to in Article 3 of the 1952 U.S.-Japan Security Treaty granted the U.S. military impunity from Japanese law and therefore conferred extraterritorial status. This meant that U.S. military personnel were able to conduct military operations without the hassles of interference from the Japanese government and were also given free rein to commit egregious crimes such as rape without fear of punishment under Japanese law. Takada added a gendered perspective to this criticism of extraterritoriality by attacking what I call "extraterritorial miscegenation." This refers to sexual assault, prostitution, and even so-called free-will romantic relationships between U.S. military personnel and Japanese women that purportedly take place in the absence of full protection under Japanese sovereignty and often lead to the birth of "occupation babies."

Takada's speech was a harbinger of the troubled politics of sex and race that continue to haunt postwar Japan today. Her valiant resistance to racialized sexual oppression by the U.S. military certainly resonates with contemporary transnational feminist movements against militarized violence. Yet, at the same time, her reduction of the "occupation baby" to a bilateral U.S.-Japan issue problematically leaves out the entire postcolonial legacy of Japan's multiethnic empire. Behind this omission lies a story to what will become, following Takada's demands, a systematic containment of the production of the "occupation baby" in mainland Japan that is intimately connected with the elimination of its imperial legacy. The voice of this story comes from the islands of Okinawa which, as the final destination of mainland Japan's unwanted miscegenation, became the vanishing point between Japan's multiethnic imperial past and its monoethnic democratic future.

This story began when the U.S. military moved into the vacuum opened up by the collapse of Japanese empire and found an opportunity to actualize its role as a leader on the stage of world history. The coast was clear for the American hegemon; across the Atlantic, Europe waned as the center of power as it was devastated by war and deteriorated from successive waves of colonial liberation.[11] Across the Pacific, the fallen Japanese empire offered access to the infinite potential of Asian markets. The problem, however, was how to access these markets without resorting to outright colonization. Given the principle of nonterritorial aggrandizement of the Atlantic Charter (1941) and the Cairo Declaration (1943), outright colonial rule was not only politically unfashionable, but also administratively unfeasible. For a solution, the U.S. military did what any other corporation would do after accomplishing a hostile takeover: Look to its predecessor for guidance.

The U.S. military sought to reinstate a modified version of the prized project of late Japanese empire known as the Greater East Asia Co-Prosperity Sphere. In place of a spread of formal and informal colonies that were now allowed to openly display their animus for their former imperial master, came a network of U.S. military bases committed to forming a regional trading bloc centered on the reemergence of the Japanese economy. This new arrangement avoided charges of colonialism—both old and new—as the incoming U.S. military claimed to liberate each area from the clutches of Japanese colonialism in the name of ethnic "self-determination" for all peoples based upon notions of national essence.[12] What emerged was the blueprint for a network of racialized territorial sovereignties across the Asia Pacific that revolved around a core of white supremacy in the U.S. synced to the "myth of monoethnicity" (*tan'itsuminzoku no shinwa*)[13] in Japan.

The so-called occupation baby was the discursive bond that held the racial politics of the U.S. and Japan together through a process of mutual exclusion. It was shunned by the U.S. at a time when anti-miscegenation laws were still in effect in the white-supremacist American fatherland. It was also shunned by Japan at a time when the popularization of the myth of monoethnicity was instrumental in suppressing the legacy of its multiethnic empire. The outcry against extraterritorial miscegenation is but one example of the multiethnicity of Japanese empire being suppressed in the name of protecting the purported purity of the Japanese race against racial mixing with U.S. military personnel.[14] The greatest irony, of course, is that while protest appeared to attack the U.S., it was entirely consistent with the U.S. military's common interest in eliminating the residual alegality from Japanese empire, or in other words, the multitude of subjects who were ethnically, linguistically, and/or culturally heterogeneous and unable to "return" to essentialist notions of a pre-imperial identity at the tap of a magic wand. Whether coded as for or against the integrity of Japanese sovereignty, both discourses unwittingly reinforced the assumption of its ethnic purity at the expense of obscuring *how* Japan was able to shed its multiethnic colonial legacy and emerge as a sovereign state in 1952. One answer to this "how" is none other than Okinawa.

It is well known that through the 1947 "Emperor's Message," Hirohito offered Okinawa to serve as a U.S. military outpost in exchange for the eventual recuperation of Japanese sovereignty.[15] But this was only the beginning. Takada's speech delivered after the Allied occupation in 1952 was an early indication of what was to come. She continued, "In order to protect the purity of Japan, this contamination cannot be washed out until all foreign troops are turned away."[16] In the decade following her statement, activists across mainland Japan launched a largely victorious anti-base movement that was animated by protest against extraterritorial miscegenation. Chapter 1 details how U.S. military facilities in mainland Japan were reduced to one-quarter of their original size in the late 1950s, only to reappear in Okinawa where 70 percent of all U.S. military bases in Japan are concentrated even though the prefecture makes up only 0.6 percent of total state territory today. And with these facilities followed a culture of miscegenation. Today, the percentage of international marriage (between an American citizen groom and Japanese national bride) and mixed heritage birth (between an American citizen father and Japanese national mother) in Okinawa Prefecture is approximately five times that of the national average.[17]

Whereas Japan was able to displace the discord with U.S. military bases onto Okinawa, I argue that the relationships engendered by sexual encounters and the resulting mixed-race offspring in these islands embody a fundamental aporia within the U.S.-Japan network of global sovereignty: Both are at once the purported evidence of Japan's victimization by the United States that bore upon their transfer to Okinawa, and at the same time, both are the impediments to Okinawa's ability to become fully integrated into a monoethnic Japan as first-class nationals. Setting aside the legacy of Japanese racism toward the "darker," "hairier," and "more barbaric" Okinawan, one can see that the mixed-race subject is an unsightly reminder of Okinawa's inability to "become Japanese,"[18] hence suggesting the reason for the choice of Okinawa as a place to concentrate U.S. military bases in the first place. And while one may certainly argue that the myth of monoethnicity has given way to a more politically correct climate of multiculturalism in the post-reversion era, the celebration of mixed-race Okinawan entertainers in Japanese popular culture today has done little to extricate Okinawa from its exceptional status. When the mixed-race queen of Japanese pop Amuro Namie sang "Never End" at the 2000 G8 summit in Okinawa, many Okinawans wondered if she was singing about the never-ending U.S. military presence on her native islands.

The question of miscegenation in Okinawa begs for an examination of the biopolitical dimensions to the U.S.-Japan network of global sovereignty. That is, what is the particular logic of population management in postwar Japan that benefited from U.S. military bases only insofar as the burden of the physical presence of the bodies that operate them was exported to Okinawa? It will be helpful to consider how biopolitics in Japan, as a continuing trajectory from the prewar era, came to terms with the postwar U.S. military basing project for the purposes of framing the rest of this book. While the U.S. military presence was useful to the continued development of the postwar Japanese economy, the next section resurrects discussions on biopolitics put forth by Marxian scholars in prewar Japan to suggest that miscegenation posed a threat to the continued growth of the Japanese middle class formed along the lines of patriarchal monoethnic normativity.

Biopolitical State

The variety of biopolitics referenced in this book is perhaps closest to the thread Michel Foucault explored in his 1978–1979 *Birth of Biopolitics* lectures delivered at the Collège de France. It was there that he brought biopolitics most intimately into the heart of sovereignty and illuminated a groundbreaking theoretical shift from sovereignty keyed to reason of the state (*raison d'État*) to sovereignty keyed to reason of the market, or what I call a "biopolitical state."

After the 1917 October Revolution, mounting economic unrest threatened states around the world with instability and drove a fundamental reconsideration of the relationship between the state and capitalism from the perspective of a new political actor that Foucault, in a larger trajectory, would go on to identify as the population. In this vein, he traced developments in the United States amidst the Great Depression to the U.S. military occupation of the Anglo-American German Bizona after World War II. The crisis that assaulted Japanese empire, however, was already unfolding over a decade earlier. Japan was hit with a series of rice riots in 1918, the emergence of Korean independence movements in 1919, and mass unemployment on an unprecedented scale after the manufacturing boom of World War I.[19] How would Japan amend the relationship between the disproportionately large number of farmers and small and medium-sized enterprises on the one hand, with a small handful of giant *zaibatsu*[20] that monopolized capital on the other, precisely at the moment when Japan was being inundated with colonial surplus populations from the corners of its empire?

Living these historical conditions in real time, Marxian scholars in Japan such as Uno Kōzō and Tosaka Jun started to theorize biopolitics long before Foucault, even if they did not use the term. Uno reconceptualized the "law of population" (*jinkō hōsoku*)[21] by problematizing the limitations of "finance capital" and its perceived corrective, i.e., the "controlled economy" (*tōsei keizai*) of a socialist state.[22] Because capitalists assumed a constant reserve of labor power ready for consumption, they paid little heed to unemployment in times of recession and dismissed it as a problem to be corrected by the "mechanism of the commodity economy."[23] But when economic depression threatened social unrest on a global scale, the continued flow of labor power could no longer be taken for granted. The reproduction, management, and commodification of labor power became a central conundrum for the biopolitical state. The conundrum, he argued, is that capital is contingent on labor power for its continued operation, but at the same time "labor power cannot be produced as a commodity by capital."[24] How would this "impossibility" (*muri*) be overcome?

Uno argued that the state needed to assume the role of organizing the population for the commodification of labor power through "social policy" (*shakai seisaku*),[25] or what Michel Foucault would go on to identify as "institutional frameworks"[26] over twenty years later. This is the first characteristic of a biopolitical state. He writes that "states were naturally compelled to intervene to some degree" to the "vast number of unemployed workers" since it could "no longer simply leave it to the mechanism of the commodity economy."[27] In this context, Tomiyama Ichirō and Katsuhiko Endo have respectively argued that the state intervened with spending policies to regulate the production of surplus populations in agrarian villages[28] and foster the development of small and medium-sized enterprises as the "primary absorbers of the relative surplus population" through "industrial policy" and "administrative guidance."[29] Ken C. Kawashima and Tomiyama have respectively shown how surplus populations from

Korea and Okinawa became racialized as cheap labor against the formation of an ethnically "Japanese" middle class.

Yet, while social policy was essential, Uno himself writes that "it could
not provide a fundamental solution to the problem."[30] When taken to the
extreme, social policy could result in a controlled economy of a socialist
state such as that of Nazi Germany that ended in ruins.[31] In his study on
the development of social policy in the interwar period, Katsuhiko Endo
reads Uno alongside Tosaka Jun to trace the emergence of a second, more
essential component of the biopolitical state. That is, "socialism as idealism,"[32] or the ideological structure of a different kind of "socialist state"
that serves a "new form of capitalism."[33] Common to Uno and Tosaka is
an emphasis on the formation of a middle class that overcomes the contradictions of capital present in everyday life through service to the ideal of a
Japanese state. At the risk of being reductive, this means that the middle
class took upon itself the task of managing the reproduction of labor power
in service to the state for capital.

Tosaka argues that the Japanese middle class was at the heart of the ideological form of "Japanism" (*Nipponshugi*) that inspired wartime fascism.
Not only was it the primary beneficiary of social policy, but it came to see
the biopolitical state as an ideal that would protect it from the greed of
monopoly capitalism and, hence, internalized the need to protect it from
perceived threats. In this way, Tosaka, in a similar vein as Foucault, introduced the biopolitical mechanism of social defense. Foucault wrote that
the "[p]olice is a set of interventions" that "ensure that living . . . can in fact
be converted into forces of the state," or in other words, ensure that all life
"will be effectively useful to the constitution and development of the state's
forces."[34] In his essay on what Tosaka called the *"spirit of policing,"*[35]
Kawashima goes a step beyond Foucault and shows not only how the police
function shifted to transform the act of living into a state force, but also
how this function came to be internalized by the masses, or what he calls
the "massification of the police, and the policification of the masses."[36] For
Kawashima, the police function dispersed throughout the masses, aimed
to care for and discipline life so that certain populations deemed "unpro-
ductive and superfluous to capitalist production . . . did not interrupt the
process of commodifying labor power. . . ."[37] Endo further articulates this
deadly mechanism as the "working class desire to become a member of a
community of the same that enables the State to utilize violence against
those who are 'different,' and who threaten to cause social disorder. . . ."[38]
This means that the "working class" targets life that is unintelligible to the
biopolitical state as a matter of its own survival. By doing so, Tosaka

writes that "[f]ascism is precisely the political mechanism that" ironically becomes useful to "monopoly capitalism" by taking "advantage of the petit bourgeois, or the middle class in the broad sense."[39] This is why he locates the heart of fascism in the "various medium-scale farmers, or the rural middle class" that subscribed to idealist notions surrounding "feudalism" such as "agrarianism" and "familialism."[40]

It is at this juncture that biopolitics intersects most intimately with the sovereign decision: Capital is contingent upon the integration of something both irreducible and external to it (i.e., labor power), just as sovereignty is contingent upon the integration of something both irreducible and external to it (i.e., the alegal). The commodification of labor power comes together with the sovereign decision to translate an unintelligible life force into units of "difference" that become intelligible to the state for consumption. In this way, the sovereign decision is not monopolized by the state, but as Stephen Legg writes in his rendering of the biopolitical dimension of sovereignty, it becomes the "prerogative of the swarming sovereigns within the population."[41]

While the ascent of the Japanese middle class had already set afoot before the end of the war, the economic reforms of the Allied occupation expedited correctives to the limitations of Japanese empire and allowed for its full-fledged emergence in the postwar era. The passage of the 1945 Labor Union Law that guaranteed workers the right to organize, engage in collective bargaining, and strike,[42] and measures taken in 1946 to dissolve the *zaibatsu*[43] widened the possibility for workers to take on a central role organizing capitalist production. In an essay written one year into the occupation, Uno identified the reemergence of biopolitics under the name "industrial democratization."[44] He argued for a two-way street in which the worker weighs in to the production process and, by doing so, becomes vested in seeing that capital makes returns to the very workers responsible for its growth so as to avoid the catastrophe of unemployment. Hence, more than simple state intervention into industries from above, he argued for a "management of capital by the state [that] is surveiled and reined in by a powerful organization of workers."[45]

In this way, Uno not only provided a preview, but also a biopolitical backstory to what Chalmers A. Johnson would go on to call the "developmental state"[46] that intervened into industry in order to achieve "substantive social and economic goals,"[47] or what Bruce Cumings would go on to discuss as "administrative guidance" that shaped prewar colonial society as much as it did postwar Japanese society.[48] As Johnson notes, these industries were interfaced with social policies starting with the "three sacred treasures" of the lifetime employment system, the seniority wage system, and enterprise unions that made the success of the industry integral to the very stability of the worker's life. Work, then, was not a nine to five job, but an economic expression of nationalism for which they were quite literally willing to die for through overwork or *karōshi*. Hence, as subject and object of industrial production, work became a holy mission for the state, for the company, and for the family—that is, the Japanese middle-class family as the very locus of the reproduction of labor power at its most literal level.

Scholars such as Johnson and Cumings have tracked the continuity of state-implemented economic and social policies from the prewar to the postwar period. Although not comprehensive, the implementation of major institutional frameworks designed to foster a mutually beneficial relationship between the U.S. military and the Japanese economy are traced in this book, with focus on the management of sex around U.S. military bases. While it is useful to understand how these institutional frameworks became implemented from above, this book does not address them as part of a comprehensive empirical history. Rather, this book contributes a study of the second component of the biopolitical state: how sovereign power dispersed through the Japanese middle class governed by norms of mono-ethnicity continued to target life unintelligible to the state from below as a *cultural* problem. Of course, the life that this book is most interested in is Okinawan life and, more specifically, Okinawan life at its most extreme point of unintelligibility—in the embrace of miscegenation.

The *alegal* that names this book, hence, is not just a state that is excluded from sovereign power, but it is more fundamentally a form of life that exists in a condition of unintelligibility to the biopolitical state. Furthermore, this unintelligibility is not reduced to the finality of a death sentence. In other words, *Alegal: Biopolitics and the Unintelligibility of Okinawan Life* is not an elegy that laments the tragedy of a people excluded by sovereign power. Certainly, Okinawans have endured unspeakable acts of violence and continue to live with them in their daily lives. Yet, as Ariko Ikehara writes, Okinawans "neither reject nor accept their lives, but cope with and negotiate the mundane in making life possible. . . ."[49] To cope means to develop a strategy for living in the here and now, or what Ikehara calls a negotiation with the "mundane."[50] This book looks in unexpected places to articulate this philosophy of coping so distanced from the ideal of the state that it is compelled to enhance its life force by other means. It traces the excess of a life force that cannot be contained by the state, the capacity of that life force to transform the world in the absence of self-determination, and the attempt to reclaim autonomy from the biopolitical state that monopolizes it.

Chapter Breakdown

Chapter 1 on mainland Japan in the 1950s and Chapter 2 on Okinawa from 1945 to 1952 contextualize the respective responses to U.S. military bases in both locations in terms of debates surrounding sex work that catered to the U.S. military. These two chapters act as complementary opposites: Chapter 1 depicts the success of Japan's anti-base protest as symbolic in structure, while Chapter 2 depicts Okinawa's failings of the same as allegorical in structure. Chapter 1 specifically shows how activists and politicians in mainland Japan launched a largely victorious anti-base movement in which they protested "extraterritorial miscegenation" as the racial contamination of the Japanese nation through the literary genre of reportage. It reads this reportage alongside Tosaka's description of protest toward private prostitution in the context of prewar Japan, where he located the formation of "familialism" (*kazokushugi*) as the symbolic substitution of the family for the state. Chapter 2, by contrast, shows how Okinawans, surviving in a vacuum of sovereignty in the immediate postwar, had no choice but to eke out life with an all-encompassing U.S. military presence. It shows how their historical failure to be included in the biopolitical order in the prewar era informed a tenuous and duplicitous attitude toward sovereign power in the postwar era. Okinawans did not experience a sense of loss of sovereign power that was assumed by mainland Japanese interlocutors discussed in Chapter 1, but rather a continuing fear of being excluded from the biopolitical order in which they were exposed to the ongoing brutalities of death and sexual violence. This fear informed an instrumental obedience to the legal order that could be reinforced just as easily as it could be disarticulated. Instead of judging Okinawan complicity or resistance to the postwar order from the seat of sovereign power, Chapter 2 reads the failure of recognition by, and failure of identification with, sovereign power in terms of Benjamin's notion of allegory. Allegory, for Benjamin, is the antidote for symbol, and it attempts to forge a different relationship with transcendental power. It does not assume that Okinawa's failure to become sovereign subjects before the law is disempowering, but instead seeks to reclaim the field of Okinawa's alegality implied by failure as the place of the political.

Chapter 3 on Okinawa during the period of the all-island struggle from 1952 to 1958, and Chapter 4 on Okinawa during the reversion era from 1958 to 1972, both show the limitations of resistance toward an assumed single-state imperialism and instead depict Okinawa within a U.S.-Japan led postwar regionalism. These two chapters are also complementary in that both describe how workers in the base towns centered on the sex industry became impediments to the Old Left's attempt to unify behind a Japanese ethnic nation (Chapter 3), and the New Left's attempt to unify behind a Japanese proletarian class (Chapter 4). Chapter 3 reads the sex worker as a lumpenproletariat subject who constantly fails representation before the state, and it reads the potentiality for this kind of subject to inspire political transformation amongst the masses through the story of Okinawa's underground communist party. Chapter 4 reads literary and filmic representations of the sex worker allegorically in order to question the ways it is possible to hear her speak. It shows how the one segment of Okinawan society that came to be despised for its inability to be mobilized into anti-military protest became the very spontaneous agents who led a moment of unplanned anti-military violence during the Koza Riot.

During the period between 1972 and 1995, discussed in Chapter 5, the complicity between U.S. militarism and the Japanese political economy became unavoidably clear and prompted many Okinawans to conceptualize a different kind of autonomy unmoored from promises of the Japanese state. This was also a time when the anti-prostitution law went into effect in Okinawa, and mixed-race individuals born to U.S. military personnel and Okinawan women started to come of age and speak for themselves. In place of self-determination that is predicated on the stability of a unified self or unified nations as the precondition for individual agency or state sovereignty, Chapter 5 considers a different sense of agency implied by morphing matter. This refers to the material dimensions of Okinawa as a borderland of the Pacific, where bodies continually mix. It does this through a close reading of a rare published mixed-race memoir to show how the author documents her failure to unify as a subject before the state. This failure leads her to a different way to appreciate her life, not as a material object that unifies as a subject before the state, but in the character of its mutability that disengages the force of sovereign power. In this way, life comes to *matter* for herself and not for the state.

CHAPTER I

Japan in the 1950s: Symbolic Victims

This chapter addresses sexual labor in service to the Allied forces in postwar Japan through the 1950s. Although the Japanese government organized prostitution for the Allied forces in 1945, it was abolished in less than six months because the U.S. military favored its operation in the sphere of the free market. So-called private prostitution, however, was already fraught with a history of controversy stemming from its operation during the Japanese empire. Here, this controversy is read through a 1935 essay written by Kyoto School philosopher, Tosaka Jun, entitled "An Analysis of the Restoration Phenomenon." In this essay, Tosaka showed how ethnic nationalists considered private prostitution inimical to the Japanese family system that formed the basis of the middle class. In fact, it was in this context that he theorized fascism as the logic of substitution, whereupon the family came to symbolically stand in for the larger society or state through quasi-religious feelings of "primitivism" or "mysticism." This chapter examines the postwar reincarnation of this kind of ethnic nationalism through reportage that focused almost obsessively on the private prostitute and repeated the logic of substitution of the Japanese family for the state. That is, the sex worker, again, came to symbolize the victimization of Japan by

"Western" capitalism, this time figured in terms of the imperialism of the U.S. military basing project in Japan. This reactionary ethno-nationalism registered on various points of the political spectrum and informed a largely successful anti-base movement in the late 1950s. Concerned with the social stability of Japan, the United States shut down many mainland bases and concentrated them in Okinawa.

Unmanageable Sexual Labor

The question of postwar sexual labor in service of the U.S. military was a question about the emergence of a postwar biopolitical Japanese state. How would the state care for its population in service to the U.S. military while not only recuperating lost economic power, but also taking it to new heights? Both states were unsatisfied with their respective solutions: The United States would not be managed by Japan's state-licensed system of prostitution, and Japan would not be liberalized by America's regulatory system of private prostitution. In other words, this story starts with the rapid rise and fall of the Recreation and Amusement Association (RAA) in 1945 that followed the prewar model of state-licensed prostitution and continued with the privatization of sex work through the emergence of street-walkers, called "*panpan*," before ending with a large transfer of U.S. military bases to Okinawa.

In preparation for the arrival of the occupation troops, sex topped the Japanese political agenda directly after the war. Japanese frightened of the "ghosts of the 'Nanjing Massacre'"[1] now feared not only the same sexual violence they unleashed onto the conquered in China, but also the precedent set by territories Japan left vulnerable to American invasion, such as Okinawa and Manila, that would translate into sexual violence for Japanese women. Accordingly, on August 18, 1945, just three days after surrender, the Police and Security Section of the Home Ministry sent a message to all police departments "Regarding the Establishment of Special Comfort Facilities for the Occupying Forces."[2] This resulted in the formal establishment of the RAA on August 29, 1945,[3] backed by a 100 million-yen budget equally split between business investors and the Japanese government.[4] Ikeda Hayato, then director of the Finance Ministry's tax bureau and later prime minister credited for realizing Japan's "economic miracle," approved the budget with the statement "100 million yen is a bargain if it can protect the pure blood of the Yamato race."[5]

In many respects, the RAA was an extension of the system of state-licensed prostitution (*kōshō seido*)[6] instituted shortly after the establishment of the Meiji state. The Japanese government issued licenses to establishments engaged in the sex trade from which it then collected taxes. The women often came from the poorest sectors of Japanese society and were circulated throughout Japanese empire along with its expansion. No different from other empires, Japan exported this system to its colonies where not only Japanese women, but also colonized Taiwanese and Korean women were pushed into the trade. After the 1937 Nanjing Massacre, Japan's system of state-licensed public prostitution quickly organized into the so-called "comfort woman" system in which Korean, Taiwanese, Chinese, Southeast Asian, Japanese, and Dutch women were forced into brutal sexual slavery for the Japanese Imperial Army during the Pacific War. Then shortly following defeat, the RAA replaced its precursor and forced Japanese women to serve not the Japanese, but now the Allied forces. Instead of coercing mostly colonized women to serve a multiethnic Japanese empire, Japanese women were now mobilized as a "breakwater of flesh" (*nikutai no bōhatei*)[7] to protect the "racial purity" of the Japanese population. Class also became a factor as Japanese officials targeted destitute women[8] who had lost their families and homes as a result of selective air raids that gutted poor neighborhoods while leaving wealthy homes and buildings available for the incoming occupation forces.[9] In an official RAA statement, recruits were "to protect and cultivate the racial purity (*minzoku no junketsu*)" of the Japanese people for "a hundred years in the future" and become the "unseen subterranean pillar that holds up the foundation of the postwar social order."[10] Deputy Prime Minister Konoe Fumimaro had similarly requested the superintendent general to "Please protect the daughters of Japan."[11]

At its height, about 70,000 women serviced the RAA.[12] Despite its popularity amongst the soldiers, the RAA was short-lived. In January 1946, less than six months after its establishment, the Supreme Commander for the Allied Powers (SCAP) issued a memorandum stating "The maintenance of licensed prostitution in Japan is in contravention of the ideals of democracy and inconsistent with the development of individual freedom throughout the nation."[13] That same month, the Police and Security Section of the Home Ministry ordered that RAA be officially disbanded with 55,000 prostitutes in service.[14] SCAP was reluctant to participate in state-licensed prostitution because, simply put, it looked bad. As Lisa Yoneyama has convincingly argued, managing the trans-Pacific politics of sex was integral to the emergence of a Cold War regime centered on a system of "Anglo-American-centered international security," whereupon the U.S. touted democratic norms of a free nation in order to justify its elimination of an "absolute evil."[15] Patronizing organized prostitution was difficult to pass off as a moral virtue. And, as if to corroborate this point, Michiko Takeuchi has similarly shown how the RAA was damaging to the United States, which was engaged in ideological warfare with the Soviet Union as it jockeyed for the role of global leader.[16]

In addition to ideological concerns, RAA was also taxing the health of the soldiers with venereal disease (VD) sharply on the rise. But, in economic terms, the abolition of state-regulated military prostitution paved the way for the privatization of the sex industry. As John Lie writes, "[p]rostitution was . . . not abolished but simply continued in a new privatized form."[17] The U.S. military needed prostitution to occur in the sphere of the free market where it could wash its hands of institutional responsibility.

First, in response to the prohibition of sexual slavery, the security chief of the Home Ministry reiterated on February 22, 1946, that "lewd acts committed by an individual's free will" were a "different matter."[18] On November 14, 1946, the Yoshida cabinet designated "special areas for restaurants" (*tokushu inshokuten no chiiki*) which were really a cover for prostitution without formal legal recognition.

Second, the privatization of the sex industry further shifted from management by private industry to self-management. The attempt to manage and contain the mobility of sexual labor gave way to the iconic *"panpan"* or sex worker who took to the streets. In contrast to the history of socioeconomically and geographically limiting prostitution to certain sectors of Japanese society, these streetwalkers came from more diverse backgrounds and were afforded more liberty to navigate the terrain on their own accord. As Sarah Kovner assesses in her study on sex work in postwar Japan, "One reason the panpan phenomenon was so disturbing was that it appeared to mean that any woman—even an educated, middle-class mother or daughter—could find a place in the sex industry."[19] Surveys conducted during occupation corroborate this assessment as well. According to a 1948 survey of two hundred streetwalkers, those who had either started or graduated from elementary school, middle school, high school, and post-secondary school figured in at 27.5 percent, 18 percent, 47.5 percent, and 5.5 percent respectively.[20] As the survey notes, different from sex workers confined to brothels, the entrepreneurial streetwalkers capitalized on a high level of intellectual and English language skills to manage negotiations directly with patrons. The streetwalkers' self-cultivated abilities yielded higher profits that were retained by the worker. Making more than their brothel counterparts,[21] they took their profits and reinvested in themselves by buying the latest fashion and cosmetics. Robert Kramm estimates that there were between fifty thousand and seventy thousand sex workers who catered to U.S. military personnel in Tokyo alone during the occupation period.[22]

Certainly, the streetwalker was a nuisance to public sanitation as the U.S. military and the Japanese police attempted to crack down on them by hunting them down and subjecting them to forced VD inspections. But while much has been said about the brute institutional power that bore down on the lives of these women, there is also an argument to be made about the bottom-up formation of a Japanese middle class that saw the streetwalker as a social threat. This was not an entirely new phenomenon, but as discussed in the next section, Tosaka Jun had already started to consider how the so-called private prostitute was targeted by Japanist ideologues integral to the formation of a middle class in the mid-1930s.[23]

The Family as the State

In 1935, Tosaka Jun published a piece of social commentary on prostitution that would go on to become part of his well-known *Japanese Ideology*. Earlier that year, a group of brothel owners attacked abolitionist forces who worried that the state's public involvement with licensed prostitution (*kōshō seido*) looked bad in the eyes of "Western civilization."[24] The brothel owners instead praised the glory of preserving this purportedly native tradition, pitched as an extension of the traditional Japanese family system (*kazoku seido*),[25] and gestured toward the criminalization of private prostitution.

In his commentary, Tosaka was not shy to point out the "comical" irony of this nostalgia for a precapitalist past when it was not only produced by, but was also an aid to, monopoly capitalism in Japan.[26] For him, there was no temporal continuity from the feudal family system of the Tokugawa era to Japan in 1935, but only an attempt to force social cohesion amongst the multitudinous masses whose communities had been cataclysmically uprooted by capitalism. Far from antagonizing capitalism, their collective fantasy of the days past actually enabled it by providing a logic of social cohesion as servitude to the state that not only aided in the organization of labor power for consumption, but also provided foot soldiers from the countryside to fight in its imperialist wars. Hence, instead of examining the contradictions of capitalism through historical materialism, an emerging middle class indulged in a historical idealism that assumed a "transhistorical" (*chōrekishitekina*) Japanese essence rooted in a primitive past.[27] Whereas prostitution should have been addressed as a problem of poverty amongst "proletarian farmers in shackles,"[28] it was instead recuperated as the patriarch's ability to manage his family as a "symbol" (*shōchō*) or "metaphor" (*hiyu*)[29] of the state's ability to manage its people.

Here, Tosaka's evocation of symbol is closely linked to Schmitt's concept of sovereign power. If the sovereign, as defined by Schmitt, is "he who decides on the exception,"[30] then the sovereign becomes a symbolic stand-in for God: The decision is a performative act that sutures the gap between an entity that is both *of* the people (and therefore must abide by the law), and an entity that is simultaneously *above* the people (and therefore capable of deciding when a special exception can be made to the law based on faith in God). Symbol, as well, is characterized by a gap between the sign and the referent that is sutured by transcendental power. For example, in his reading of the notion of symbol in Benjamin's *Trauerspiel*, Lutz Koepnick writes that these "metaphorical substitutions disrupt or transcend the given continuum of meaning, fueling it with external significance, and thereby elevating it to some higher poetic stance."[31] Here, the sovereign as a stand-in for God interrupts the secular "continuum of meaning" by virtue of appealing to the "external significance" of transcendental power, whereupon it becomes elevated "to some higher poetic stance." The important insight here is that the burden of interpreting the gap—of the individual capacity to connect the dots between two points of sign and referent—is surrendered to transcendental power. Koepnick continues:

> According to Benjamin's *Trauerspiel* book, symbolism ultimately becomes complicit with myth because it hides the very mechanism of signification upon which it is based. As it invokes totality and closure, classical symbolism seeks to transcend time and history, thereby displacing the anguish of life with images of stabilized harmony and eternal perfection.[32]

According to this passage, symbol, along with myth, "hides the very mechanism of signification upon which it is based," or in other words, hides the fact that it is denying the individual the agency of interpretation and feeding the people preassembled narratives that seductively glow with the phantasmagoria of "stabilized harmony and eternal perfection."

Of course, different from Schmitt, Tosaka is not writing of a sovereign entity that rules the masses, but sovereignty of a biopolitical state, whereupon the decision becomes "prerogative of the swarming sovereigns within the population."[33] Reading the piece carefully, we can see that Tosaka notes the state's intervention into the population as state-licensed prostitution,[34] but places his analytic emphasis on how power operates from the bottom-up on the level of symbol. In this way, he writes that the familialists relied on "hermeneutic expression" (*kaishaku hyōgen*) to argue that the attack on the family system was really an attack on society and, by extension, the state. This "idealistically (*kan'nentekini*) alleviates the trouble" caused by the "problem of unemployment and poverty" that encroaches upon the "family system."[35] In other words, the contradictions of capital that present in the here and now are "alleviate[d]" or deferred to a higher power, i.e., the Japanese state in the image of the feudal family system that is to be recuperated from the past as "*fukkoshugi*"[36] (restorationism) toward a utopian future. He describes the logic of substitution in detail as follows.

> In a family, for example, two members who are of two hearts and two bodies can be of one heart and one body, or one heart and two bodies. That feeling is beyond analytic explanation and must be completely intuitive and immanent. While the logic in which two different things can be directly and intuitively thought to be one is completely that of symbol or metaphor, it is as if the logic of familialism was such that the family is nothing more than a metaphor for society.[37]

The feeling of communion in the intimate sphere of family life is substituted for a feeling of communion amongst members of society, or as he states elsewhere, subjects of the state.

Here he suggests that the substitution is sutured by a "religious feeling" that is found in "mysticism" (*shinpishugi*) or "primitivism" (*genshishugi*).[38] And while he agrees that Japan is different from liberalist states founded on Rousseau's social contract, the "primitivism" of the former is nonetheless common to the "naturalism" (*shizenshugi*) of the latter in its "historical idealist content."[39] It is in this sense that he argues that while Japan may be more socialist than individualistic, it nonetheless subscribes to the same liberalist tenants of idealism.

Against the popular assumption that Japanese fascism was defeated alongside the military defeat of imperial Japan, Tosaka's linkage of fascism to liberalism as socialism is useful in tracing the triad's reemergence in the postwar era. While fascism was replaced by democracy (or what Nomura Kōya will go on to call "democratic colonialism," as discussed later), the ethos of social cohesion and servitude to the state was not only alive and well in the postwar era, but reinvigorated in modified form. For example, Chalmers Johnson cautions against assuming that the "Japanese consensus" integral to Japan's well-known "industrial policies" that drove its postwar economic success is rooted in an essentialist cultural trait. Rather, he attributes it to the "mobilization of a large majority of the population to support economic goals" during the 1930s.[40] The biopolitical state that was in gestation during interwar Japan was now guided through a safe delivery in the postwar era. Emerging as the developmental state that works closely with the middle class for economic prosperity, socialism had now found new ground for expression.

Understanding this continuity is crucial for contextualizing the implications of extraterritorial miscegenation in the postwar era. As Tosaka showed with the attack on private prostitution in the 1930s, the attack on the streetwalker had immense, perhaps unsurpassed symbolic value. An examination of anti-base reportage in the next section shows how the issue struck the heart of the middle class by most directly affecting its children. Not only could any middle-class woman potentially become a streetwalker, but reportage incited the fear that any middle-class child living around the numerous military bases throughout mainland Japan could be adversely placed under her cultural influence to the detriment of the entire nation's future. In this way, the streetwalker became a powerful symbol for the victimization of the Japanese family as a stand-in for the victimization of the state by the U.S. military.

Anti-Base Reportage

At the end of an almost seven-year occupation, Japan was released from the censoring eyes of the Allied Powers and overcome by a wave of social unrest expressed most powerfully through the trope of extraterritorial miscegenation. A *Washington Post* article indexed this new discursive trend by stating "Japan's independence was signaled by a rash of articles critical of the Occupation. A favorite theme was illegitimate children fathered by occupation soldiers."[41] This topic was particularly popular in anti-base reportage, a literary genre invested in the nonfictional depiction of experience designed to speak truth to power in service of political protest.

Reportage itself was part of what Toba Kōji calls the "1950s age of the document" that witnessed a proliferation of documentary films, photography, and reportage art.[42] Within the literary reportage genre, Toba catalogs the documentation of protest in various social movements from dam construction to opposition to U.S. military base operations.[43] The earliest years of 1952 and 1953 that I focus on here describe the U.S. military as infringing on Japan's sovereignty and document the impact the U.S. military bases have on the everyday lives of the Japanese people as a cultural problem.

Kanzaki Kiyoshi, a central figure in the early anti-base reportage movement who quickly became an authority on U.S. military prostitution, opens *The Town That Sells Its Daughters* by characterizing the U.S. military base presence in Japan as a form of colonialism. He writes, ". . . to protect children from an environment that has been quasi-colonized is to protect Japan's future and to do the work of completing the independence of the race (*minzoku*)."[44] Similarly, editors of *Children of the Bases* quickly follow suit and argue that ". . . Japanese nationals who have long looked down upon the Asian races have fallen into a new colonial condition" vis-à-vis the U.S. military.[45] This "new colonial condition" resonates closely with the 1951 Japanese Communist Party (JCP) manifesto which designated Japan as a "colony/dependent state."[46] It depicts Japanese sovereignty wounded by colonialism that results in the successive loss of autonomy over the economy and then society. This trickle-down erosion is what foregrounds the trope of extraterritorial miscegenation within anti-base reportage as a manifestation of colonial violence that had penetrated Japanese society to its innermost core.

Inomata Kōzō, a Socialist Party politician, provides a concrete definition of the violation of Japanese sovereignty in his coauthored book *Camp Japan* very early on in 1953. He writes that the grounds for U.S. military extraterritoriality in Japan can be found in the Administrative Agreement referred to in Article 3 of the 1951 U.S.-Japan Security Treaty. As commonly known, the U.S.-Japan Security Treaty was signed just hours after the San Francisco Peace Treaty that terminated the Allied occupation and formally actualized Japan's independence as a sovereign state. The Security Treaty allowed for a continued U.S. military presence in Japan, and the Administrative Agreement (renewed as the Status of Forces Agreement in 1960) stipulated the specific terms of the arrangement. According to Article 17 of the Agreement, members of the U.S. armed forces, including its civilian components and dependents, fall under the "exclusive jurisdiction" of the United States when arrests are made on "all offenses which may be committed in Japan." Under such circumstances, the "United States service courts and authorities shall be willing and able to try and, on conviction, to punish all offenses."[47] Inomata and others make their case for the existence of extraterritoriality based on the second and third points regarding the arrest and prosecution for criminal offenses in which the U.S. military is guaranteed virtual impunity from Japanese law. The aim of extraterritoriality in the Security Treaty was to allow the United States to treat Japan not as a state, but as a military base that could be freely used without the entanglements of the law. As General Douglas MacArthur of

SCAP stated, the "entire area of Japan must be regarded as a potential base for defensive maneuver with unrestricted freedom reserved to the United States as the protecting power through her local commander. . . ."[48]

Unlike the San Francisco Peace Treaty that was rigorously debated in the Japanese Diet, Prime Minister Yoshida Shigeru failed to introduce the content of the U.S.-Japan Security Treaty as required by Japanese law. In fact, he was only given the details of the Security Treaty in English the night prior to its signing, whereupon his advisors worked on a Japanese translation.[49] He took it upon himself to sign the treaty as the sole representative of Japan without anyone outside his immediate circle knowing the content. According to Inomata, this was the moment that "Japan lost its total independence."[50]

Kimura Kihachiro, also a politician from the Socialist Party, argues that this compromising of Japanese sovereignty subsequently led to "economic extraterritoriality." He writes, "With no autonomy after the so-called 'Accords,' we lost our independence and fell under the rule of America's military economy which can be assessed in one word as a [military] 'base economy.'"[51] As he points out, a base economy is not simply the local accommodation of the military while the state maintains its overall economic autonomy. Rather, it is an overhaul of the entire economic infrastructure in support of military basing operations.

To support his claim, Kimura argues the "postwar resolution funds"[52] that Japan paid annually to the occupying forces for the purchase of goods and labor amounted to extortion that contributed to Japan's rampant postwar inflation.[53] The procurement of goods for the U.S. military also altered the inherent structure of the Japanese economy so that its main directive was skewed toward the needs of the U.S. military, particularly during the Korean War. This not only led to the "loss of autonomy in the Japanese economy,"[54] but also tied it directly to U.S. political interests. Finally, he describes Japan as a "military colony of America" which "castrated the autonomy and independent spirit of the Japanese nation"[55] by "preserving Japan's feudal and monopolistic institutions."[56]

If the erosion of political sovereignty led to a loss of economic autonomy, then reportage detailing the realities of military base life revealed how the social fabric of Japan was unraveled to the core: "Just as the Japanese economy in its entirety is a base economy, Japanese society in its entirety is a base society."[57] In a society of military bases, not only are farmers displaced from their land and forced to open up businesses that cater to the agent of their displacement, but they must also facilitate a local base economy centered on the sale of sex. Hence, the rally against extraterritoriality quickly became expressed in the most visually explicit, sensational, and immediate form as a movement against U.S. military prostitution.

Following the arguments against political and economic extraterritoriality, I call this phenomenon "extraterritorial miscegenation." In this first sense, it refers to miscegenation that occurs under conditions in which it is assumed that sovereignty is either absent or compromised. With the loss of sovereignty, Japan was afforded little to no legal recourse in cases of sexual violence. This fostered widespread resignation to the perceived threat of sexual violence and incited appreciation for the need of sex workers who supposedly "sacrifice themselves for ordinary women."[58] Economic extraterritoriality provided the structural conditions for a booming sex industry around the U.S. military bases that made significant contributions to the economy. As a banker remarked in a speech on the economy of Sasebo, a major U.S. military base town in Nagasaki Prefecture: "We shouldn't despise the streetwalkers, we should thank them. According to my calculation, they earn approximately $1,000,000. This money circulates according to the dictates of economic principle and serves the people of Sasebo."[59] Not only did women earn money through the various forms of fraternization, but the entertainment establishments and housing areas that accompanied the sex trade created a local economy centered either directly or indirectly on it.

However, we get a fuller sense of what is implicated by extraterritorial miscegenation in other parts of the texts. Regarding political and economic extraterritoriality, reportage assumes a set form: It provides information to buttress the repetitious political slogan of sovereignty violated. However, it switches form when suggesting that the effects of extraterritorial miscegenation are detrimental to the reproduction of Japanese society. The social fabric of Japan, as a purported patriarchal monoethnic state, starts to unravel as it loses its ability to mobilize its own children into the postwar national effort. Hence, many works such as *Children of the U.S. Military Bases* draw heavily on quotations, essays, or poems from children because they argue that "youthful eyes are able to keenly see through the problem."[60] The narrative structure of unmediated language that speaks truth to power allows the reader to directly wrestle with the contradictions the children face, to feel the weight of innocent yet refreshingly clear criticism of the U.S. military, and also to decry an ominous Japanese future.

For example, a second-grade elementary school girl from Yokosuka states she "wants to become" a streetwalker because they "always appear fashionable" and "get a lot of money and chocolate from the Americans."[61] However, a male high school student has different feelings when he sees a "streetwalker breastfeeding her baby, and then moves on to call on clients as her husband walks away nonchalantly with the baby on his back." For him, she encapsulates "contempt and pity, poverty and the problem of evil, and contradictions within society."[62] In any case, the streetwalker is so ubiquitous that children "play around, pretending to be *panpan* and pretending to kiss."[63] One sixth-grade elementary school girl from Sasebo thinks this inappropriate role play is the "*panpan*'s fault" and states that "it would be nice if they would just hurry up and go away."[64] Another third-grade elementary school boy from Yokosuka writes that the woman who rents from his house "creates huge disturbances" with the soldiers, causing him to get "so upset" that he "can't study anymore."[65] Whether out on the streets, at home, or at school, these children impart a sense of urgency in an imagined community of parental readers to improve the social conditions in which they come of age. It is consistent with other media portrayals in which, as Kovner notes, the *panpan* is presented as a "threat to the nation and its children."[66]

Finally, the purported racial contamination of the Japanese population is depicted as the final frontier in a long line of violations. A sixth-grade elementary school girl from Tottori Prefecture writes:

> We have two of them [*panpan*] at our house. Two of my classmates come from homes that rent out to them as well. The mixed-race children who are born between the *panpan* and soldiers go to daycare with my younger brother and younger sister. These are the characteristics that define our village.
>
> Next year, these mixed-race children will enter elementary school. . . . I don't remember the exact number, but it is something like 2,000. I can't believe we will be studying alongside this large number of mixed-race children in the same school.[67]

Through the logic of substitution, these mixed-race children are a stand-in for their parents' controversial relationship and are not seen as deserving of the same rights to participate in society, starting with the right to an education. A life beyond the conditions of their birth is foreclosed in the future.

One middle school boy from Yokohama writes that the "8 million yen" G.I.s leave behind each month during their R & R from the Korean War is good for an impoverished Japan, but "the [mixed-race] humans they leave behind are not appreciated."[68] Even in her sympathy, a middle school girl from Aomori Prefecture reifies the assumption of racial purity by lamenting the tainting of blood flowing through the veins of young Japanese women.

When the U.S. military exercises are done
children are given gum and pocket money, and [the G.I.s] seek
    out the dwellings of young women.
As [one] wonders if this is okay,
blood is tainted
and [a woman] is made to have a baby.
How pitiful that baby.[69]

An essay written by a middle school boy from Aomori Prefecture speaks of the other side of such sympathy by depicting mixed-race children as un-welcome intruders in the population that should be contained.

If the status quo continues, then I worry that all of Japan will be over-taken by mixed-race children within the next few years. American G.I.s and the *panpan* will turn the present Japanese race into an American-Japanese hybrid . . .

If mixed-race children continue to be born, and if American culture is integrated [into Japan] without careful thought, then I suppose that the unique Japanese culture handed down to us from our ancestors will disappear. We need to protect Japanese history and Japan's unique beautiful culture.[70]

Here the child evokes an ancestral Japanese culture encroached upon by the "American G.I.s" in a similar way that the Japanists evoked a primitive culture encroached upon by "Western enlightenment." Furthermore, the implication of the disappearance of Japan's racial purity and the erosion of its native cultural forms replicates Takada Nahoko's linkage of the "oc-cupation baby" to the atomic bomb described in the Introduction. If it seems that the claim is duplicated, it is: Takada had in fact referred to re-portage on prostitution in her statement. The intertextuality between re-portage and political speech speaks to the authority this genre of writing carried in the formation of policy in Japan.

Yet, at the same time, the child suggests that the problem of extrater-ritorial miscegenation is not only about the violation of sovereignty from above, but the way it interferes with cultural production from below: "We need to protect Japanese history and Japan's unique beautiful culture." The child hits on a critical theoretical slippage. Is the streetwalker vic-timized by the top-down violence of American imperialism, or is she so-cially excluded by the bottom-up violence of an emerging working class that seeks repossession of the sovereignty to collectively manage the re-production of its own labor power? Just as Tosaka showed how the threat of the private prostitute to the family system was symbolic of Japan's victimization to "Western enlightenment," the threat of the streetwalker to families attempting to recover from the war was symbolic of postwar Japan's victimization to the U.S. military. By reporting the "fact" of miscegenation in reportage—as opposed to depicting it in fiction—the degradation of the Japanese family was allowed to most directly substitute for the victimization of the Japanese state. In short, postwar anti-base reportage was deeply invested in reporting the *fact* of oppression as part of a cultural project that sought to turn the postwar *fiction* of a patriarchal monoethnic Japanese state into a reality.

The Proletarian Arts

Although miscegenation was certainly portrayed in works of fiction,[71] the topic loomed undeniably large in reportage. What was it about the figure of the streetwalker that took so readily to this genre?

Historically, reportage has roots in the proletarian arts movement in Japan. Shortly after writers in Europe such as Egon Erwin Kisch called for a proletarian art based on documentary in the mid-1920s, Japanese report literature (*hōkoku bungaku*) and documentary literature (*kiroku bungaku*) emerged. According to Kurahara Korehito, one of the leading communist literary theorists of the time, the purpose of this genre in Japan was to empower the masses to take literature into its own hands as its creators and compare their experiences of struggle with one another. All this was to be accomplished through the imperative to "accurately document revolutionary reality."[72] But how was it possible to determine exactly what this "reality" was?

Debates on literary realism were integral to the development of proletarian realism by members of the Federation of Japanese Proletarian Artists (herein referred to as "NAPF") that formed in 1928 and dissolved in 1934. A prominent member of NAPF, Aono Suekichi, points out that the documentation of everyday reality is nothing new to Japanese literature, as it had been a characteristic of naturalism at the turn of the century. However, whereas the "artistic objective of the theory of naturalism is the reproduction or copying of reality" as it appears in a static moment, proletarian realism understands the temporality of reality as pregnant with potentiality toward the future.[73] Specifically, writers must document with a "purposive consciousness" (*mokuteki ishiki*) from the standpoint of the future of "proletarian class struggle."[74]

This development of a class, as opposed to individual consciousness, is central for Kurahara as well. Determining which fragments of everyday life to document should not be determined by individual consciousness as stressed in naturalism, but from the standpoint of a collective class consciousness. He argues that the "human" cultivated in the arts here is not a generalized abstraction, but a "total 'human' of the proletariat that only emerges through class struggle."[75]

Here we can detect the influence of Georg Lukács. He is important because he illustrates how the cultivation of the "total 'human' of the proletariat" plays out in a distinction between reportage and realist literature. Lukács calls for the formation of class consciousness of the proletariat as the only thing that "can point to the way that leads out of the impasse of capitalism."[76] Specifically, he argues that the "worker can only become conscious of his existence in society when he becomes aware of himself as a commodity."[77] Hence, for Lukács, as well as the proletarian realists, the role of literature is to de-reify reality by revealing the driving forces of history invisible to consciousness. On this point—of presenting the particularity of the fact in reference to the totality of class relations— the proletarian realists in Japan and Lukács agree that reportage can share much with realist literature.

Anti-base reportage is no exception in its affinity with proletarian realism. Reports compiled from across the country work to overcome regional difference and foster not prewar "class," but now postwar "national" consciousness. The voices transpire as innocent and, at times, contradictory; yet this tension is presented as the growing pains in the developmental process of becoming, and does not undermine its overall ideological message. Finally, reportage cannot be more specific in revealing the stakes of Japan's biopolitical future, because much of the genre is told through the voice of children or describes the effects U.S. militarism had on their lives. The reproduction of labor power was a national crisis to be shared with individuals across Japan.

However, the impasse between the two genres, one based on fact and the other fiction, is encountered in the "*way* that facts and their interconnections are combined, i.e., the particular and the general, the individual and the typical, the accidental and the necessary."[78] In "Reportage or Portrayal?" Lukács charges that reporting the facts alone results in the "unportrayed subjectivity of the author" who attempts to "convince by reason alone"[79] through a "(scientific) reproduction of reality."[80] In other words, it is lacking in the "dialectical interaction" between a purportedly

objective reality and subjective consciousness that literature can more effectively cultivate. The "proletarian revolutionary writer," on the other
hand, "always has in mind the driving forces of the overall process"[81] and
constantly seeks to uncover the totality of class relations. The people must
be led by ideals established by the intelligentsia.

Kurahara criticized report or documentary literature on similar grounds.
He wrote that writers who merely record the facts cannot adequately "serve
as educators of the masses."[82] He argues that while it is impossible to sum-
marize (*gaikatsu*) a human belonging to a different class, occupation, age,
sex, and so on, it is possible to create an "artistic type" amongst writers of
those various categories.[83] This "type" does not simply record things as
they are, but in the "process of its germination."[84] In the case of both writers, reality is not something that is grasped in the moment, but something
that retroactively comes true through the process of positing its totality
in a future yet to come.

It is in this context that Lukács writes of a definitive difference between
the two genres with respect to the lumpenproletariat. For him, the appearance of the lumpenproletariat in reportage detracts from the ability to
grasp the totality of the social process and instead only myopically focuses
on the tragedy of state violence as a singular event.

> Firstly, the exposure of the bourgeoisie's repressive apparatus, which is
> made with good revolutionary intent, is given a false emphasis
> politically. It appears all-powerful and invincible. What is missing is
> the struggle and resistance of the working class. The proletariat is
> depicted as the impotent object of the judicial system. Indeed, in most
> cases what we see are not genuine representatives of the class, but
> rather characters who have already been worn down and had the life
> beaten out of them, people incapable of resistance who have fallen into
> the lumpenproletariat. Even where workers in struggle do become the
> object of the judicial machinery (e.g. the Cheka trial in Leipzig), they
> are still mere objects of the system, and their class-conscious and
> combative attitude cannot find effective expression.[85]

Reading anti-base reportage against this passage, we can see that its characters are "depicted as the impotent object of the judicial system," or more
specifically, the impotent object of international law as nationals belonging to a dependent state subservient to the United States. Here, the state
is one that works in service of capital by exhausting the "people" to the
point where they are "incapable of resistance" and fall "into the lumpen-

proletariat." By focusing on such "impotent objects," reportage "gives false emphasis politically" because its singularity is disconnected from the totality of class struggle.

Rather, Lukács implies that it is only by positing the fictional totality of a revolutionary future that the worker can escape the fetish of reality assumed by reportage and embrace a more authentic consciousness in which he or she becomes an empowered subject—not "impotent object"— of struggle. He points to the formation of a different kind of sovereignty through artistic production: the ability to translate the specificity of the fact into the fictional totality of class struggle as a condition of the formation of a working class.

When considered in this context, then, anti-base reportage suggests a complementary combination of both elements. While Lukács was interested in going beyond exposing the "bourgeoisie's repressive apparatus" as "all-powerful" by pursuing revolutionary struggle with the working class, anti-base reportage remained fixated on showing the "all-powerful" victimization of the Japanese state to the U.S. military. It followed the JCP two-stage program in which Japan must first overcome U.S. imperialism that infringes upon its sovereignty in order to subsequently approach the problem of class struggle within Japan. In this sense, the streetwalker as lumpenproletariat subject was instrumental in staging Japan as an "impotent object." At the same time, its all-inclusive scope of not only problematizing the lumpenproletariat, but doing so through the voice of children, allowed for a substitution of the family for the state: The dire future of the Japanese family was equated to the dire future of the Japanese state. Here, the idealism of mythological time of what Tosaka called "restorationism" snuck in past the materialism of historical time. In other words, by protesting the sexual predations of the U.S. military on Japanese women, many essentialist claims about the existence of "Japanese culture" as a transhistorical ethnic substratum emerged in the process. In this context, the sex worker as the lumpenproletariat could only exist as a threat to the formation of a biopolitical state or object in need of rescue. The assumption of her violation by an external foreign entity produced the inner space of "Japanese culture," which took as its primary concern the inability to properly reproduce itself according to norms of patriarchal monoethnicity.[86] These norms, in turn, were integral to the formation of a Japanese middle class. And as was the case in interwar Japan, the formation of the middle class was not divorced from the politics of population management in Okinawa.

Securing Okinawa for Miscegenation

As the authors of the various anti-base reportage texts show with convincing detail, the United States is indeed guilty of compromising Japanese sovereignty at certain historical junctures. This is not my dispute. Rather, my point is that it is one moment in a larger historical development of biopolitics in which Foucault traced the emergence of an overlapping but irreducible economic register that "steals away from the juridical form of . . . sovereignty."[87] This is a sovereignty that makes state interventions into the population from above, but more so, it is shaped from below by the people who have come to govern themselves internally according to reason of the market. Although the overwhelming tendency in contemporary Okinawan studies is to lodge Okinawa as the unfortunate scapegoat of Japan's subservience to the United States, a growing number of people from the grassroots to academe have been articulating the ongoing effects of Japanese colonialism, manifest in its overwhelming concentration of U.S. military bases in Okinawa, as an everyday practice of racism in Japan.

Two contemporary scholars of Okinawa, Gavan McCormack and Nomura Kōya, represent aspects of these positions respectively. McCormack, who popularized the client state thesis in the context of Japanese studies,[88] suggests that Japan has been subject to the rule of the Liberal Democratic Party (LDP), which is backed by bureaucratic elites and disconnected from the "popular, grassroots, democratic movement."[89]

By contrast, Nomura argues that Japanese democracy, perfectly compatible with colonialism, is responsible for the Japanese state's disproportionate concentration of U.S. military bases in Okinawa. He writes:

> What is not so easily understood are the "progressive" or "conscientious" Japanese. They have the nerve to say, "All Japanese nationals should be equal." If that is the case, then shouldn't we expect they equally bear the burden of the U.S. military bases? I often hear voices that declare, "I oppose U.S. military bases in Japan! I oppose the U.S.-Japan Security Treaty!" While they have carried on repeating this phrase, sixty years of sticking Okinawans with bases have gone by, and even more years will probably go by in the future. How will they take responsibility for having forced bases onto Okinawans for so long? Do they propose to have Okinawans put up with them for the eternal and everlasting? Moreover, do not all Japanese, whether they support or oppose the U.S.-Japan Security Treaty, enjoy the benefits of not having to bear the burden of military bases?[90]

Here, Nomura critiques what he calls "democratic colonialism." Over and above criticism of U.S. imperialism, he draws attention to the fact that a majority of the Japanese population not only supports the U.S.-Japan Security Treaty, but the Japanese electorate has voted for an administration that keeps U.S. military bases concentrated in Okinawa. This in itself is not incongruous with McCormack's client state thesis. The difference, rather, is whereas McCormack emphasizes the servility of Japanese politicians and bureaucrats to the United States at the top, Nomura focuses more on how the Japanese people engage in the democratic process from below. Interestingly, both argue for a more faithful rendering of popular sovereignty in Japan. McCormack suggests that the international community should respect the popular sovereignty of the Okinawan people who oppose bases.[91] Nomura thinks that Japan should respect the popular sovereignty of its own people, or in other words, if the Japanese electorate has voted to support the U.S.-Japan Security Treaty,[92] then it should follow through its own democratic process to a tee and equally distribute U.S. military bases throughout the state of Japan instead of concentrate them predominantly in Okinawa. In short, Nomura picked up the argument for *kengai isetsu* developed by Okinawan women at the grassroots.[93] "*Kengai isetsu*," literally meaning "move [bases to a location] outside the prefecture," is an argument that calls for equal distribution of U.S. military bases throughout the Japanese state (inclusive of Okinawa) as a separate issue from support or opposition to the U.S.-Japan Security Treaty.

Needless to say, the appearance of Nomura's book in 2005 was not well received. His Fanonian-style language was certainly shocking to Japanese intellectuals and activists concerned with the so-called question of Okinawan. After all, as we shall see in subsequent chapters, Okinawa had become the holy grail of progressive Japanese politics by the reversion era. Yet it was not simply his fiery tone that ruffled feathers, but the fact that he had hit on the nature of the postcolonial problem manifest in Okinawa as Japanese fascism formed through the democratic process from below. This is what he meant by "democratic colonialism." Instead of pinning Okinawa's dream for equality on toppling an intangible beast who rules from the bureaucratic heavens above, he affirmatively took Okinawa's failure to achieve the Japanese dream of equality and allowed it to work for itself by rotting in the belly of the beast. He did not turn away from the Japanese state in pursuit of another ideal, but he persisted in the here and now by turning toward the state in order to allow its own contradictions to antagonize itself. That is to say, he worked to antagonize the state from the inside instead of appeal to an ideal to criticize it from the outside. As a result, he unmasked Japanese liberalism with the unexpected demand to make good on its promise.

Despite the controversial reception of Nomura's book, what was said could not be unsaid. Okinawa's Pandora's box had been opened. Although it is unlikely he had read Nomura, Hatoyama Yukio, just four years later in 2009, legitimized the argument for *kengai isetsu* in his historic bid for prime minister from the opposing Democratic Party of Japan (DPJ), where support from the Okinawan voting district was crucial.[94] It took a Japanese prime minister to legitimize what a handful of Okinawan women from the grassroots and a marginalized Okinawan sociologist had been saying all along. Soon *kengai isetsu* had become *the* political platform in Okinawa, at a time when opinion polls confirmed overwhelming disapproval of the construction of new U.S. military facilities in northern Okinawa. In this political climate, Okinawan journalists such as Yara Tomohiro started to uncover the hitherto unquestioned history that led up to the disproportionate concentration of U.S. military bases in Okinawa. It is this history, told below, that stitches together anti-base reportage, the effects of the subsequent anti-base movements that raged throughout Japan in the late 1950s, and the destination for mainland Japan's unwanted U.S. military bases and its accompanying miscegenation: Okinawa.

After the war ended, the occupying Allied powers moved into approximately 100,200 of the 741,300 acres of land formerly occupied by the Japanese military. Then, after Japan gained independence in 1952, the Allied powers confiscated an additional 234,000 acres of land with the aim of expanding their operations during the Korean War.[95] In opposition to these additional land confiscations, and combined with the ability to freely criticize the United States after the end of occupation, the anti-base movement quickly gained momentum.

The first spark flew from the proposed confiscation of land in the fishing village of Uchinaba (Ishikawa Prefecture) in 1952. Popular protest led by directly impacted locals inspired other areas facing land confiscation such as Asamayama (Nagano Prefecture) and Myōgiyama (Gunma Prefecture). Not only did Uchinaba locals succeed in having the land returned to the people in 1957, but demonstrators in Asamayama and Myōgiyama ended in total victory as the U.S. and Japanese governments abandoned plans for land confiscation entirely.

In May 1954, the United States requested land confiscation for the expansion of Air Force operations in the additional five locations of Tachikawa (Tokyo), Yokota (Tokyo), Kisarazu (Chiba Prefecture), Niigata (Niigata Prefecture), and Itami (Osaka). Itami was later changed to Komaki (Aichi

Prefecture). Kisarazu was returned to the Japanese Self Defense Forces in 1958, and Niigata and Komaki were returned to the people in 1958.[96] The anti-base struggle in Tachikawa made history when seven protesters were prosecuted for illegally entering the base.[97] Nonetheless, operations in Tachikawa effectively ended in 1969, and it was returned entirely in 1977. One of the only locations that did not end in failure for the United States was Yokota.

The overwhelming success of the anti-base movement in preventing new land confiscations put pressure on locations with existing military bases. That is, "'If new locations are met with protest," then areas such as Camp Fuji, already rife with base culture, "felt the pinch" to take on the burden.[98] Although there was protest in base towns that had sprung up immediately after the war, Camp Fuji was plagued more intensely with division and contradiction than other areas facing new land confiscation. This is why Shimizu Ikutarō, an editor of the aforementioned *Children of the U.S. Military Bases*, stated that "Uchinaba is still a pure virgin" as compared to areas that were already made into "sluts (*abazure onna*) who parasitically live off the U.S. military."[99] On the one hand, protest was turned into spectacle when an elderly local woman threw her body in front of a gun at a Camp Fuji firing range.[100] On the other hand, "places that bring in large revenue from renting out rooms to prostitutes" around Camp Fuji were reported to "welcome many G.I.s even while they worry about the effects of public morals on the children."[101] Approximately 10 million yen was brought in monthly from businesses catering to G.I.s, and after they left in 1956, the village was only able to collect 10 of 20 million yen in taxes biannually.[102]

Yet even with the gulf between "resisting subjects" who reject U.S. military bases unconditionally and "petitioning subjects" (discussed in Chapter 3) who implicitly accept them given the right conditions, the anti-base movement was still largely successful. To its advantage, it coincided with restructuring within the U.S. military after an armistice was signed in 1953 to bring fighting to an end in the Korean War. Under the leadership of Dwight D. Eisenhower, a president who went on to warn the United States of the "military-industrial complex," the Department of Defense was pressured to streamline its budget. It responded with a greater reliance on nuclear weapons which allowed for troop reductions in the army, along with pressure on its allies to prop up their own defense forces. Left behind were the marines that would provide backup support in the event of a sudden security threat in the still volatile Korean Peninsula. But not for long. The marines in Fuji and Gifu were transferred to Okinawa in 1956, despite strong protest already raging throughout the island, as will be examined in Chapter 3.[103]

By this time, the United States had become increasingly wary of growing anti-military sentiment in Japan. Yoshida, the sole Japanese signatory of the U.S.-Japan Security Treaty, lost power to the incoming prime minister, Hatoyama Ichirō, in 1954, who succeeded in restoring relations with the Soviet Union and improving relations with China, much to the apprehension of the United States. Not only were leftists gaining force through the anti-base movement, but their choice rhetorical maneuver of condemning extraterritorial miscegenation had now also become adopted by Japanese ultraconservatives. For example, future prime minister Nakasone Yasuhiro declared the following in the Diet in 1954:

> Is handing over a Japan to our children and grandchildren that is stationed with a foreign military, overtaken by hundreds of military bases, and overrun by mixed-race children and *panpan*, something we can afford to be patient about?[104]

The United States became increasingly concerned whether Japan could secure "overseas markets and domestic economic policy" if the conservative base essential to the U.S.-Japan partnership crumbled.[105] The further concentration of U.S. military bases in Okinawa—this time the marines—provided a convenient solution to this conundrum.

Yet it is not as if the United States never considered other options besides Okinawa. Even though the United States Department of Defense was considering moving the U.S. Army 1st Calvary Division and a marine unit to Guam, it quickly switched to the more expedient Okinawa in 1957 by order of President Eisenhower, who came to an agreement with Prime Minister Kishi Nobusuke. The newly elected Kishi was under popular pressure to eradicate U.S. military bases because of public outrage over the murder of a Japanese woman by an American soldier that year, known as the Girard Incident.[106]

The problem that the United States ran up against in postwar Japan was that complaints of the erosion of political sovereignty, voiced forcefully through the trope of extraterritorial miscegenation, threatened its ability to secure Japan as a key economic partner in the Pacific essential to the United States. Unlike the U.S. occupation of Iraq after 2003, when the shameless lust for neoliberal capitalist pillage rendered concerns about Iraq's sovereignty little more than a careless afterthought, the United States was literally invested in the maintenance of Japanese democracy.

From 1954 to 1960, the number of U.S. troops in Japan dwindled from about 180,000 to 46,000. The area occupied by U.S. military facilities shrank from approximately 334,100 acres in 1952 to approximately 82,800 acres in 1960, or approximately one-quarter of its original size.[107] While the U.S. military diminished its presence, the Japanese economy continued to boom. Productive capacity recovered to its prewar level by 1955.[108] In 1960, Prime Minister Ikeda Hayato—the former director of the Finance Ministry's tax bureau mentioned earlier who approved the 100 million-yen budget for the RAA in 1945—announced his "income-doubling plan" and realized Japan's economic miracle.

Japan was able to enjoy economic prosperity with a significantly reduced burden of U.S. military bases. Japanese sovereignty largely protected the population from the adverse effects of its postwar institutional arrangement facilitated by the U.S.-Japan Security Treaty. Although South Korea initiated an adoption campaign to neutralize its mixed-race problem that went on to flourish in the 1960s, no such campaign made headway in Japan, with only a handful of mixed-race children being adopted out to the United States by 1956.[109] On the one hand, the United States had certainly cultivated a white man's burden ideology under the guise of humanitarianism by the 1960s that facilitated transnational adoption. But on the other hand, in Japan, the mixed-race issue was largely contained as a social problem in the late 1950s with the help of the anti-base victory and widespread economic prosperity, thereby allowing it to continue to promote a policy of assimilation into mainstream Japanese society, which had been recommended by Colonel Crawford Sams, the chief of the Public Health and Welfare Section of SCAP since 1948.[110] In short, Japan secured itself *from* miscegenation by securing Okinawa *for* miscegenation.

CHAPTER 2

Okinawa, 1945–1952: Allegories of Becoming

In contrast to the symbolic structure of Japan's victimization depicted in Chapter 1, this chapter positions Okinawa in terms of an allegorical structure of becoming. What this means, in advance, is that although Okinawans have historically tried to "become Japanese," they have chronically failed to do so. While even the "Japanese" ultimately fail in the impossible quest for authenticity, this chapter is concerned with a more specific kind of failure: the capability of cultivating an Okinawan middle class that internalized the need to organize labor power in service to the state. Allegory, as described by Benjamin, is an antidote for symbol; it is that which interrupts the idealism implied by the promise of sovereign power. Allegory is that which fails, and as such, this chapter reads the struggle to internalize the interests of the Japanese state in the immediate postwar allegorically.[1]

This chapter starts with a brief prehistory to the biopolitics behind Okinawa's failure. In the prewar years, Okinawa was treated as an exception to the biopolitical order as neither a Japanese colony nor an equal part of the Japanese state. This exceptionalism continued into the postwar years as Okinawa was again treated as neither a U.S. military colony nor an equal part of the Japanese state. Though the U.S. military, as the machinery for a new form of empire, was certainly vested in reinserting Okinawa into capitalist relations, its economic recovery and development were subordinated to its utility as a U.S. military fortress that allowed for the reemergence of mainland Japan as the regional economic leader. Yet, while this meant that Okinawa was subject to less institutional intervention aimed at improving the economy, it also meant that it was richer in an alegal life force concerned with survival in the here and now.

This chapter traces the establishment of the postwar sex industry amidst these exceptional conditions. Different from biopolitical concerns of preserving a newly imagined monoethnic state in mainland Japan, the formation of the sex industry in postwar Okinawa was ominously informed by the fear of continued exclusion from the biopolitical order. I read this fear in terms of the ambivalent structure of becoming that inspired an instrumental obedience to the legal order. In other words, Okinawans danced precariously on the razor's edge of fear in which they could fall just as easily on the side of anarchistic insurgency as they could on the side of fascistic collaboration.

Yet the purpose of this chapter is not to pass judgment on minority subjects who "resisted" or "collaborated." Rather, in line with an allegorical reading, it is to suspend the structure of judgment altogether. Allegory, as opposed to symbol, is not grounded in the exclusionary force of the decision, but seeks to exaggerate the sovereign failure to decide and embrace the motion of liminality. I argue that it was the alegal life force implied by this liminality that the U.S. military aimed to contain by integrating Okinawans into the legal order as "petitioning subjects." That is, far from coercing Okinawans into sexual slavery, the U.S. military imposed economic sanctions on the base towns in the form of off-limits orders if they could not manage the spread of VD. This set them up to be subjects who petition the U.S. military for their "right" to conduct business with the U.S. military. What the U.S. military had to gain was not only allowing Okinawans to assume the burden of managing the spread of VD, but more important, the ability to manage self-determining subjects who recognized the legal order of occupation.

A Biopolitical Prehistory

In order to understand Okinawa's precarious position within the postwar Japanese biopolitical state, it is necessary to go back to the prewar period. In thinking about "a birthplace of biopolitics"[2] in the larger context of Japanese empire, Katsuhiko Endo and Tomiyama Ichirō[3] have both paid special attention to theorizations on the "regional economic sphere" (*kōiki keizai-ken*) that first emerged in the early 1940s in the context of the Greater East Asia Co-Prosperity Sphere. As witness to the 1920 collapse in the global sugar industry, Uno Kōzō, in particular, saw possibility in the regional economic sphere as a way that Japanese empire could shield itself from the unpredictability of the free market. This required a radically different relationship between the metropole and the colonies. In this regard he wrote, "the colonies must also be developed as a member of the regional economic bloc" according to the "standards of domestic relations" and "must not be developed with the aim of producing commodities for the global market in which colonial economies are sacrificed."[4] In short, he envisioned the integration of the colonial economies into the national economy as a dynamic regionalism that could offset local imbalances through some sort of overarching monitoring rationality that he had yet to identify.

For Uno, the regional economic bloc was very much a project in the making. However, as Tomiyama notes, it had an underside as it developed out of the 1920s that Uno neglected to mention: Okinawa. Wendy Matsumura recuperates its position in Uno's essay by showing how the "state wanted Taiwan, not Okinawa, to take the lead in making Japan self-sufficient in sugar" because it was easier to enforce "coercive policies" in the colony where it would have been "too burdensome" in Okinawa.[5] What this means is that the sugar industry was developed in the Japanese colony of Taiwan (and as Tomiyama adds, the Japanese mandated territory of the South Sea Islands)[6] while it was allowed to collapse in the Japanese national territory of Okinawa Prefecture as part of a calculation for overall regional economic success.

Yet, at the same time, even though Okinawa was not "colonial" enough to coerce into submission to state-implemented policies, it was also not "national" (Japanese) enough to be privy to state-implemented policies that aimed to solve the agrarian crisis domestically. As Tomiyama writes, "different from other agrarian areas" within the Japanese state, Okinawa was not subject to spending policies to "stave off the [formation of a] surplus population."[7] He continues:

> . . . Okinawa did not form a circuit in which its agrarian villages could be mediated by the maintenance and organization of the surplus population. Therefore, the agrarian surplus population was not so much an industrial labor reserve that could be drawn from or deposited into, but it consequentially had to take on the characteristic of being a surplus population that flowed out unidirectionally.[8]

In the absence of this "circuit" or "mediation" in Okinawan agrarian villages (i.e., in the absence of institutional frameworks of a biopolitical state), the surplus population had little staying power and flooded mainland industrial centers such as Osaka in the 1920s, where migrant workers met widespread discrimination. These workers were seen as "'unsanitary,' 'insane,' 'lazy,' and 'uncivilized,'" and their labor power was valued less on the market. Through a "lifestyle improvement movement" (*seikatsu kaizen undō*), they aimed to rid themselves of their ethnic markers in hopes of attaining a better life.[9] Tomiyama writes, "everyday acts from the bodily act of chatting in the Okinawan language, to ways of cooking and child-rearing became surveilled as the basis for the determination of labor power."[10] Important here is that the codification of labor power was not dictated by the state, but that it was the "prerogative of the swarming sovereigns within the population."[11] This meant that not only mainland Japanese, but also Okinawans themselves, surveilled other Okinawans to the point where they often attempted to conceal their ethnicity. In this way, the alegality of Okinawa's labor power as a force of life that was not "mediated" by "management or organization" was translated or codified into ethnic markers in the most intimate spheres of everyday life.

Treating Okinawa differently from colonial territories, such as Taiwan and the South Sea Islands, and its workers differently from both farmers and industrial workers in mainland Japan, moreover, led to a Japanese government–implemented system of aid and relief that acted as a sort of patch on Okinawa's alegality floating in an ambiguous space between both.[12] The Okinawa Relief Bill that passed through the House of Representatives in 1925 was the prototype for the "Okinawan promotion and development regime" institutionalized as the Okinawa General Bureau and housed within the Japanese government today, as discussed in Chapter 5. At the time, it functioned to have a community that was excluded from the biopolitical order—and hence fraught with the possibility of rebellion— come before the law as "Japanese national subjects" to ask for economic assistance in order to survive hardship that it was often blamed for creating.[13]

These historical conditions informed the experience of the Battle of Okinawa and its postwar aftermath of military occupation. The constant fear of being excluded from the biopolitical order spurred the endeavor to "become Japanese" not only in the workplace, but also on the battlefield. Take, for example, the following excerpt from a letter sent by an Okinawan soldier fighting for the Japanese Imperial Army in Papua New Guinea to his son on his birthday.

On the dawn of victory in the Greater East Asia War, we Okinawans as humans will be treated equal to the Japanese. Hence, if we too win this battle, we can go to Japan and live[14] a peaceful life with our families.[15]

It is significant that the soldier uses the same word "live" or *seikatsu* that was the object of the "movement to improve life" amongst Okinawan workers in the 1920s. His experience of discrimination within the Japanese state presses him to victory in the hopes of attaining a better life, thereby encapsulating what Naoki Sakai calls "imperial nationalism"[16] amongst ethnic minority subjects in empire.

In contrast to the symbolic structure of Japanism, I read this structure of becoming Japanese allegorically. The key difference between the symbolic structure of Japanism that asserts communion with the state and the allegorical structure of becoming Japanese that betrays the failure of such communion is in their respective relationship to transcendence. Modern-day allegory is commonly associated with fables in which animal characters convey a moral to a story. Important, here, is the visual aspect of allegory and the relative proximity (as opposed to symbolic distance) of the sign that is substituted for the referent. A fox is a stand-in for a cunning individual because a fox is a cunning animal. What you see is relatively close to what you get. Benjamin himself introduced allegory through ideographs such as hieroglyphs, but more importantly, rebuses or emblems used in baroque *Trauerspiele* or tragedy plays. As he states, "the written word tends toward the visual"[17] and interrupts phonetic orthography. With the use of alphabetic writing systems, however, what you see is not what you get, but language signifies through the transcendental structure of symbol. In contrast to the proximity between sign and referent in allegory, the distance between sign and referent in symbol is sutured by faith in an extralinguistic (transcendental) power.[18] In other words, the alphabetic script does not immediately correspond to the thing it signifies but is predicated on our faith in the system of signification to give it meaning. Allegory, then, is the re-emergence of a potentiality of language not anchored to faith in a transcendental power that gives it meaning, but a more direct and immediate form of signification that grounds its own meaning in what it already is (versus what it promises to become), however imperfect that may be. In other words, because the sign is relatively close to the referent, it constantly thwarts the appeal toward a transcendental power to suture the gap.

In the absence of this suturing power, we are left with a multiplicity of signs or images that say little other than what they already are. This leads to the crisis of not being able to organize multiplicity into a unified narrative. Benjamin writes:

> As those who lose their footing turn somersaults in their fall, so would the allegorical intention fall from emblem to emblem into the dizziness of its bottomless depths. . . . [19]

Here, Benjamin points to those foreclosed from access to the heavens who "turn somersaults in their fall." The "fall from emblem to emblem" is dizzying because there is no stable ground to bring them together in unity.

Reading the failure to become Japanese allegorically does not assume a transcendental power that gives meaning to Okinawan life; it displaces the seat of judgment in which Okinawans are evaluated according to their faith in this ideal as collaborators or insurgents. Instead, as we shall see in the next section, we can only track the dizzying movement from one subject position to another as the "allegorical intention" to ground the meaning of life by virtue of what it already is and not what it promises to become. The intentionality here is not that of a self-determining subject that opposes sovereignty from a position of externality, but the intentionality of movement that disarticulates the bordering effects of sovereign power.

The Specter of the "Comfort Woman"

The Battle of Okinawa and its aftermath is not a story of Okinawa being violently thrown outside of sovereign power. It is a story of suspending Okinawa in a liminal space that is ambiguously legal and extralegal at the same time, exposing it to the lawmaking violence of sexual assault, and then interpreting the Okinawan fear of this violence as the desire to be repatriated back into the law.

Fighting in the war itself did not polarize the friend/enemy distinction characteristic of Schmitt's constitution of a field of political homogeneity that establishes the ground for conflict.[20] Quite the contrary, it was not clear whose side Okinawans were on. Okinawa was officially a part of Japan. Yet it became the only site within the state encroached by land battle that was designed to hold off infiltration into the mainland where the emperor resided, thus warranting it the name "disposable castaway stone" (*sute ishi*). As a result, over one-quarter of the island's population was lost, and approximately 90 percent of the homes and buildings were destroyed.[21] Okinawans, particularly those indoctrinated with the ideology of imperialized education (*kōminka kyōiku*) that emphasized loyalty to the emperor, were torn between the paralyzing fear of the "American beasts" they were told would ruthlessly rape women, and the Japanese imperial forces that killed Okinawans as "spies" for speaking in their native tongue. This constant state of ambiguity, punctuated by the omnipresent clarity of violence, was intensified by a mix of Korean and Taiwanese colonials mobilized into the imperial Japanese war effort. In addition to the soldiers, these included "comfort women." Okinawa, again the exception, was the only area within the state of Japan that housed "comfort stations" for the imperial forces. In respect to the "comfort stations," Okinawa was neither an "outer territory" (*gaichi*) of the official colonies nor an "inner territory" (*naichi*) of the Japanese metropole; rather, it was a "semi-outer territory" (*jungaichi*) in between both.

As briefly mentioned in Chapter 1, the "comfort woman" system was instituted by the Japanese imperial forces after the atrocities of the 1937 Nanjing Massacre. An estimated two hundred thousand women from the corners of Japanese empire were confined to "comfort stations" in areas where the Japanese Imperial Army engaged in combat. Approximately 130 of these "comfort stations" were set up during the Battle of Okinawa, purportedly to deter the rape of Okinawan women by imperial Japanese soldiers and encourage the Okinawan population to commit to the war effort against the invading Allied forces.[22] However, this confusing setup only muddied already murky waters as many Okinawans questioned the designation of "semi-outer territory" against the historical backdrop of its second-class status within the state of Japan.

In *"Comfort Stations" as Remembered by Okinawans During World War II*, Yunshin Hong puts her finger on the pulse of liminality that ran through the confluence of various colonial subject positions such as the "comfort woman" and Okinawan civilians during the Battle of Okinawa. Theoretically, she traces this liminality through a genealogical reading of Foucault's "race war." Particularly in his 1975–1976 *Society Must Be Defended* lectures given at the Collège de France, Foucault articulated the conjunctural emergence of race and sovereignty: Race war functions to homogenize the multiplicity within each warring state so as to reinforce the assumption of juridico-political sovereignty supposedly common to both.[23] In her reading, Hong argues that "the 'battlefield' for 'excluded subjects' who are not included in the social contract . . . is not limited to a simple battlefield between two states."[24] What she is referring to here is the warring that goes on within states, even as they confront other states in conflict. In this way, she looks past the complementary binary of those who lament defeat or celebrate liberation on both sides of the battlefield and instead focuses on those who "hesitate" (*tomadō*) in between.[25] In order to challenge the mythic narrative structure of struggle, sacrifice, and cathartic birth of a unified national community, Hong instead dwells on a radical moment of indecision that runs through the wartime "comfort woman." She writes:

> What did the Korean soldiers who fought as "imperial subjects" for imperial Japan, and the Korean "comfort women" who were designated as beings who gave "comfort" to the Japanese soldiers, witness in the end? After confronting death on the battlefield in Okinawa, was it the joy of a fatherland liberated [from Japanese colonial domination]? Or was it sorrow that accompanied the fall of the Japanese empire? . . . [26]

Okinawa, for her, is a productive place to reconsider postwar characterizations of the "aggressor" versus the "victim" implicit in both Japanese-American and Korean-Japanese histories because of its continuing liminal position as neither a colony nor fully part of the Japanese state. Okinawa is precisely that which does not allow for closure.

By focusing on this space of liminality, Hong makes a critical intervention into the sovereign decision that remains constant amidst regime change from Japanese empire to U.S. military occupation. Schmitt's definition of sovereignty as "he who decides on the exception"[27] is predicated on homogeneity on both sides of the battlefield. Under this assumption, "comfort women" are sacrificed in order to preserve the norm, i.e., the purity of Japanese women. The problem, of course, is that the norm here—i.e., "Japanese women"—are really Okinawans who also shuttle precariously back and forth across the boundaries of the law.[28] The contrast between the exception and the norm breaks down, thereby rendering the justification of the exception for the sake of the norm questionable.

Hong argues that it is this breakdown that both animates the constitution of the law and also renders it vulnerable. On the one hand, precisely because Okinawans ambivalently identified with the "comfort women" as subjects excluded by the law, they more desperately sought refuge within the law. She suggests that it was this fear that motivated the reincarnation of the wartime "comfort station" in the postwar "to [secure] rest and recreation for the U.S. military as a buffer to the violence."[29] Here, the exceptional sacrifice of some Okinawan women in order to protect the rest was predicated on the instability—and not the stability—of the norm. The distinction here is subtle yet crucial. The exception was made not to preserve the preconstituted homogeneity of the norm amongst those who are complacent, but to stabilize the radical heterogeneity of the norm amongst those who were afraid.

In his indirect challenge to Schmitt,[30] Benjamin closed in on the sovereign's vulnerability. As Samuel Weber writes in his reading of Benjamin's *Trauerspiel*, the "sovereign and exceptional decision is justifiable . . . only insofar as it provides the conditions for the reappropriation of the exception by the norm."[31] Far from being an uncontested assertion of sovereign authority, the exception is contingent on the norm's ability to restore it to a field of homogeneity. This is because if there were no normalcy, there would be no conditions for the possibility of the exception in the first place that gives rise to sovereignty. Precisely because of this vulnerability, the state of exception resorts to a highly aesthetic show of power that reinforces both the charismatic authority of the sovereign as a superhuman and the so-called normal citizen that it purportedly protects.

Certainly, the spectacle of violence invokes fear. However, Hong's text delivers when she disallows this fear to be articulated in terms of a stable subject position vis-à-vis a specific state sovereignty. As witness to the "comfort stations," did Okinawans feel relief that Korean women were being sacrificed for Okinawan women? Or did they feel anxiety that this could also happen to them? Did they feel pity for the Korean women abused by the imperial Japanese soldiers, or envy that at least they were afforded food rations as military affiliates? This line of questioning should not be read as a replacement for the question of war responsibility of Okinawans,[32] but rather as a fundamental reconsideration of the nature of the law. Hong's text comes alive with the movement of one conflicting emotion cascading into another. In adumbrating this ambiguity, she does not succumb to the authority of sovereign power that seeks to limit an articulation of fear in terms of one's position before a preexisting law, but instead points to the moment in which the sovereign attempts to ground its violence through the monopolization of liminality itself. The function of the sovereign spectacle of violence is to produce a fear irreducible to the law while simultaneously allowing for its reappropriation by the norms—norms that constantly attempt to contain liminality in a unified representation.

However, when this reappropriation is interrupted, there is no resolution to the violence, but only a continual haunting. As a kind of allegorical intention, haunting deploys a different mode of representation that interrupts the superhuman leap into transcendence as such. Whether a performance of political sovereignty that decides on exceptions to the law or an artistic sovereignty that decides on exceptions to meaning attributed to the sign, haunting presents a fundamental antagonism to the ability of the sovereign to make an ecstatic flight to the limits of the order for the purpose of folding its excess back into the internal community of shared meaning.

This is precisely what is at stake in reading the "hesitation" of "comfort women" at the end of the Battle of Okinawa who could not decide if they were joyous or devastated. Sovereignty loses nothing through a tragic critique of their exclusion from the law, but it reveals its vulnerability and intense paranoia the moment they fail to become intelligible through the grammar of the law. As suggested in Benjamin's "Critique of Violence," what offends the state is not the citizen's abuse of the law, but rather the "mere existence outside the law"[33] presented by both.

The complexity of "comfort women" interrupts the idealistic leap toward sovereign power, leaving their excess to come pouring down with the force of a "cataract."[34] Incapable of taking flight to the heavens, they are left no other recourse but to haunt the land of the living in a restless liminality. In place of the transcendental mode of symbolic representation (i.e., myth) comes an allegorical presentation before another. With the dead suspended on earth, the theatrical stage of the spectacle spills over into the audience, where the spectator is wrested from his or her role of passive onlooker. This is why, in pursuing her analysis of "how the space of the 'comfort station' changed Okinawa internally," Hong shows that the Okinawans were always *watching*.

> For me, the some 130 "comfort stations" do not speak to the intensity of the "victimization," but rather to the hypothesis that they were an existence that profoundly affected everyday life in Okinawa. . . . This kind of "politics of death" does not just affect the "Korean comfort women," but also those who "witnessed" her.[35]

Hong delineates how it was impossible to ignore the presence of "comfort women" in Okinawa. Not only were civilians ordered to surrender their private houses as "comfort stations," but their operation was highly dependent on Okinawan labor.[36] Simply put, they were part of everyday life. Yet, as Hong points out, postwar accounts of the U.S. military in Okinawa often occlude how these experiences with "comfort women" went on to inform life in the camps after civilians were captured.

The function of the camps was to establish a new spatial order in Okinawa. Upon the official invasion in April 1945, Admiral Chester W. Nimitz declared that "All powers of the Government of Japanese Empire are hereby suspended" and "final administrative responsibility are vested in me as Fleet Admiral. . . ."[37] In place of the old legal order, Nimitz established a civilian administration that he emphasized was "a necessary part . . . of destroying Japan's power of aggression."[38] Part and parcel of this strategy was to capture and confine civilians to what the U.S. military referred to as "refugee camps."[39] By June 1, 1945, 284,625 people were confined to these camps.[40] Although the space of the camp was recognized under international law by provisions of the 1907 Hague Convention that upheld the belligerent's right to exercise military governmental powers, it was still conceptually and legally ambiguous. Nimitz ordered that Okinawans should be treated as "ordinary Japanese subjects." This meant that they were designated as enemy civilians in combat and not afforded the rights and privileges of liberated peoples under international law like the Koreans and Taiwanese.[41] Okinawans were both Japanese and not Japanese at the same time.

Stories of rape in the camps are voluminous. Although there were only approximately twelve reported cases of rape from April 1 to June 30, 1945 (which includes reports by five male victims), oral testimony suggests that sexual violence was a daily occurrence.[42]

It was in the space of the camp that Okinawans began to exercise a nascent form of government under the direction of the U.S. military. The provisional Okinawa Advisory Council formed in August 15, 1945, with 128 representatives from the thirty-nine camps,[43] and it was soon followed by the Okinawa Women's Alliance (*Okinawa fujinkai rengō*) that became gravely concerned with sexual violence. At this time, Okinawans chose to refuse social relations with the U.S. military by asking that anti-fraternization regulations be kept in place.

The U.S. military initially adopted anti-fraternization regulations out of concern for their own soldiers because it recommended that "all civilians be treated with suspicion."[44] Fraternization was also potentially a "matter prejudicial to the health of the soldiers" as a conduit for the spread of VD.[45] However, after they determined that, aside from an isolated incident where an Okinawan "threw a knife (fortunately with poor aim at an American sailor)," there was no other case of "personal violence attempted against any member of the occupying forces," and they argued for a repeal of the regulations.[46] It was rather Okinawans who protested its repeal, hoping to keep the G.I.s away from women. The military report states:

> There was one additional factor of great importance, and that was the constant preoccupation of large numbers of American soldiers abroad with creation of opportunity for illicit sexual relations, a matter prejudicial to the health of the soldiers, to the morals of the community, and to the maintenance of dignity and order. The presence of a high concentration of negro troops on the island and the unfortunate fact that the negro troops were the greatest offenders against the honor of the native women, and the further circumstance that

civilians themselves expressed a reiterated desire to have the regulations kept in force resulted in enforcement of anti-fraternization regulations on Okinawa when they were in force nowhere else in the world.[47]

The U.S. military accounted for the Okinawan repulsion to fraternization by pinning it onto the "high concentration of negro troops on the island." Yet the politics of minority sexual relations on the side of the U.S. military obfuscates another politics of minority sexual relations on the side of imperial Japan: Okinawan women were both afraid of being made into U.S. military "comfort women" like their Korean counterparts for the imperial Japanese military and also afraid of being targeted as "spies for the U.S. military" by Japanese imperial soldiers for fraternizing with the Americans. In other words, they continued to calculate the repercussions of sexual relations with U.S. military soldiers *through an imperial Japanese gaze.* In the end, Hong succeeds in showing the difficulties of parsing this fear and attributing it to either the American or Japanese military, and instead delineates an omnipresent fear of racialized sexual violence vis-à-vis the institution of the military itself.

Sexual Violence on the "Forgotten Island," 1945–1947

Fighting on the island came to an end in mid-June 1945, and by the Potsdam Declaration of July 1945, it was determined that "Japanese sovereignty should be limited to the four home islands of Honshu, Hokkaido, Kyushu, Shikoku and to such minor islands as we determine."[48] In discussing the future, a subcommittee of the House Naval Affairs Committee initially recommended in 1945 that the United States "take outright" Okinawa.[49] Others favored placing the Ryukyus under a trusteeship because it would appease the 1941 Atlantic Charter declaration in which signatories "seek no aggrandizement, territorial or other,"[50] and the 1943 Cairo Conference in which "[t]he Three Great Allies . . . covet no gain for themselves and have no thought of territorial expansion."[51] President Harry S. Truman presided over the issue by stating the Ryukyus would be placed under a trusteeship until a peace treaty could be forged with Japan at a later date.[52]

Leaving the disposition of the Ryukyu Islands without clear definition only worsened its problems. Since the U.S. government did not know whether it would keep the islands in the long term or return them to Japan, it did not develop its economic infrastructure and political administration as extensively as it did in the mainland. As a result, the Ryukyu

Islands became a "dumping ground for Army misfits," and crimes involv-
ing American soldiers were rampant."[53] The soldiers were not only incom-
petent and unmotivated, but miserable from boredom and the sweltering
heat.[54] Heinous crime and sexual assault, in particular, became such a problem that Major General Fred Wallace threatened the death penalty in a
vain attempt to curb the instance of rape.[55]

In addition to the "misfits" were black soldiers and the more cheaply
contracted Filipino Scouts. The U.S. military was pressed to make use of
its minority population and started to integrate African Americans into its
ranks. This was not only a response to pressure coming from within the
United States for racial equality; internationally, the United States was also
wary of the fact that "Japanese propagandists have . . . made the most of
the anti–Negro discrimination" and realized racism would only hurt
American interests abroad.[56] The Tenth Army that invaded Okinawa contained a large number of black units, and the all-black 24th Infantry arrived in Okinawa from Saipan in August 1945.[57]

In April 1946, Lieutenant Commander James Watkins noted that "fear
of cruelty, rape, and violence replaced respect for American authority," and
he recommended the withdrawal of blacks to "avoid further compromising the American position in the eyes of the Okinawans."[58] While the
24th Infantry left Iejima for Gifu and Osaka on January 28, 1947,[59] their
departure did little to reduce sexual violence.[60] In their place came 2,339
Filipino Scouts of the 44th Infantry Regiment on January 23, 1947.[61] Some
suggested the Scouts were more dangerous than African Americans, as
purportedly evinced by the American director of public safety crime statistics.[62] As the first postwar editor in chief of *Uruma Shimpo*, Ikemiyagi
Shūi, wrote, the Scouts "unleashed resentment from the atrocities experienced in the Philippines at the hands of the Japanese military onto the
Okinawan civilians."[63] The Filipino Scouts left Okinawa in 1963.[64]

In this way, Okinawa quickly became a contact zone for the bottom
ranks of the U.S. military, racial minorities, and colonial subjects. On the
one hand, the hauntings of two empires, both American and Japanese, converged in a space in which sovereignty was left without clear designation.
Okinawa, as such, existed as a vacuum of sovereignty haunted by liminal subjects who struggled with ghosts that found no easy way to
transcendence.

With the potential for the confluence of these hauntings to disarticulate the colonial order, the U.S. military both provided the conditions for
and subsequently policed minority-to-minority sexual violence. Okinawans
were exposed to violence that continually overwhelmed the parameters of

the law on the one hand, while it attempted to enforce the law so that sexual violence was interpreted as illegal for racial minority subjects and extralegal for majority white subjects in the military on the other. In other words, minorities were stripped from an above-the-law authority and repatriated back into the legal order as criminals.

As Okinawans started to return to their villages after October 23, 1945, to a now U.S. military occupied Okinawa, sexual violence continued to terrorize their everyday lives. M. D. Morris, a former U.S. military affiliate, writes:

> Stories of [G.I.s] sneaking into civilian dwellings and raping women were told on a daily basis . . . For American G.I.s, occupied Okinawa was an area of extraterritoriality. Women could not go outside with ease. Even if they stayed in their dwellings, they did not know when a G.I. would find his way inside.[65]

In some villages, the threat of sexual violence was so acute irrespective of the patrolling military police (MP) that villagers formed their own neighborhood watch (*jikeidan*). If a G.I. slipped through the barbed wire to enter residential areas, the neighborhood watch would ring bells to signal women to smear their face with charcoal and hide in their closets or under their floorboards.[66] According to the group for pre-treaty settlement of loss and reparation, there were seventy-six reported crimes against women between 1945 and 1949.[67] In 1946, approximately 61 percent of the attacks came while civilians were farming or doing laundry.[68]

Since men of all ages—adolescent, conscription age, and elderly—were mobilized into the war effort, a disproportionately larger female population was left behind in the postwar to care for underaged, elderly, or incapacitated dependents.[69] With chronic sexual violence threatening women on the one hand, and the responsibility to save their families from starvation on the other, many were driven to prostitution. Morris continues his account with the development of a so-called willing submission to the soldiers as follows:

> . . . there were local girls in sufficient numbers who were willing, for a consideration, to entertain the soldiers' wants. Naturally any such traffic could not be organized officially. But for the common good, some wiser, saner heads worked out of an off-the-record arrangement whereby all interested girls were assembled in a single area in which drinking, money, medical examinations, and an orderly movement of actually thousands all were controlled closely without creating any disturbance from the outside. After duty hours, military buses from several areas unofficially would take and return the troops. For a while

> this appeared to be a satisfactory solution. Then some chaplains and
> others had the bus service prohibited from *stopping* at the area in
> question. The buses continued to run, and slowed down to a low-gear
> crawl, so that all would be able to leave and enter without mishap. . . . [70]

The "willing" mentioned here were bartering sex for clothing, cigarettes, and canned food because Okinawa still had not returned to a currency-based economy. Prostitution unfolded haphazardly against the backdrop of this unorganized field of circulation.

For the U.S. military, the rise of prostitution created a VD crisis that severely hampered the productivity of its troops. It responded by passing a series of proclamations in March 1947. First was Special Proclamation No. 14, "Prostitution Prohibited with Members of the Occupation Forces." Special Proclamation No. 15, "Venereal Disease Control," called for the establishment of clinics to treat VD, isolation of infected patients, the requirement for all health care providers to report all cases of confirmed or suspected VD, and compulsory treatment. Special Proclamation No. 16 declared "Female Sex Slavery Prohibited" for girls under the age of eighteen. Similar to the "prostitute hunting" that occurred in Japan, these proclamations used the Ryukyu police to capture women who were suspected of carrying VD and subjected them to forced treatment and hospitalization. Despite the acute shortage of doctors on the islands, they were ordered to prioritize the containment of VD. For example, Teruya Zensuke found it particularly troubling that he was forced to become a VD tracer when he returned to the Ryukyu Islands in December 1947. He writes, "Even though the demand for physicians was so acute that I was desperate for any help I could get, I was given the assignment to become a 'VD Tracer' that did not require a physician's [qualifications] and was subsequently branded a VD doctor."[71]

In this period, Okinawa is often referred to as the "Forgotten Island," after the well-known *Time* magazine article attesting to subhuman conditions, international apathy, and U.S. military neglect.[72] The goal was to establish the supremacy of U.S. martial law in Okinawa at a time when the prospects for long-term occupation had not yet been determined.

Birth of the Sex Industry, 1947–1952

Relying on the might of the U.S. military to enforce the law, however, was not a practical strategy for long-term occupation by a country claiming to "make the world safe for democracy." It needed to contain the field of alegality that allowed for the interplay between liminal subjects through more fundamental measures: the creation of a labor force that would come to autonomously manage sexual relations. In this way, the management of sexual relations in Okinawa took a turn as Okinawa approached the "reverse course" of occupation and emerged as the "Keystone of the Pacific."

Political talks were rekindled by mounting fear of the spread of communism in 1947. Terasaki Hidenari, advisor to the emperor, relayed the following message to SCAP, General Douglas MacArthur, in September 1947 regarding Okinawa:

> The Emperor hopes that the United States will continue the military occupation of Okinawa and other islands of the Ryukyus. In the Emperor's opinion, such occupation would benefit the United States and also provide protection for Japan. The Emperor feels that such a move would meet with wide-spread approval among the Japanese people who fear not only the menace of Russia, but after the Occupation has ended, the growth of rightist and leftist groups which might give rise to an "incident" which Russia could use as a basis for interfering internally in Japan.[73]

The emperor's offering was quickly utilized by the United States as the discrepant positions between its military and Department of State started to come together in 1948. George Kennan of the Department of State released "PPS/28: Recommendations with Respect to U.S. Policy Toward Japan" on March 25, 1948, after a series of meetings with General MacArthur. "[A]t this point," the report reads, the "United States Government should make up its mind . . . that it intends to retain permanently the facilities at Okinawa, and the base there should be developed accordingly."[74] This decision was a direct result of a solidified U.S. policy toward Japan in which primary importance was placed on "the achievement of maximum *stability* of Japanese society." Specifically, this was to be obtained by "(a) A firm U.S. security policy" that became the U.S.-Japan Security Treaty; "(b) An intensive program of economic recovery; and (c) A relaxation in occupational control, designed to stimulate a greater sense of direct responsibility on the part of the Japanese Government."[75] Okinawa was directly referenced in this recommendation as MacArthur suggested that "by properly developing and garrisoning *Okinawa* we can assure the safety of Japan against external aggression without the need for maintaining forces on Japanese soil."[76] Specifically, this entailed Japanese economic recovery without the need for U.S. bases in Japan. In this configuration, the transnational network of sovereignty and capital that made allowances for the exceptionalism of martial law traversed the region globally, while it simultaneously converged through the bodies of women locally.

These developments made it clear that Okinawa's economic recovery was secondary to mainland Japan's. In "Okinawa and American Imperialism," Kokuba Kōtarō, the future leader of Okinawa's underground communist party (discussed more in Chapter 3), argued that "U.S. military economic policy in Okinawa" at this time was not "simply a 'colonial policy' in the classical sense" of the term.[77] Rather, it was to "stabilize political rule" on the islands while preparing for the "restoration of Okinawa's economic union with mainland Japan alongside the restoration of Japanese monopoly capitalism."[78] In the absence of a long-term economic policy, Okinawa's economy was temporarily sustained through economic aid. Quite simply, as Kokuba notes, the U.S. military feared that without such measures to placate the islanders, Okinawa would become susceptible to communism.[79] Similar to how the Okinawa Relief Bill acted as a patch to Okinawa's exclusion from the biopolitical order in the 1920s, the Government Aid and Relief in Occupied Areas (GARIOA) kept the Okinawan economy afloat in the early postwar years. GARIOA went into effect in late 1946[80] and peaked in 1950 before the economy started to temporarily stabilize through U.S. military base construction in 1951.[81] While base construction attracted some sixty-three thousand base workers at its peak in 1952 that bolstered short-term economic reconstruction,[82] the boom more fundamentally served the long-term reconstruction of Japanese industry. The U.S. military turned away from foreign construction companies to accept bids from mainland Japanese companies.[83] Not only did they earn dollars that funneled back into the Japanese economy, but of equal importance, they acquired technological know-how on construction from the U.S. military.[84]

In 1940, 74.22 percent of the working population was involved in agriculture and forestry versus 58.12 percent by 1950. This 16.1 percent difference was predominantly accounted for by the introduction of a new category of military labor (*gunsangyō*), which represented 15.05 percent of total labor.[85] This entailed a displacement of farmers from the countryside to quickly emerging U.S. military base towns. Around these base towns, the U.S. military instituted a series of institutional frameworks that first, foreclosed the possibility of economic self-subsistence that was not linked to U.S. military base construction and operation; second, cruelly denied this narrowly defined space of possible circulation when Okinawans could not provide sexual services to the discretionary or sanitary standards demanded by the U.S. military; and third, created Okinawan "petitioning subjects" who asked for their so-called right to participate in a market centered on the sex industry.

As described earlier, Okinawans were confined en masse to camps during the war, and then allowed to repatriate to what was left of their villages after October 1945. As many G.I.s stationed in Okinawa during this time testify, no one thought there were bases on a place called "Okinawa"; they thought "Okinawa" itself was a military base. Needless to say, this total occupation of Okinawan land distorted the economy. The poorly thought-out American policies devoted approximately one-fifth of its arable land to military purposes "with no regard for its economic value" by 1949.[86] Additionally, the influx of Okinawan repatriates from various corners of the Japanese empire compounded the acute food shortage.

Goyeku Village (later known as Koza City, and then Okinawa City),[87] at the middle of the main Okinawan island, quickly became the center of these contradictions. Since two-thirds of the land was occupied by the U.S. military, farms were displaced and small businesses sprung up in their place. Furthermore, the population increased on the remaining one-third of the unoccupied land as it more than doubled from 8,481 in 1940 to 18,431 in 1950, and then nearly doubled again to 35,283 by 1955.[88] Encircled by the U.S. military, it became a site of widespread sexual violence as well as an active hotbed for prostitution.

With VD on the rise, the U.S. military responded in June 1949 by issuing the institutional framework of the notorious "one-mile limit" that prohibited native structures within one mile of any dependent housing or military billet of a hundred or more soldiers in the Goyeku Village.[89] Since a one-mile radius around the massive U.S. military settlements encompassed most of Goyeku Village, farmers and small businesses were cut off from their livelihood. Conflicting opinions arose amongst the leadership on how to respond. Goyeku Village councilman Ōyama Chōjō, who would go on to become Koza City mayor from 1958 to 1974, stood by villagers who hoped Goyeku would eventually return to farming. However, he was overshadowed by Goyeku Village mayor Shiroma Seizen, who represented the interests of advocates for a base town that would serve the needs of the U.S. military.[90] In order to convince the U.S. military to remove the one-mile limit that strangled the village, Shiroma understood that he must first conduct a prostitution sweep, euphemistically called the "movement to reinforce sanitation and elevate morality" (*eisei kyōka dōgi kōyō undō*), that took place through August and September 1949.[91]

The sweep, however, was said to have triggered a series of unexpected events. In his personal history, Shiroma claimed that at least one African

American soldier burned down a civilian house just north of the current Okinawa City Hall in retaliation to the sweep.[92] This was near the location where the black unit took up residence. He wrote that Okinawans were helpless to extinguish the blaze as the G.I. also exchanged gun fire with the MP.[93] Despite the shock of the military government, he suggested that "they (*karera*)" were undeterred and rode into the village in a jeep as a show of force sometime later. Hearing rumors that Shiroma's own house would be targeted next and his daughter would be taken, he sent his wife and child into hiding.[94] In response, the U.S. military posted two MPs to guard his residence and even gave Shiroma a pistol to carry.

The minority subject figured into the staging of a "bad" world of sexual violence, prostitution, and crime that served as a contrast to a "good" form of international exchange. Shiroma directed these two parts well. He was not just a politician, but also a skilled translator who had intimate insight into military government culture—including its racial politics. As a former English teacher, he was quickly mobilized by the U.S. military in 1945 to translate newspapers and interpret for military officers.[95] In his capacity as mayor, he worked well with Major General Josef R. Sheetz, who left Korea to take up the post of military governor in Okinawa on October 1, 1949, and promised democratic improvements to preexisting military rule. Both were invested in ending the anti-fraternization policy in order to encourage the infusion of U.S. dollars into the Okinawan economy. Individually, Sheetz's agenda was to make long-term occupation more palatable to Okinawans by representing military personnel as good neighbors dying to spend dollars that were burning holes in their pockets.[96] As for Shiroma, he was motivated by the desire to have a central swath of land in Goyeku, around Goya Crossing, returned from the U.S. military so as to avoid splitting the village into two. This area, as he explained, was a trouble spot that invited crime because it was the site of storage facilities, parking lots, and residences of the black unit.[97]

Together, the two conceptualized a city plan for a "business center." This was a proposal to create a "recreation center" (*gorakujo*) where "Americans and Okinawans [could] engage in upright and healthy business" by exchanging U.S. dollars for goods and services in shops, restaurants, movie theaters, and so on.[98] Although Shiroma was involved in its conceptualization, the bid could have gone out to any base town throughout Okinawa. Sheetz toured the island in early December to gauge interest and also sell the idea as a model for the entire island. However, he was not very convincing, since he was quickly accused of promoting the establishment of "prostitution districts" throughout Okinawa.[99]

Shiroma backed Sheetz by insisting that his vision for a business center would be modeled on textbook-like scenarios of international exchange. In fact, he claimed that because of his explicitly anti-prostitution stance, Goyeku again faced retaliation as the number of rape incidences increased.[100] Sheetz finally granted Shiroma the bid, and on December 8, 1949, Koza was released from its off-limits designation. It "opened up as a commercial town for U.S.-Ryukyuan friendship"[101] and took the name "Business Center Street," known today as "Park Avenue." Sensitive to criticism, *Uruma Shimpo* was compelled to start off the introduction of Business Center Street with the defensive subheading "Let's Do Away with Misconception." The first few lines read:

> The establishment of the Business Center is a place for light-hearted, virtuous, and sound business as well as amusement[102] between Americans and Okinawans, but naysayers of the entertainment district[103] went so far as to hold a forum and espouse their misconception of the problem as a military-appointed prostitution district. According to the governor's comments yesterday at the assembly, the major general told him that "[t]he Business Center is a light-hearted place of amusement found in any civilized country." Nonetheless, there is an individual[104] around Naha with a misconception that it is a replica of the prewar Okinawan pleasure quarters[105] who is rousing up opposition. This is truly unacceptable.[106]

The opening of Koza was followed by a lifting of the off-limits restriction in Naha in January 1950. The *Okinawa Times* reported the G.I.s "look forward to meeting the young Okinawan ladies on the street."[107] After seeing how off-limit areas profited from the infiltration of G.I.s into the community, northern Okinawa also petitioned to lift the Okinawan ban. According to Ikemiyagi Shūi, village leaders justified their request to the U.S. military by stating, "contact with Americans would promote democratization," "friendship with American officers would edify English-language studies," and "friendly relations would heighten the level of trust between the villagers and American officers."[108]

However, Katō Masahiro suggests that the Business Center campaign was a cover for the informal establishment of "comfort facilities" (*ian shisetsu*), more informally called "entertainment districts" (*kanrakugai*) or "special drinking districts" (*tokuingai*), that facilitated prostitution.[109] Shiroma Seizen, the aforementioned mayor of Goyeku Village, Shiroma Eiko, vice president of the Women's Association, and Shima Masu, the so-called mother of social welfare who worked in the Goyeku Village after the war, met with a Major General Alvan C. Kincaid in August 1949 to discuss the problem. Hokama Yoneko recalls:

> He[110] said, "It's difficult to be concerned with the sexual problems of the soldiers . . ." We made a case for self-discipline amongst the soldiers and the withdrawal of special women.[111] He responded, "Well then, let's make a special area at the fringes of town on the fields of Yaejima. This is the best way possible." We had no choice but to agree with Kincaid's opinion.[112]

In this way, Yaejima became established as a "special drinking district" (*tokuingai*) in order to contain sexual relations with the G.I.s in a secluded area of the village.

Goyeku was representative of similar developments unfolding throughout Okinawa. In August 1949, local municipalities were petitioning the military government to establish "U.S. military comfort stations" (*Beigun ianshisetsu*) in Koza, Naha, Maebaru, and Ishikawa.[113] Their objective was explained by the following article.

> Considering the need to prevent VD that has rapidly increased in the postwar era, the assembly has discussed the moral propriety for the need of dance halls or other comfort amusement establishments from every angle. In particular, the Ōgimi public sanitation chief has worked on a plan with this as the only way to suppress VD, and is currently furthering talks with the police department. However, the governor has stated that the establishment of this kind of pleasure facility should be further examined as a social policy issue. All types of documents are currently being gathered. Establishment of a special area for amusement is almost entirely supported by men and opposed by women.[114]

The police suggested that "the problems of rape, murder, assault, and arson by G.I.s are all caused by the male/female issue."[115] Here, the reference to "arson" potentially alludes to the incident in Goyeku after the prostitution sweep.

The issue was contentiously debated at a town hall forum in Naha on September 30, 1949, amongst the Women's Association, the Okinawa Civilian Administration, political party representatives, priests, and youth group representatives. In particular, it was Senaga Kamejirō of the Okinawa People's Party (*Okinawa Jinmintō*, herein referred to as "OPP")—the future Naha City mayor (1956) that earned the title of "troublemaker"—who expressed his opposition to the U.S. military through the issue.

Senaga stated that dance hall is merely a beautiful name for a prostitution district considering it institutes a system for monitoring syphilis. Hence, speaking from a position [that advocates] the protection of human rights and women's liberation, he expressed his absolute opposition.[116]

As seen in mainland Japan, Marxist politicians such as Senaga who were antagonistic toward U.S. military occupation had quickly taken up the issue of prostitution. Senaga and the OPP had covert ties to the JCP since the former's inception in June 1947,[117] and starting in April 1949—just four months before the town hall forum—the OPP had become openly critical of the U.S. military.[118] The OPP was empowered to show its true colors because of the widespread unpopularity of the military government that had both temporarily halted the distribution of food rations and arbitrarily raised the prices on food from late 1948 to early 1949.[119] Senaga attempted to ride this wave of discontent in order to attack the formation of a sex industry. However, he stumbled on a critical rift that would continue to run through postwar Okinawan society. Discontent amongst farmers and base town workers was not always congruous, as we shall see in subsequent chapters.

Shiroma and the police chief reluctantly supported the establishment of the entertainment districts as the lesser of two evils. The article continues:

The Goyeku Village mayor and Koza police chief both contested the wretched conditions of the middle district [where Goyeku was located], and supported the establishment of a breakwater [of the flesh] that would preserve the social peace by gathering prostitutes in one area as a policy for preventing the depravity of the youth and harm to the residents.[120]

Quickly, the issue became polarized and set the tone for the rest of the occupation. Shima captured the essence of the dilemma.

These two positions were representative of the debate that took place that day. Both were serious arguments. Residents living around the bases, however, were troubled by the fact that ideals could not solve the very real problem at hand. This debate took place in every corner of Okinawa, and finally, everyone was resigned to accept the establishment of a special drinking district.[121]

Headlines for the *Uruma Shimpo*, directly after the town meeting, made the exact same characterization: "The Great Dilemma of the 'Entertainment District': A Debate between Ideals and Reality."[122]

This put Sheetz in an awkward yet desirous position. Okinawans were poised as subjects who petition for their right to prostitute while Sheetz was poised as the authority who bestows the privilege for Okinawans to prostitute themselves. Yet, in light of the 1947 special proclamations, he was at the same time compelled to publicly display his outright opposition to prostitution. In actuality, the distinction between the "good" areas for international exchange and "bad" areas for prostitution was rendered defunct. After the off-limits ban was lifted in areas throughout Okinawa, there were an estimated seven thousand sex workers in Okinawa by 1950,[123] and the number of VD cases skyrocketed. Syphilis cases rose 583.8 percent (111 to 759), gonorrhea cases rose 112.5 percent (711 to 1,511), and chancroid cases rose 980 percent (10 to 108) from 1949 to 1950.[124]

Around this time in early 1950, off-limits orders were reinstated and started to take on new meaning. The U.S. military prohibited its personnel from entering certain restaurants, bars, brothels, or hotels if they were suspected of being a source of VD.[125] Because this was tantamount to an economic sanction, Okinawan business owners were put in a position to petition for the removal of the order by eradicating VD and improving sanitation in their establishments. Again, the U.S. military did not mandate prostitution through the legal order, but rather prohibited it. Instead, the off-limits orders shifted the problem of controlling VD to the Okinawan people by explicitly linking it to the economy.

On November 24, 1951, Deputy Military Governor Robert S. Beightler drafted a letter to Higa Tatsuo, the governor of the Okinawa Guntō, underscoring the severity of VD with veiled threats of more off-limits orders.[126] In response, the Okinawa Guntō government established a "VD Prevention Committee" on November 29, and VD policy committees were established at the local level throughout Okinawa in December. They identified the *gaishō*, or streetwalker, as a conduit to transmission and subsequently put pressure on these women to work in the entertainment districts where they could be monitored and directed to submit to medical exams.[127] The committee worked closely with health centers that were established throughout the island earlier that year in 1951 to promote education and regular examinations.[128] In this way, the U.S. military conveniently allowed Okinawans to do the work of controlling the spread of VD and police streetwalkers into entertainment districts by intrinsically linking the management of sex work to the economic stability of the entire island.

As the sex industry became established as a social phenomenon in U.S. military–occupied Okinawa, its discourse was secured by anchoring it to conceptions of free will. Prostitution was either justified by the "local girls in sufficient numbers who were willing . . . to entertain the soldiers' wants"[129] on the one hand, or condemned because they were forced to "prostitute themselves to G.I.s as a means of 'living' and 'eating'" on the other.[130] That is, whether or not that will was respected or violated, the sanctity of a self-determining will was nonetheless posited. In this register, U.S. military strategy was to highlight Okinawan agency and downplay any instance where the political opposition could dig up evidence of slave-like exploitation to criticize the draconian force of the U.S. military.

By freeing ourselves from the constraint of this register, however, we can alternatively ask what is at stake with the emergence of this type of subject. As Kokuba had analyzed, the goal of the U.S. military was to "stabilize political rule" over Okinawa in the absence of a long-term economic policy so it could be prepared for a later reunion with Japanese monopoly capital. In this context, the ultimate aim of U.S. military governance was not to protect or violate the free will of Okinawans, but rather to allow for the emergence of the technology of what Tomiyama calls a "petitioning subject."[131] As "petitioning subjects," Okinawans not only produce goods and services, but they produce themselves as subjects before the law. In this sense, merely exposing U.S. military rhetoric as a trick to violate the autonomy of Okinawan women does not step outside of the register of free will, but unwittingly reproduces it. The ultimate goal here was not to negotiate for more autonomy and better protection of the inviolable human will, but it was to produce subjects who negotiate within the channels of the law. As a result, it depoliticized the field of alegality in which Okinawans were fraught with the contradictions of a "will" that was simultaneously compromised, even as it was exercised.

A petitioning subject is a precarious one who must ask for things because it has little to nothing. These social conditions were different from mainland Japan, where the middle class came to internalize the need to reproduce labor power for capital in service to the state, as discussed in Chapter 1. Certainly, while there was similarity in that both positioned the sex industry as a deterrence to sexual violence, suggested that exposing children to the social phenomenon of prostitution was detrimental to their upbringing, and generally discriminated against the women, there was also a conspicuous difference. While Okinawans were well aware of the racial dynamics of the sex industry that catered to the U.S. military, there was sparing to no mention of miscegenation as racial contamination of the population in need of preventative measures until around 1956, when popular sentiment shifted toward reversion to the Japanese administration amidst the all-island struggle (discussed in Chapter 3). For Okinawans, the debate on the formation of the sex industry was informed by an intense fear of sexual violence and the desire for dollars to escape destitution. Because Okinawans were failed subjects before the state, the U.S. military, particularly after the arrival of Sheetz in 1949, sought to contain this field of alegality by incorporating them into the legal order as self-determining subjects with the temporary promise of dollars that would come with base construction on the eve of the Korean War. And as we shall see next, the attempt to contain this field of alegality led to disastrous consequences for Okinawa's ability to embrace the birth of its mixed-race children.

Impossible Descendants of the Future

The first mention of mixed-race children I was able to locate was in a handwritten *Okinawa Times* article dated August 13, 1948, entitled "Pleas for Abortion Knocking on the Door of Underground Doctors." Different from mainland Japan immediately after the end of occupation, these children were not articulated in terms of the racial contamination of the population that must be preemptively contained in order to preserve the purity of the race. Rather, in accordance to the primary goal to "stabilize political rule" in Okinawa by getting Okinawans to recognize the legal order, the lives of mixed-race children were superimposed onto a grid of legal intelligibility in which they did not fit and hence became existences purportedly in need of erasure.

When a forty-nine-year-old man was arrested for suspicion of performing an illegal abortion, it became known to the authorities that it was not an isolated case, but a growing social phenomenon amongst mostly unmarried women who could not bear the consequences of having a mixed-race child. The article reads:

> The women were outraged at the investigator's assertion that they
> exchanged their chastity for material goods from the military and
> instead proclaimed they were living in pure love. They were all
> unmarried and ranged from ages 20 to 25. But when they thought of
> the reality of childbirth, they didn't know what else to do, and ulti-
> mately resorted to the crime for which they candidly apologized
> before bursting into tears.[132]

Prostitution and "pure love" are posited at opposite ends of the same legal continuum. The former is stigmatized as the illegal activity of women who gave in to the temptation of "material goods" while the latter is poised as choice that longs for formal recognition by the law.[133] The women are reported as preemptively aborting because of the "reality of childbirth" in which their children would not only be born out of wedlock, but also doubly stateless. In the first sense, Okinawa was already legally in limbo as it was severed from the Japanese administration, and in the second sense, Japanese nationality could only be conferred through patrilineal lines until the large number of stateless children in Okinawa compelled Japan to reform its nationality law to include a mother's right to confer nationality to her child in 1985.[134] These children were literally unintelligible to the state in the most concrete sense of the law.

Another woman resorted to infanticide after she realized the child whom she birthed was not the child of her husband.

> Soon after getting married this past June, Maemura Hiro (age 22, pseudonym) . . . gave birth to her first child. When she realized it was an illegitimate child with the skin of a foreign race, she was arrested three days after delivery for suffocating and murdering the child in her underarm as she breastfed it.

The corporeality of this woman whose body breastfeeds her newborn is horrifically disconnected from her conscious actions that can realize no possibility for a racialized "illegitimate" birth other than death. Not only is the soul torn asunder, but the bodily enclosure of the (native) mother/(mixed)child unit that continues postpartum through breastfeeding is severed with the razor-sharp boundary-inscribing violence of infanticide; the mother must cut out the part of her body that is of a "foreign race," thereby disallowing the possibility that the baby can be an extension of herself.

Continuing with quotes from individuals who blame the women for their "irresponsibility," a male researcher pointed out that "these women face a crisis that cannot be handled by the old morality due to the drastic changes in the [postwar] environment." At the same time, he thought "they should be blamed for the irresponsibility of taking a new life." The Shuri Youth Group president thought that the public was "too lenient toward the 'social cancer' of the times." A female worker from A. J. Futenma Camp sympathizes with the women because it is "a sad reality of the postwar era" and at the same time admits they are a "nuisance" to "the numerous working women" who "protect their purity" because they are categorically "scorned" by society.[135] Such excerpts from this massive article betray a schizophrenic rhythm. The article is incapable of processing emotions that overflow with the incommensurability between the racialized body and law in one instance, and rigidly prescriptive normative values in another.

The *Uruma Shimpo* published statistics on mixed-race children in a September 23, 1949, article entitled "A Colorful Assortment of Mixed-Race Children: Most Numerous of Caucasian Descent." The article describes them as "born either as a crystallization of international love that transcends borders or by accidental misfortune," encapsulating the two polarities between life legitimated by and excluded from the law. Significantly, this article appears amidst the widely contested debate on the establishment of "entertainment districts."[136]

These initial writings on miscegenation spoke of the need to blanket Okinawa with a legal intelligibility in the immediate postwar when Okinawa's position in the Cold War order was still in flux. But amidst this initial encounter, where multiple worlds collided in the space of postwar Okinawa, what was important was the cultivation of a petitioning subject, or a self-determining entity that recognized a sovereign power who decides. It was the form of this decision, as a power that suspends the movement of liminality, that incapacitated Okinawan women from claiming their mixed-raced children as the progeny of Okinawa.

When Ifa Fuyū (1876–1947), the so-called father of Okinawan studies, wrote just one month before his death in 1947, "[t]he only choice Okinawans have is to throw themselves before the will of their descendants after them,"[137] it was unlikely he had mixed-race children in mind amongst these "descendants." But what is significant is that Okinawans were not only incapable of deciding their own political future, but "they themselves [were] in no position to command their descendants to be in possession of it."[138] Ifa expressed disillusionment toward the field of representation in which the conditions for the possibility of autonomy could find articulation, but could only exist as a haunting "without a voice and without a figure."[139] Neither in death nor in life would Okinawans find transcendence to the other world, but the dead would comingle amongst their descendants, imbuing them with the hope for a future that the dead themselves could not decide. It is precisely in the inability to determine Okinawa's future that mixed-race children remained the potential children in a dream of a different kind of liberation.

CHAPTER 3

Okinawa, 1952–1958: Solidarity under the Cover of Darkness

Chapter 2 argued that the objective of the U.S. military was, for the time being, to establish a legal order in postwar Okinawa recognized by self-determining subjects at a time when its position within the Cold War regime was only starting to materialize. While fear of racialized sexual violence incited an identification with the law, it was nonetheless a tenuous one that could fall apart just as easily as it came together. The post-1952 era was a testament to the need for something more than a legal order rooted in fear amongst a war-torn people, namely, a long-term plan to care for the population so as to maintain governance in Okinawa. GARIOA had already peaked in 1950 and dwindled thereafter. The U.S. military needed Okinawa to be as economically self-sufficient as possible, if not to avoid the burden of economic aid, then to avoid communist aspirations amongst the dissatisfied islanders. The problem, however, was that it took over an Okinawan economy that was neglected by Japan and did not achieve such aims on its own accord from the prewar era.

This chapter charts the position of the sex industry amidst mass social protest as the U.S. military struggled to reintegrate the Okinawan economy from 1952 to 1958. On the one hand, a wide range of workers speaking in different island tongues (*shima kutuba*) flooded into the main island around base towns from Okinawa's peripheries. On the other hand, the U.S. military was compelled to confront the issue of compensation for the use of land confiscated during the war in addition to new confiscations after 1952. Amidst this radical heterogeneity of the postwar, base construction workers successfully carried out the first postwar workers' strike, farmers ignited the "all-island struggle," and the Ryukyu Legislature was winning seats by political radicals backed by the communist-influenced Okinawa People's Party (OPP). If Okinawans were to recognize the legal order, then they would publicly protest for reversion to the Japanese administration through legal channels of the democratic process. Unfortunately, this was not the political message that the U.S. military wanted to hear. It not only responded with outright political repression, but also issued off-limits orders to base towns centered on the sex industry that paralyzed the Okinawan economy. While the OPP opposed the formation of the sex industry, there is little evidence to suggest that they were able to infiltrate these communities and mobilize them into public forms of protest as they did construction workers and farmers. Yet these base town workers were not only integral to the economy, but to the understanding of sex, race, nation, and class in Okinawa's mass resistance. How was it possible to continue with popular resistance against the U.S. military under the banner of an "all-island struggle" when a significant part of the island refused to protest the very patrons that frequented their businesses?

This chapter addresses the sex worker as a subject who could not be mobilized under a political platform before the state, i.e., the lumpenproletariat. I argue that the lumpenproletariat is neither inherently subversive to nor inherently complicit with U.S. military oppression. Rather, an examination of the lumpenproletariat repositions politics as the interplay between a radical heterogeneity (i.e., alegality) attuned to the immediate struggle for life and political representation oriented toward an idealistic goal in the future. The all-island struggle of this period was more than just a struggle for land against U.S. military confiscation; it was a struggle to reclaim the power of resistance in an unofficial and nonpublic form that was opened up by OPP's underground communist party after the U.S. military shut down other official possibilities for political expression. It was under this cover of darkness that we can locate moments of solidarity between women involved with G.I.s and Okinawans resisting U.S. military repression. Additionally, it was this solidarity that was compromised by off-limits orders that polarized Okinawan society and drove them into political factions by making a public spectacle of "pro-

Japanese reversion activists" who came up against "pro-American base town workers."

In the end, I argue that what divided Okinawan society was not so much how the U.S. military pitted various interests against each other as it was the displacement of an understanding of representational politics as an instrumental expression of heterogeneous interests. In this sense, OPP played into the polarizing tactics of the U.S. military by pushing an ethno-nationalist identification with the Japanese state. It was this "spiritualis-tic" (*seishinshugitekina*) ethno-nationalism, much like the "mysticism" or "primitivism" described by Tosaka in Chapter 1, that fostered the biopolitical imperative to eliminate miscegenation in the base towns for the sake of an idealistic communion with Japan in a utopian future.

The Lumpenproletariat

The postwar social landscape radically changed in the 1950s as Okinawa was transformed from a countryside filled with farmers to a handful of larger base towns bustling with workers who built and serviced U.S. military bases. After plans for long-term occupation solidified at the end of the 1940s, the Okinawan economy that was sustained by GARIOA shifted to an economy sustained by "base income" that reached an all-time high in 1953.[1] Workers came from Okinawa's peripheral islands such as Amami, Ishigaki, Miyako, and Yaeyama. Of these islands, a large number came from Amami, which was officially part of the southernmost islands of Kagoshima Prefecture, but was occupied (similarly to Okinawa) by the U.S. military until it reverted to the Japanese administration on Christmas day in 1953.[2] Workers also included returnees from the corners of the now collapsed Japanese empire. They built military bases, serviced base operations, and of course flooded into the base towns centered on the sex industry.

Hayashi Yoshimi, a member of the Amami Communist Party, worked closely with General Secretary Senaga Kamejirō of the OPP and organized military base workers. Hayashi was the behind-the-scenes leader of the first postwar large-scale workers' protest known as the Nippon Road Company (*Nippon Dōrosha*) strike on June 5, 1952. Most of the 143 workers came from Amami[3] and demanded a 30 percent pay increase, back pay, paid leave for injury or sickness, and better dormitory living conditions.[4] Senaga, who was a member of the Ryukyu Legislature, brought the spirit of the strikers' public demonstrations onto the stage of representational politics and won overwhelming public support. On June 11, the legislature unanimously passed a resolution of support. As the *Okinawa Times* reported, this was an invitation to the "100,000 Ryukyuan workers" to protest the U.S. military; 2,000 throughout the islands, in fact, participated in a rally outside of Naha Theater on June 15.[5] Soon thereafter on July 11, the Ryukyu Legislature also passed a law that enabled workers to unionize.[6]

The U.S. military was also facing problems with landowners. When the 1952 San Francisco Peace Treaty went into effect, the U.S. military was compelled to legitimize its claims to the land it confiscated during the war and its aftermath. It accomplished this with Article 3 of the treaty, which stipulated "the United States will have the right to exercise all and any powers of administration, legislation and jurisdiction over the territory and inhabitants of these islands. . . ."[7] Accordingly, the U.S. military issued Ordinance No. 91 (Authority to Contract) and agreed to retroactively pay rent from June 1, 1950, to April 27, 1952, at a rate of 1.08 B-yen for one tsubo. Additionally, it proposed a twenty-year contract.[8] However, 1.08 B-yen at the time was about the equivalent of a pack of cigarettes, and the lengthy contract gave cause for concern about the future.[9] How would these families eke out a life in postwar Okinawa without farmland? Because of the confiscations, Okinawans already lost 24 percent of their arable land.[10] Furthermore, they were compelled to make greater use of it because returnees from the empire had increased the population by 21 percent.[11] Land was precious, food was scarce, and the future was uncertain. As a result, only about nine hundred of fifty-seven thousand families (1.6 percent) complied with the terms of the ordinance.[12] If one considers that each family had about five members—the average at the time—then this means that about half of the entire Okinawan population was at odds with the U.S. military ordinance.[13]

Additionally, the U.S. military demanded more land. While there was little resistance in confiscating land when Okinawans were struggling to survive the war and immediate postwar aftermath, the political climate had changed by 1952. To legitimize the confiscations, the U.S. military issued Ordinance No. 109 (Land Acquisition Procedure) on April 3, 1953, that provided terms for acquiring new leases, including the ability to take private land with armed force in the case of noncompliance.[14] Aja and Mekaru of Mawashi Village were taken in April 1953, Gushi of Oroku Village in December 1953, Maja of Ie Village in March 1955, and Isahama of Ginowan Village in July 1955.[15] These land confiscations were dramatic. With "bulldozers and bayonets," they often tricked farmers into signing documents they did not understand and burned down their houses at gunpoint.

In the wake of open resistance, the U.S. military resorted to outright political repression. In 1952, the military's governing body, the U.S. Civil Administration of the Ryukyus (USCAR), established and surveilled the civilian Government of the Ryukyu Islands (GRI) that was organized into three branches (executive, legislative, and judicial): the chief executive who was appointed by USCAR, the Ryukyu Legislature whose members were elected through popular vote, and the supreme court. Okinawans were allowed to express their democratic will through its only electoral channel, the Ryukyu Legislature.[16] Senaga suggested that the new political infrastructure was tantamount to a "puppet government."[17]

Yet, even with the high degree of USCAR control, Okinawans still voted on an overwhelmingly anti-U.S. military platform led by a coalition between the OPP and Socialist Party (*Shadaitō*) in a special election to fill a vacated seat belonging to the middle district (*chūbu chiku*) on April 1, 1953. The candidate, Tengan Chōkō, won a landslide victory supporting repeal of Article 3 of the San Francisco Peace Treaty (quoted earlier); reversion to the Japanese administration; opposition to colonization and continued occupation; the immediate enactment of the labor law; opposition to land confiscations; the overthrow of the USCAR appointed chief executive of the GRI, Higa Shūhei; and public elections for the same position.[18] After the opposing Democratic Party (*Minshūtō*) took advantage of the political repression by presenting USCAR with evidence of a purported scandal, the victory was rendered null and void.[19] More than an incidental election to fill a vacated seat, it became known as the "Tengan Incident" and was emblematic of the political repression of widespread opposition to USCAR voiced through the democratic process.

Perfectly orchestrated to fall on the eve of the April 1 election, USCAR issued an off-limits order on establishments catering to U.S. military personnel on March 29. Different from the 1950 off-limits orders that aimed to contain the spread of VD, Deputy Governor David A. P. Ogden of USCAR hinted that these new orders were related to "anti-American thought."[20] What this means is that the U.S. military now positioned the businesses in the base towns as instruments of political manipulation. Concerned with the economic impact of the order, a resident from the entertainment district of the Shintsuji Town of Oroku contributed the following article to the *Ryukyu Shimpo*.

> If the off-limits continues for another month or two, I think there will
> be a number of bankruptcies in the Yaejima District of Koza and
> Shintsuji Town of Oroku. Particularly in the middle district, I think

90 percent of the residents live dependent on the U.S. military. People are incited to satisfy the ambitions of a few anti-Americanists who sacrifice our livelihood.[21] They don't understand the feelings of the middle district residents. Yet the crisis is not limited only to the middle district. The aftershocks are felt throughout the Ryukyus and threaten the livelihood of all Ryukyuans with collapse. If the off-limits are semi-permanent, then all of the Ryukyus shall be assaulted with an economic crisis within a few months.[22]

Although the OPP protested the formation of the sex industry in Okinawa, this article suggests that the so-called anti-Americanists named here were not able to infiltrate the base towns. The author writes of a rift between the "ambitions of a few" who incite the masses with public protest and the base town workers most immediately concerned with making a daily living (*seikatsu*). In simple terms, this means that the immediate life of base town workers was sacrificed on the altar of the protestors' higher ideals. In more complex terms, however, it pushes the theoretical problem of what to do with those who fail to be politically organized, i.e., the lumpenproletariat. Despite the rich heterogeneity amongst the workers and farmers, they were still able to find a voice through the democratic process before the law. The workers of the base towns, however, were not.

Marx classifies the lumpenproletariat as a form of pauperism within the relative surplus population, below the floating, latent, and stagnant populations. Even within the category of pauperism, the lumpenproletariat exists at the bottom as "vagabonds, criminals, [and] prostitutes."[23] As such, it is a peculiar segment of the population for Marx. Ernesto Laclau points out that the other categories of unemployment surrounding the lumpenproletariat are still "functional to capitalist accumulation because the competition of the many workers for the few jobs pushes down the level of wages, and in that way, increases surplus-value."[24] What he means is that the industrial reserve army is predicated on the assumption of an unemployed population that sustains competition for a few jobs, thereby pushing down wages and increasing the rate of profit. In this way, it maintains a "functionality within the system, and as a result, these people are still part of a 'history of production.'"[25] However, the lumpenproletariat is different in that it is unintelligible to capital; it is not part of capital's future commodification of labor power; or as Laclau writes, it is a "heterogeneity which cannot be subsumed under a single 'inside' logic."[26] This points to a heterogeneity—that this book names as the alegal—that cannot be easily mobilized into the official "history of production," either as its workers or as its dissidents.

Here, one may certainly be justified to argue that, contrary to Marx's assumption, the "prostitute" as the "actual lumpenproletariat"[27] is in fact not external to the history of capitalist accumulation, but as the author of the article quoted earlier suggests, a driving force that has the potential to "threaten the livelihood of all Ryukyuans with collapse." While this gendered analysis is important, my concern here is not the "lumpenproletariat as a class or group that can be defined sociologically" as a problem of "occupation or income level."[28] Rather, I am interested in the lumpenproletariat as a potentiality omnipresent across disparate groups. It is in this way that Tomiyama argues that the industrial reserve army is based on a "faith relation" (*shinyō kankei*) in which the unemployed are assumed to be ready and waiting for mobilization into production. By describing it as a "faith relation," however, Tomiyama dislodges the facticity of the industrial reserve army and underscores the mechanism through which it comes to be—that is, through the management of the lumpenproletariat as "the limit where the potential of labor power for capital can turn into an impossibility."[29] The lumpenproletariat is the limit where the "faith relation" breaks down and marks the constant threat of crisis; it is an interruption in the teleological view of history. In this way, Tomiyama does not position the lumpenproletariat as an exception to the rule, but shows how the history of production normalizes itself by categorically excluding the lumpenproletariat. This is why he does not write about the lumpenproletariat as an absolute outside of history—as if its place has already been decided—but instead describes it as a "place of language that searches for a future."[30] Writing the history of the lumpenproletariat, as an unstable category that can turn into a crisis for capital just as easily as it can ensure its continued operation, is a performative process (i.e., that "place of language") that does not lead to a teleological end but "searches for a future" in the process of its articulation.

The question of the base town worker as a lumpenproletariat subject, then, is how to write its history without silencing it in the name of giving it a voice, but allowing the articulation to be an open-ended and transformative process. This is crucial to representation before the state and the lumpenproletariat as un-representable heterogeneity because it opens up the possibility for social transformation when not tethered to state recognition. This is the power of the lumpenproletariat and the alegal: It is not in denying the existence of the state or plotting for its collapse, but in cultivating a life force that exists in its own right removed from the imperative for state recognition. This is a life force that does not have a lifetime to wait in hopes of recognition, but embraces itself in the here and now. This is precisely the possibility that was opened up when Okinawans exhausted the official channels for protest; resistance was driven out of the blinding light of sovereignty and into the rich darkness of the underground. In the next section, I discuss the possibilities opened up by OPP's underground communist party, led by Kokuba Kōtarō, which fostered social transformation through unofficial channels.

The Underground

After the off-limits orders in April 1953, Okinawa's political landscape only became more dismal. In March 1954, USCAR announced plans for a lump-sum payment on lands for which the lease period was projected to be over five years. Okinawan anger was driven to a breaking point after a U.S. congressman erroneously suggested USCAR was catering to the Okinawan desire to sell their land to the U.S. military.[31] In response, the Ryukyu Legislature unanimously passed the well-known "Four Principles for Solving the Military Land Problems" (herein referred to as "Four Principles") resolution on April 30, 1954. It stated that (1) the United States should renounce the purchase of land and the lump-sum payment of rentals; (2) just and complete compensation should be made annually for the land currently in use; (3) indemnity should be paid promptly for all damage caused by the United States; and (4) no further acquisition of land should be made, and the land that was not urgently needed by the United States should be restored promptly.[32] At the same time the resolution was passed, the GRI, Ryukyu Legislature, Mayor's Association (*shichōsonchōkai*), and Federation of Landowners (*tochirengōkai*) formed the Council of Four Organizations (*yonsha kyōgikai*). Despite their various motivations, they unified across the political spectrum. Since Okinawa had exhausted the available channels for political redress, the Council of Four Organizations decided it had no choice but to trump USCAR altogether by going over its head to directly appeal to the United States Congress. The results of this mission would not be known until 1956 (discussed later as the Price Report). Until then, Okinawa was left with its hands tied politically.[33]

In the wake of the Four Principles, Ogden responded with a full-scale Red Scare in Okinawa. In May 1954, he blamed any public opposition to USCAR policy on communism. By October, USCAR targeted the OPP by arresting its members, including Senaga.[34] In Okinawan historiography, this period is known as the "dark ages" in which the possibility of expressing the will of the people through legal channels was foreclosed. The leading historian of contemporary Okinawa, Arasaki Moriteru, argues that these "dark times of repression and plunder . . . became the fertile ground for the people's struggle" and "planted the seeds for the eventual explosion that became the all-island struggle."[35]

Mori Yoshio makes an important intervention to this received historiography by filling in the blanks between the "dark times"—where political speech was repressed—and its "explosion" as the all-island struggle after the 1956 Price Report. He does not assume a natural developmental trajectory from one to the next, but instead depicts a dance between unrepresentable heterogeneity (i.e., the alegal) irreducible to the state and political representation before the state. To this end, he demonstrates how Senaga intentionally and masterfully manipulated these two registers: the unseen on-the-ground work that incited the heterogenous masses and the channeling of this energy into a political platform before the state. Specifically, he tracks the relationship between Hayashi Yoshimi (the aforementioned member of the Amami Communist Party and behind-the-scenes leader of the Nippon Road Company strike), who pushed for the formation of an underground or "nonlegal" (*higōhō*) communist party[36] in Okinawa; Senaga, who capitalized on-the-ground protest on the public platform of the Ryukyu Legislature; and Kokuba Kōtarō, who worked as the leader of the underground communist party in its actualized form, from 1954 to 1957, after Senaga was arrested and Hayashi was deported to Amami during the Red Scare. Whereas Senaga saw the utility in an underground communist party as it existed for representational politics, Kokuba's commitment to the underground enabled him to cultivate a deep suspicion of Senaga's spiritualistic ethno-nationalist pro-reversion politics that would later take Okinawa by storm and engulf the base town as its enemy.

Kokuba was a student of economics at the University of Tokyo when he became involved in the movement for Okinawa's reversion to mainland Japan.[37] Upon his return to Okinawa, Hayashi had already successfully convinced Senaga to start construction of an OPP underground communist party after the success of the Nippon Road Company strike in 1952.[38] Kokuba quickly learned that its role was to augment the OPP by covertly infiltrating the pockets of society that the OPP could not reach publicly. This shed light on the character of the OPP as a true people's party of the masses that was radically different from the JCP in mainland Japan.[39]

Kokuba turned to the farmers of Isahama in 1955, who were suffering an "intense sense of isolation" in their struggle against land confiscations by USCAR.[40] Although they initially rejected him, he gained their trust after working with them in the fields. He facilitated meetings between

farmers from different villages so as to build solidarity amongst them, and
then facilitated a roundtable discussion between the farmers and politicians.[41] Nishime Junji, a Socialist Party member who would later serve as
Okinawa's governor from 1978 to 1990, was deeply moved by the women
in particular, a contingency least likely to participate in representational
politics as the most outspoken in the movement. The women argued:

> While the village men may have been forced to accept [a lease that]
> came through coercion, they do not understand the pain of raising
> children. Men probably recklessly accepted thinking they can just die,
> but women aren't afforded the luxury.
>
> We are driven to madness when thinking of what will happen to
> the children. Even if we want to die, we can't when thinking of the
> children.[42]

The women were resolute in their rejection of negotiations with USCAR
because the futurity of the land was connected to the futurity of their
children like an umbilical cord. Death was a luxury of escape that they
could not afford; instead, they were pressed to confront the immediacy of
life.

At the same time, Iejima was also facing ruthless land confiscations by
armed force. The farmers decided to sit in before the USCAR and GRI
building in Naha after their homes were burned to the ground. At this
time in March 1955, members of the underground communist party that
Kokuba had been working with in the Ryukyu Legislature sent the farmers an anonymous letter which was to be burned after it was read.[43] It
stated:

> We are in the midst of a most painful battle. This is because the
> opponent is an absolute power backed by the greatest military force
> ever. No matter how much they appeal to military force . . . the U.S.
> military's land seizures rob humans of life and rob humans of the
> freedom to live. This cannot be rationalized by anything. . . . This is
> where their weakness lies. The people of Isahama and Iejima who are
> risking their lives expose these unjust acts and weakness. Their call to
> arms is not an act of strength, but rather a manifestation of their
> weakness. . . .
>
> . . . If the struggle continues to consolidate the power of all Oki-
> nawan prefectural citizens and quickly win over the support of the
> people who love justice and humanity, then solidarity will deepen and
> alienate the American military.[44]

The beauty of this letter lies in its auto-subversion. It undermines itself, transforms, and takes on a new life. If starving farmers from an agrarian village receive a letter from faceless individuals associated with an underground communist party who combat a perceived U.S. military dictatorship, one might expect to find explicit instructions for some sort of call to arms. What? When? Where? How? Yet this letter's only instruction, "Burn after reading!," incites the reader to do the exact opposite: Ahagon Shōkō is compelled to "hold it ever more closely to [his] heart."[45] Language as a means to a greater end, i.e., the communication model, is subverted. Furthermore, it is not the authorship that gives it legitimacy, but rather its anonymity that gives the farmers a sense of the infectious nature of the agreement in which it became difficult to discern where it came from. The power of the letter gave courage to the farmers who would go on to take to the streets and lead a "beggar's march" from July 1955.

Ahagon writes that "[n]o one came up with the idea" for the beggar's march, but it organically emerged through conversation amongst the farmers. Without thinking to make a donation box, they used only what they had at hand—their hats—to collect donations as they marched across villages throughout the island.[46] In this way, they did not make something new in order to fulfill a purpose, but the materiality already surrounding them morphed into new purpose. Their march furthermore transformed the people they touched. He writes:

> Women and others listened to our plea as they shed tears. People who didn't have money with them went all the way back home to retrieve their wallets. Police officers who thought it would be unsuitable to make a donation entrusted women listening next to them to do it [on their behalf]. Also, even though they didn't do it [directly] themselves, there were Americans who donated by slipping their honeys (lovers) money.[47]

This passage is significant because it shows how women, in particular, women involved with the "Americans," were used by the representatives of institutional violence (i.e., police officers and most likely "American" soldiers) as mediators. They were useful precisely because they were thought to be the farthest removed from representational politics. This solidarity was only possible under the cover of darkness.

Mori argues that in taking on the most powerful military in the world, the farmers were armed with nothing but a public display of their own vulnerability. Instead of internalizing the shame of becoming beggars, they revealed how the U.S. military had stripped them down to bare life. As a result, they performed a "reversal of values" in which the "weak can overcome the strong."[48] It was this redefinition of strength amidst conditions of utter powerlessness that reinvigorated Okinawa's body politic. The people were no longer dominated by values determined by their oppressors. For Mori, this is the possibility of revolution cultivated within the ground, out of plain view of representational politics, which takes the title of his book, *Revolution within the Ground*.[49]

Mori succeeds in intervening in Arasaki's historiography that too quickly passes from the dark ages of political repression to a new age of popular dissent by failing to see how the work of the underground communist party prepared the soil for the people's empowerment. However, while farmers turned the idea of weakness into a weapon against itself, it still left open the question of whether or not it led to what James R. Martel calls "subversion rather than just more delusion."[50] After all, Ahagon's pacifism was very much informed by religious beliefs in Christianity.[51] Did the Nietzschean reversal of values simply reproduce the delusional hope for recognition through a universal ideal—that of a Christian-inspired nonviolence—or did it subversively dispense with the desire for redemption through a different universal ideal altogether? By valorizing nonviolent forms of protest as representative of the "Okinawan heart"[52] that perseveres to this day, there is a risk of reinscribing it as a universal ideal and imparting it with "just more delusion." Rather, as Masaki Kinjo has shown, neither nonviolence nor violence is inherently good or bad; what makes either powerful is the particular way each is deployed in relation to the state so as to reclaim the state's power over life.[53]

As the letter written to the farmers by the underground communist party suggests, the power of the farmers lies in the immediacy of their fight for survival. They succeeded in exposing the idolatry of mythic violence that does not exist to protect human life, but only exists to protect itself. In other words, while the rest of the world may believe the U.S. military exists to protect the weak—a mantra it continues to recite in the face of Okinawan protest, i.e., "we are here to protect you"—the farmers simply revealed this fallacy with their life. They did not become something other than what they already were in order to be recognized by the state, but by simply being themselves, they altered their relationship to the state. Like Benjamin's notion of allegory, they simply performed what they already were and, by doing so, infused nonhuman and human things of the world with new purpose. Instead of replacing one universal for another, they formed a new community liberated from the onus of sovereign recognition. As an unintended consequence of forgoing a polity that waits to be saved, the responsibility of the decision—however imperfect it may have been—fell upon the individual. Kokuba describes the contagious force of the people who made decisions unmoored from the clear guidance of an authority figure. He writes:

> . . . What is important is becoming unintelligible to America. In doing so, the people's movement will come forth with an explosive force. Not knowing who is behind it is the most important thing.
>
> That's why after arresting Senaga, arresting the party leaders, crushing all of the unions, incapacitating the movement for reversion, Iejima and Isahama were nothing but a second thought for them. And then before they knew it, the counterblow came from that direction, and before they knew it, it spread like wildfire. Certainly, they would try to sniff out how it was [the handiwork] of someone who did something. But no one knows. That is the meaning of having an underground organization. . . . If it is managed to function this way, then I think there is no need for something like an iron rule.[54]

Here he suggests how the law, or "iron rule," becomes superfluous. It was not overcome, but disengaged. Furthermore, women involved with the G.I.s were not alienated from this social order hidden from view of the state, but were its active agents. When Kokuba traveled from village to village every other night so as to not be detected by the U.S. Counter Intelligence Corps (CIC) that was actively hunting him down, he says it was these women who helped keep his cover.

> . . . at that time, there were people amongst the Isahama farmers called G.I. "onlies" or "honeys," and amongst them, some who went on to marry them. There were places where those people were renting rooms. When I was around, they would sometimes come and tell me "the CIC is coming now" or "the CIC was over there just now." And you know how the American military would show up bearing arms, right? About a day in advance, the G.I.s would tell their honeys "I think something's gonna go down. They're getting ready." And then, through the honeys, they would tell us agents. This is how close we got: the locals living there and the party members.
>
> In that way, I was assisted to some degree and was able to carry on the entire time while avoiding the eyes of the CIC. It must have been a surprise for the CIC because [the all-island struggle] exploded with such a bang.[55]

Women involved with the G.I.s (i.e., Okinawa's lumpenproletariat) were not indifferent or hostile to the struggle, but under the cover of darkness, they transformed into mediums and covert agents of solidarity. It was precisely because they stood in the shadow of history that they were able to help make it.[56] Different from the reportage examined in Chapter 1, and articles on Okinawa by the JCP newspaper *Red Flag* at the time,[57] the Okinawan underground communist party newspaper *For the Freedom and Independence of the Nation* is markedly absent of depictions of women who work the base towns.[58]

With the aid of the women, Kokuba was able to move in a modality "unintelligible to America." Stuck in their sovereign modes of thought, USCAR automatically assumed Okinawa would ape its decision-making process of mobilizing a collection of individual wills toward a common goal decided by a charismatic figure. The unexpected "counterblow" that came from Iejima and Isahama was the anonymity of the decision that "spread like wildfire." Released from the mediation of representational politics to deliver their will, the decentralization of power had the unintended consequence of empowering the people. They did not defer to the decision of another, but precisely because there was no identifiable authority figure, they were empowered to make the decision themselves. It was this energy that ignited the all-island struggle a year later.

Into the Blinding Light of Sovereignty

The results of the Council of Four Organizations that sent a mission directly to the United States Congress were in. After a six-member House Committee on Armed Services headed by Charles Melvin Price directly visited Okinawa, they responded with the Price Report on June 9, 1956. Although it attempted to concede with better compensation for the land, it still maintained the intention of a lump-sum payment.[59] This was the trigger that unleashed widespread protest that took the name "all-island struggle" as described here by Arasaki.

> On June 9, when the outline of the Price Report was announced,
> fifty-six of the sixty-four cities, towns, and villages throughout
> Okinawa, or more than 20 percent of the total Okinawan masses,
> united and held a residents' rally[60] on June 20. Then in Naha and Koza,
> the people[61] held a second residents' rally of 100,000 and 50,000 each
> on June 25. This was the process through which the energy of the
> people had reached a boiling point and explosively sprung into action.[62]

The momentum of the all-island struggle did not stop with the farmers, but swept across many sectors of Okinawan society that had grievances with the U.S. military. But how would this mass protest be channeled through the political process?

As we have seen, the U.S. military government (USCAR) had said "no" to the people. Okinawa's civilian government (GRI) had said "yes" to the people, but it was vetoed by USCAR and turned into a "no." And now, the United States Congress had said "no" to the people. Okinawa turned to option number four and found another gate to the law left to knock on: the Japanese administration.

Because Okinawa was boxed in on three sides, the Japanese government appeared as the only remaining gate leading to justice. On June 18, 1956, the Council of Four Organizations announced it would send four representatives to mainland Japan to plead its case. Furthermore, the Council of Four Organizations announced a seven-point platform on June 16, 1956, that was oriented toward the Japanese mainland.[63] It moved to (1) form an organized body in solidarity, (2) transcend individual interests with an ethno-nationalist consciousness to protect the land and territorial sovereignty, (3) renounce all forms of violence in resistance, (4) struggle against the policies of the United States and not individual Americans whose human rights and character must be respected, (5) eradicate all forms of criminal activity, (6) exercise self-governance amongst the people, and (7) overcome complications in strict adherence to the Four Principles.[64]

Generally speaking, support for the Four Principles was framed in terms of support for Okinawa's reversion to the Japanese administration. Popular support for reversion to Japan was already clear by 1950 and formalized with the inauguration of the Association for the Promotion of Reversion to Japan (*Nihon fukki sokushin kiseikai*) in 1951,[65] but frowned upon by USCAR throughout the years of political repression. Point two of the platform, in particular, explicitly drew a distinction between "individual interests" and "ethno-nationalist consciousness." This suggests recognition of the heterogeneity within Okinawa that was "transcend[ed]" by "ethno-nationalist consciousness." The crucial point here—particularly in light of our consideration of the position of the base town workers as the lumpenproletariat—is the way in which this transcendence takes place. As the leader of the underground communist party, Kokuba was extremely sensitive to this point and how it informed the meaning of "nationalist consciousness." For example, in an interview, he states:

What we called nationalism[66] was not a question of a feeling of
oneness that [comes with a sense of being] the same as all other
Japanese. That is the part that seems to be difficult for people to
understand.[67]

As a Marxist, Kokuba did not see the ultimate goal of revolution as the
recuperation of state power. Rather, after socialist revolution, it was assumed that the state would exhaust its utility. This is why Kokuba identi-
fies with the state as a political platform that can only instrumentally
represent the "individual interests" of the masses. In other words, the "individual interests" are instrumentally "transcend[ed]," thereby suggesting
an awareness of the inevitable *failure* of transcendence toward an all-
encompassing idealist totality.

However, this instrumental identification became increasingly replaced
with a spiritualistic one as USCAR made a spectacle of public political di-
visions by polarizing Okinawan society with more off-limits orders. Once
placed under the spotlight, Okinawans became divided as "protesting subjects," coded as pro-Japanese who protested the U.S. military, and "petitioning subjects," coded as pro-American who petitioned for their right to
participate in the base economy.

The off-limits order issued on August 8, 1956, was catastrophic. In 1955,
57 percent ($74.8 million) of Okinawa's gross national product (GNP) came
from outside sources. Of this figure, 27 percent ($20 million) came from the
purchase of "consumption goods" by the U.S. military, or in other words,
entertainment-related expenses in the base towns.[68] When students of the
University of the Ryukyus and Okinawan students in Japanese universities
planned a rally opposing the lump-sum payment in Koza, where many of
the bases were concentrated, the Okinawa Federation of Night Clubs Association (*Okinawa fūzoku eigyō kumiai rengōkai*, herein referred to as OF-
NCA) opposed the demonstration.

The next day on August 9, President Ōshiro Seiji of OFNCA issued a
petition translated into English to USCAR. I could not locate this document, but instead found a supplementary report and petition submitted
on August 13.[69] OFNCA stated that they stood by the Four Principles and
pleaded to "[s]eparate clearly Off Limits from the land problem." However,
they were not shy to demonstrate their open hostility toward the growing
leftist faction of the popular movement, in particular, the platform put forth
by the Land Protection Association at the June 18, 1956, prefectural rally.
The document:

accused Yara Chōbyō of co-opting the Land Protection with "Anti-
   American Ideology," and suggested those "Okinawan future
   leaders" and "pure-minded students" were corrupted from "being
   under the [sic] bad leadership";
boasted of their attempt to "stop the meetings and demonstrations"
   directed by Chief Yara of the Land Protection Association;
reported their resistance to representatives of the board of directors
   of the Land Protection Association;
advocated the "[e]stablishment of [sic] Pro-American underground
   organization and Intelligence . . . under the cooperation of Military
   Intelligence and CID" to counter the "people's party and other bad
   ideologists" that "have an underground organization";
articulated a plan to "stud[y] measures against" "Mr. Senaga and
   Mr. Kaneshi" as they "make an [sic] Anti-American Propaganda";
stated that they would "not call our representative Democrats legisla-
   tors from now if they don't make any reflection [sic]."

What is impressive about this document is that it shows how protesting
subjects came to appear as enemies to their own brethren who were constituted as petitioning subjects. In order to secure the right to participate
in the base economy, which essentially meant the right to sell sex, OF-
NCA was willing to go so far as to advocate the "[e]stablishment of Pro-
American underground organization and Intelligence" since they
emerged as a threat to their very survival. This is far removed from the
days when Okinawan women in relationships with G.I.s tipped off underground communist party members by warning them of CIC raids just one
year prior.

Senaga understood the off-limits order to be a desperate measure taken
by USCAR that was astounded by the "breadth and depth of the resistance
that enveloped all classes and all areas" of Okinawan society.[70] He para-
phrased the sentiments of a speaker from the base town as follows:

I know that we have to protect the land by following through with the
Four Principles. But what about life[71] today, much less tomorrow?
Shouldn't the one protecting territorial sovereignty be the Japanese
government? Shouldn't it be the Japanese people? They say that they
are our brethren, but have they done a single thing for us? I support
Japanese reversion. But wait. Isn't it the case that we don't know when
reversion will happen? How are we supposed to go on living until
then? What's wrong with relying on Mr. America to get by?[72]

The speaker repeatedly points to the here and now, "life today, much less tomorrow," and getting by in the base town instead of looking beyond to the Japanese government and Japanese people to do what both neglect to do. The statement is allegorical in structure because it interrupts the idealism of the reversion movement that makes promises toward the future and points to the failure of total unification by revealing that the "all-island struggle" really did not encompass "all" of the island to begin with. Senaga is at a loss as to what to do with these "bastards (*otoshigo*) of military colonial rule," or as he calls them, "Okinawa's 'lumpenproletariat,'" and asks when they will be "washed away."[73] By use of this verb "washed away," or "*kiyomeuru*," language commonly used for religious purification, he suggests an ethnic cleansing from contamination of a social or moral evil. He is interested in Okinawa's underground only to the extent that it can be brought up to the light of representational politics and therefore locks the lumpenproletariat in a position outside of history. This is why for him, "[t]he most horrifying thing in the world is military colonial domination . . . whereupon shameless exploitation by capital comes to bear upon those thrown outside of production and allowed to fall into prostitution."[74] In this sense, Senaga performs the sovereign power of exclusion of sex workers from a political enclosure—ironically couched in his plea for reincorporation into the Japanese administration—much like anti-base activists appealed to the elimination of the occupation baby in mainland Japan during the 1950s.

Yet, with this quotation, Senaga's ambivalence is apparent since he also demonstrates an understanding of how the base town workers instrumentally deployed a pro-American stance out of the immediate concern for making a living. The problem, however, is when an instrumental identification becomes confused with what Kokuba calls a "spiritualistic" (*seishinshugitekina*) one. In other instances, Senaga increasingly evoked a spiritualistic ethno-nationalism as he rallied against "rule by a foreign race" (*iminzoku shihai*) toward Japan in which Okinawans were "connected by blood to the fatherland."[75] Kokuba faults Senaga for crossing this line by stating that his "appeals to 'ethno-nationalism' rooted in spiritualism in 1958 lacked the power to move the Okinawan masses" toward revolution and only delivered them to the door of Japanese monopoly capital.[76] I will return to this point at 1958 in terms of the development of capitalist relations in Okinawa shortly, but first, what is significant here is how this spiritualism complicated the mixed-race issue.

Whereas Senaga only made gestures to this here, the prominent Okinawan historian, Higashionna Kanjun, lodged a public attack on the base towns framed in an explicitly spiritualistic ethno-nationalism amidst the all-island struggle. In a 1957 newspaper article entitled "Mixed-Race Children," he identified the problem specifically as the type of miscegenation that occurs as a result of extraterritoriality, and not "international marriage."[77]

> The mixed-race children that creep out of the present red-light districts are nothing but scars of war damage that have inherited the inferior genes of both parents. Of course, these children are not guilty of sin or blame. However, regarding their birth, they are nothing but the crystallization of disgrace that was not planned for nor hoped for. They will eternally be an enormous liability to society. Letting such a liability go—or worse yet, letting [the population grow] larger in numbers—will condemn our communal life to darkness. We probably have no choice but to look after those already born. But it is to our greatest dissatisfaction that in these times where a limitation on the number of births in the healthy sector of society is recommended, there is no check on these unhealthy births.[78]

And:

> When the representative petitioners traveled to Tokyo last year to advocate the Four Principles, the occupying U.S. military ordered the soldier's red light district off-limits on the grounds that it would reduce friction with the locals. Accordingly, the district's business owners fell onto hard times. When I heard them complaining that this was the revenge tactic of economic pressure, I thought as people who purport to protect the land and protect their everyday life,[79] their argument was suicidal. Rather, we became livid and felt that these types of unhealthy businesses should be completely eliminated. Nonetheless, they countered that ideals and reality are different. These kinds of businesses are proof that they have come to think it is a natural given that mixed-race children are growing in numbers every year primarily out of these kinds of districts.[80]

In these passages, Higashionna's writing is spiritualistic because the merely instrumental identification of heterogeneous "individual interests" with ethno-nationalism is replaced by the imperative for all individuals to identify with the future of an idealistic "communal life." The allegorical structure of an instrumental nationalism that is reminded of the ultimate *failure* of identification is replaced with a symbolic structure of ethno-nationalism in which the integrity of the family unit is substituted for the

integrity of the community and, by extension, state. In other words, similar
to protest against extraterritorial miscegenation in Japan, Higashionna does
not take issue with racial mixing per se, but with the racial mixing that
occurs as a result of extraterritoriality. These are the "unhealthy births"
that occur outside of the state's ability to manage the population. Furthermore, Higashionna's spiritualism, similar to what Tosaka Jun described
as "mysticism" or "primitivism," beckons forth a biopolitical mechanism
of social defense: It becomes the imperative of so-called good Japanese to
eliminate these "unhealthy births" for the sake of the entire Japanese
community. This is why Higashionna expressed his "greatest dissatisfac-
tion that . . . there is no check on these unhealthy births" and disapproved
of the thought in which "it is a natural given that mixed-race children"
grow in numbers every year.

For Kokuba, however, this kind of spiritualistic ethno-nationalism was
not only ineffective, but in fact played directly into the hands of the global
political economy after 1958. While the United States became the world's
strongest economic power after World War II, the relative strength of the
dollar propelled by military expenditures during the Korean War was losing ground. The U.S. balance of payments resulted in debt in the late
1950s.[81] Europe and Japan, which had focused on reconstructing the
war-torn infrastructure of their economies, were now transitioning into
export economies.[82] As a result, Eisenhower opened a new chapter in
the story of American empire in which the U.S. military and global
economic policy became even more intimately intertwined. This new economic policy aimed to first, integrate the economies of the United States
and its allies through free trade, and second, promote burden-sharing of
military security.[83]

In Okinawa, the political unrest from the all-island struggle combined
with the overall global trend of defense spending cuts and liberalization of
the markets of the free world resulted in a decisive policy change in the
political economy. USCAR announced the abandonment of the lump-sum
payment proposal, agreement for payment on a yearly basis, reassessment
of lands every five years, and agreement for payment of more than six times
for rent than was originally agreed upon in the Price Report.[84] This created a military base land lessor class that became immune to the spiritualistic ethno-nationalism of the all-island struggle. Kokuba argued that this
led financiers and entrepreneurs hungry for capital into believing the
trickle down of rental income could be used to fund growth in industry.
Cultivating this sector of the political economy could further neutralize
discontent in the base towns. Kokuba writes:

At the height of the "all-island struggle," the U.S. military implemented off-limits measures in which G.I.s were prohibited from
entering the entertainment districts in Okinawa's middle district
around U.S. military bases. This started to put economic pressure on
the residents who were directly dependent on base income for their
livelihood. . . . In other words, they were opposed to the Price
Report. . . . but the Okinawan economic structure replete with a social
stratum[85] considered lacking in future prospects after the loss of base
income became conspicuous as a weak point when moving forward
with an ethno-nationalist resistance movement.

In suturing this gap, some finance industries or various business
managers scraped together the residents' military land rent. Thinking
that they could exploit the capital for the establishment or expansion
of new industries, enthusiastic supporters of the lump sum payment
for military use of the land started to come forward.[86]

The "entertainment district" exemplified the "weak point" of the "ethno-
nationalist resistance movement" because the everyday life of its workers
could not sustain on spiritualism alone. In addition to the economic sanctions, the introduction of the A-sign system in 1956 also shifted the cost
of managing the spread of VD to base town establishments. Even though
the U.S. military made prostitution illegal, there were no corresponding
laws effective enough to enable the local Ryukyu police to punish offenses.[87] Hence, VD was controlled through a combination of off-limits
orders and regulations that imposed expensive standards to be "Approved,"
thereby warranting it an "A-sign" establishment. This meant that the
establishments required more startup and running capital, and drove
struggling establishments into bankruptcy.[88]

At the same time, even though the original dream for reversion to mainland Japan was rooted in a dream to return to Japan as part of a global
proletariat and not a bourgeoisie state,[89] Kokuba detected that the larger
aim of the resolution to the all-island struggle was to further the reintegration of Okinawa into the Japanese political economy. Money would not
go into supporting the growth of Okinawan industry, but it would flow
into Japan. Much of this infrastructure had already been laid by the 1952
Japan-Ryukyu Trade Memorandum that allowed Okinawa's main industries in sugar and pineapple to be subject to special treatment on exports
to Japan.[90] In other words, these industries were treated as domestic, not
foreign, from the perspective of Japan. This enabled Japanese businesses
to take advantage of the government protection of Okinawan industries

by importing sugar and pineapple at a low price. At the same time, Okinawan imports vastly exceeded exports, resulting in a balance of payments deficit. Furthermore, 70 to 80 percent of the imports were consumption goods, and not materials for the promotion of industry. The gap was offset by base income; base income, as Kokuba argued, centered on the entertainment industry.[91] In this way, Kokuba formulated what would become known as a "colander economy" (*zaru keizai*).[92] Dollars that flowed in from the U.S. military bases passed through the hands of Okinawans and into the coffers of Japan as Okinawans used the dollars to purchase consumption items from the mainland. Takazato Suzuyo added a feminist analysis to this tripartite arrangement: "Japan came to the end of the war by using its 'Okinawan' daughter as a breakwater of flesh and then subsequently sold her body to gain economic prosperity."[93]

In order to further win over the industrial sector, USCAR implemented a series of ordinances to open Okinawa up to the global economy in September 1958. Ordinance No. 11 encouraged foreign investments in the Ryukyus,[94] Ordinance No. 12 encouraged foreign trade,[95] and Ordinance No. 14 regulated the conversion of the B-yen military notes to U.S. dollars.[96] While the aim of the 1958 ordinances was to encourage investments in Okinawan industries, Kokuba understood as early as 1962 its limitations.[97] Without production subsidies from Japan, he saw little hope for their development.[98] Indeed, as he predicted, imports continued to far surpass exports,[99] leaving the difference to be offset by the base economy.[100] As others have noted, tertiary industries (tourism, restaurants, transportation, retail, and the service industries) came to dominate the structure of the Ryukyuan economy with renewed vigor.[101] Although the Ryukyus were technically open to foreign investments globally, imports and exports were largely to and from Japan.[102]

In place of substantial economic development, the United States instead created yet another type of petitioning subject. The United States Congress directly passed Public Law 86–629, "An Act to Provide for Promotion of Economic and Social Development in the Ryukyu Islands," that provided a legal basis for "improving the welfare" of the Ryukyu people through economic aid.[103] This was reinforced by the Ikeda-Nixon Joint Statement of 1961 in which the United States agreed to increase funding of the Ryukyus and also accept funding from the Japanese government in preparation for the eventual reversion to the Japanese administration.[104] In 1962, GRI received significantly increased aid from the United States and newly introduced aid from the Japanese government.[105] This aid concentrated primarily in funding educational facilities and public works.[106]

By 1971, a year before the reversion, aid from the Japanese government was more than double the aid from the United States.

The spiritualistic ethno-nationalism, which Senaga (and the JCP before him) hoped would resist capitalism, ironically went on to become the voice that petitioned for Okinawa's reintegration into the Japanese economy. Even though the workers and farmers were pitted against the base towns—giving the illusion of a binary between pro-Japanese protestors and pro-American petitioners—Kokuba understood that this dialectic could be readily sublated. In order to "break through this 'imperialist' ideology generated by Japanese monopoly capital and the 'utilitarianism' of Okinawa's local capitalists," Kokuba argued for an "organization of workers and farmers based on class into a revolutionary movement."[107] The possibilities and limitations of this new class-based movement through New Left activism, along with its implications for the base towns, is the topic for the next chapter.

CHAPTER 4

Okinawa, 1958–1972: The Subaltern Speaks

In Chapter 3, I showed how the simple pro-Japanese versus pro-American national binary was complicated by fundamental shifts in the global economy. The economic policy changes of 1958 triggered a second, more substantial exodus from Okinawa's peripheries to U.S. military base towns in pursuit of dollars. This era also marked the emergence of the New Left, both globally and in Japan, and the development of its thought in Okinawa as a critique of the Old Left's ethno-nationalism.

While class solidarity seemed like a progressive step beyond the trappings of Marxian ethno-nationalism, a number of Marxist activists started to question New Left assumptions of a "single-state imperialism" against which the "Japanese proletariat" was to resist. Taking into account the differing Leninist internationalist model of imperialism, critical Marxian activists such as Kawata Yō and Matsushima Chōgi questioned the middle-class assumptions about a "Japanese proletariat" and drew connections between the regionalism of the Greater East Asia Co-Prosperity Sphere and a renewed trans-Pacific regionalism that emerged in the postwar period. Paying attention to Okinawa's historical exclusion from the biopolitical order, Matsushima particularly defined the "Okinawan proletariat" as a social stratum that constantly failed to be represented by the state.

Instead of assuming that the failure of class representation is an impediment to resistance, this chapter repositions it as a valuable clue. It reads portrayals of base town women in reportage and documentary film in order to show the possibilities of their failed representation. It also shows the real-life possibilities of an allegorical reading of the world through a remarkable moment of insurgency amongst base town workers during the 1970 Koza Riot. Those very subjects who had hitherto shied away from public protest were able to celebrate a moment of open anti-military violence precisely because of the absence of any sort of political mobilization. Hence, I ultimately show how the failure of representation does not necessarily lead to the weakening of politics, but instead points to the possibility of a different relationship to the political itself.

Koza, a Trans-Pacific Borderland

During the reversion era, from 1958 to 1972, Okinawa became a borderland between the United States and the Asia Pacific. It was the hub of the Vietnam War through which multiple worlds, each engaged in their own internal struggles, passed. It was the turf on which white supremacy and Black Power clashed, the launching pad for the Vietnam War and anti-war protest amidst reconceptualizations of Pan-Asian solidarity, and the ground upon which debates on global capitalism were rehashed. Base towns such as Koza City (formerly Goyeku Village) quickly became a central nodal point that facilitated a proliferation of these rhizomatic entanglements. Hence, Koza's formation is the story of a borderland. Here, we will examine the kaleidoscopic overlapping of differences as these multiple worlds of the United States, Japan, and Okinawa converged through the expansion of the base towns.

Farmers throughout the prefecture flooded into Koza in search of the dollars brought in by the 1958 economic reforms and entered the labor force of the U.S. military base economy. Okinawa's internal ethnolinguistic multiplicity was collapsed into the base towns whereupon it writhed restlessly under the new heading of a working class enslaved to the American dollar. Often these migrant workers could not immediately identify as "Okinawan" much less as "Japanese." They came to establish and/or work for dry cleaners, pawn shops, general stores, and of course, the entertainment industry. Interviewees of a Koza oral history project paint a picture of this exodus whereupon migrant island peoples flocked to Koza in pursuit of the American dream in Okinawa.

> People from all areas of Okinawa gathered around Koza's Business Center Street. These were not just people from Koza, but they also came from Naha, Itoman, Kadena, northern Okinawa, and peripheral islands like Miyako and Amami. They settled down on this land with dreams of success and continue to live here as pioneers from that time. The economic promise of Koza drew in the impoverished *Uchinānchu*[1] of the day. The entertainment industry that serviced U.S. military personnel and its affiliates, bars, and such emanated with a gaudy charm and drew people in. Americans jostled together in this gathering from all corners of Okinawa and created a *champurū*[2] culture.[3]

Amidst this social transformation, workers flooded into base towns such as Koza that sprung up around the sex industry, referred to here as "*fūzoku eigyō*." As workers filled into these spaces in search of work, they were met with American-style racial segregation; the internal diversity of one group collided with the internal diversity of another. Because fights immediately erupted as soon as whites rubbed elbows with blacks in Yaejima bars, Yaejima and the Business Center Street became designated as white neighborhoods while the nearby Teruya became designated as a black neighborhood.[4] Many African Americans claimed the space themselves by calling it the "Bush" or the "Four Corners."[5] According to one estimate, by 1969 there were approximately ten thousand black G.I.s in Okinawa; six thousand of them were ardent supporters of the Black Power movement and two thousand were members of the Black Panther Party.[6]

Okinawan bar bouncers, known as "Boys," became implicated in the maintenance of these boundaries, as they understood its economic implications. Higa Sadanobu narrates the following in an oral history.

> There were black versus white brawls. If a white person came to the black neighborhood by chance, he would get jumped by black people. It's the same if a black person came to the white neighborhood. Moreover, when the Boys got involved in black versus white altercations, the Boys from the black neighborhood would join forces with the blacks and the Boys from the white neighborhood would join forces with the whites.[7]

In recognition of the place of the base town in maintaining racial segregation, U.S. military soldiers attempted to desegregate by threatening offending bars with off-limits orders. One Koza resident recalls the following:

Since brawls would immediately ensue if [blacks and whites] came face-to-face with each other, we A-sign business people were deeply troubled and hence put up "no blacks" signs. The reality is that fights ensue when black people are let into an establishment frequented by white people. We put the signs up because our establishments would get trashed. [Our actions] were interpreted as discriminatory because it was right before reversion when discrimination against blacks was facing scrutiny in the U.S. We were subject to off-limits orders. If we put up a "no blacks" sign, then our A-sign designation would be taken away.[8]

Above concerns with the larger implications of racial discrimination, the speaker focuses on how blacks challenged racial boundaries to the detriment of good business by intentionally sitting in white-designated bars for prolonged periods of time with only one beer on their tab so that "whites would stop coming and [the bar] would get hijacked by blacks."[9]

The racial politics amongst people of the base towns was also complicated by gender and national difference. In 1972, Okinawa's future governor, Ōta Masahide (1990–1998), foregrounded the problem of Okinawa's sex industry in terms of the deteriorating position of women after the indigenous Ryukyu Kingdom became absorbed into the modernizing Japanese state. Drawing from Ifa Fuyū and Majikina Ankō's *Okinawan Women's History* (*Okinawa joseishi*) and Sakima Kōei's *Meditations on Female Politics* (*Josei seijikō*), he contrasted the modern form of Japanese state sovereignty with a dual structure of male/female sovereignty under the Ryukyu Kingdom in which sovereignty of the female court (*onnagimi*) took precedence over the male court (*otokogimi*). This soon changed, however, with the demise of the Ryukyu Kingdom. Patriarchal social relations were inscribed within the process of Okinawa's assimilation into the Japanese state.[10] Women commonly fled catastrophic domestic situations into the arms of pimps who took on their monetary debts in exchange for bondage into a form of indentured sexual slavery.[11] Debts grew as the women were charged interest; penalized for taking days off; and charged for supplies such as toiletries, clothing, and bedding, in addition to room and board. If they attempted to escape, they risked being caught by watchmen at the airport or harbors who brought them back with additional debt tacked onto their account.[12] Hence, as is the case with colonialism in general, gender inequality amongst Okinawan men and women was part and parcel of the unequal relationship between mainland Japan and Okinawa before the war.

Despite the gendered implication of Okinawa's precarious relationship to Japanese sovereignty, anti-prostitution campaigns were couched in pro-reversion rhetoric of equal protection under the Japanese constitution. While Japan had just passed anti-prostitution legislation in 1956 that was implemented in 1957, petitions for similar anti-prostitution legislation by the Okinawan Women's Association (*Okinawa fujin rengōkai*) in 1958 were not well received. Initially, anti-prostitution campaigns were designed to eliminate a social evil that plagued Okinawa's youth with bad influence.[13] But after feminist politicians and activists from mainland Japan, such as the suffrage leader Ichikawa Fusae,[14] visited Okinawa, it was recast as a human rights issue.[15] Under this rubric, women's groups addressed the conditions and rights of prostitutes as well as the movement to revise Japanese nationality laws in order to accommodate stateless mixed-race children born to Okinawan mothers and U.S. military fathers.[16] Director of the Women's Congress of Japan (*Nihon fujin kaigi*) and future House of Councillors politician Shimizu Sumiko addressed the issue as follows.

> . . . the problems women in Okinawa have come to face under the U.S. administration is a structure of oppression that is two or three times worse than what women in the mainland face. . . .
>
> Albeit incomplete, in the postwar mainland, there was a period where the administration encouraged women's liberation, and in some way or another, managed to inculcate the spirit of human rights into the constitution.
>
> However, for Okinawa, which is deprived of such things, women are sacrificed. Accustomed to an obedient way of life, their human rights are trampled on through prostitution and their slave-like bodies are confined; they are resigned to the idea that debt upon contract [with their pimps] is unavoidable.[17]

Shimizu views the women as "slave-like" and links the recuperation of their autonomy to protection under the constitutional democracy of the Japanese state. Yet this is a state sovereignty that Japan recuperated at the expense of allowing Okinawa to become a U.S. military fortress.

The inability to account for Okinawa's precarious position vis-à-vis Japanese state sovereignty in the anti-prostitution campaign was compounded by the absence of an analysis of the political economy. Although prostitution was opposed by most sectors of Okinawan society, conservatives representing the Ryukyu Legislature argued that it would be impossible to outlaw because Okinawa "has bases."[18] What this meant more explicitly was that it was integral to the Okinawan economy. Shimabukuro

Hiroshi argued that sex work was Okinawa's largest off-base industry by 1970. He estimated that it generated $50.4 million per year compared to the largest official off-base industries in Okinawa: sugar ($43 million) and pineapple ($17 million).[19] Joined by four other organizations active in the reversion movement, the anti-prostitution lobby at least succeeded in prompting the Ryukyu Legislature to instigate a series of studies in 1964. As of 1969, the police department reported approximately 7,385 suspected prostitutes in Okinawa.[20] This pointed to about one in forty to fifty women ages ten to sixty.[21] Furthermore, anti-prostitution legislation was put into place on July 10, 1970, although it was essentially useless because there was no social welfare infrastructure to assist the women and their children until after Okinawa was incorporated into the Japanese administration in 1972.[22]

In showing how the various categories of race, gender, and nation—each fraught with internal contradictions within—collided in Koza's base town, my aim here is to show how its workers became a highly contested site precisely because of their ambiguity. The more they pushed the boundaries of each category, the more there was a compulsion to determine their position before the law. Furthermore, the more these issues became politicized, the more they retreated into the shadows. The attempt to forge class unity clashed with the base town workers. Not only is this New Left archive still somewhat taboo within Okinawan studies,[23] but no one has been able to directly engage it with the question of sexual labor. Yet, as the Okinawan activist Matsushima Chōgi acknowledges,[24] base town workers were so central to debates during this time that it was impossible to work around them. In the next section, I show how the New Left's assumption of class solidarity failed to breach the foundational problem of alegality that the base town workers embodied.

Class Struggle

As early as 1962, Kokuba Kōtarō's writings marked a deep cleft in the reversion movement. He challenged his readers to reposition an ethnonationalist struggle against American imperialism as a class struggle in which Japanese monopoly capitalism collaborates with American imperialism. Yet Kokuba was not part of a social movement or mainstream intellectual current. He was ousted by the OPP in 1959, fled to mainland Japan, and had little connection to the arrival of New Left thought in Okinawa. Although remarkably close in trajectory, the *Ryūdai Marukusu shugi kenkyūkai* (University of the Ryukyus Marx Research Group, herein referred to as "*Maruken*") came together in 1961 and became one of the first social formations that integrated New Left thought and activism into Okinawa. The group's leader, Yamazato Akira, wrote of the emergence of *Maruken* as a result of the disillusionment with Senaga's OPP politics. Even though both the JCP and Senaga had identified Japanese capitalism as complicit with American imperialism, their adherence to the two-stage thesis prevented them from apprehending it theoretically. Both insisted upon a national unification of Okinawa and Japan first; the messy matter of capitalism would be dealt with later.

Kokuba, *Maruken*, and others who would come to be aligned with the New Left, however, criticized the primacy of national struggle as a sort of political opportunism that gained force in the blind spot of theorizing a new form of militarism wedded to transnational capitalist exploitation. Yamazato charged that Senaga's "vassal state policy" "failed to capture the sense of crisis imbued in the people." This is why, he argues, Senaga's campaign "fell apart without allowing for the spontaneous formation of an organization and consciousness."[25] Okinawans were not becoming complicit with the U.S. military because of a lack of ethno-nationalist sentiment; it was because resistance toward economic hardship was transforming Okinawans into a new type of "petitioning subject": Okinawans who petition the Japanese government for "industrial subsidies"[26] to protect Okinawan industries within the Japanese national economy. Far from Okinawans becoming pro-American and anti-Japanese, they were being aligned by the United States to "request for a return to the Japanese administration" through economic interest.[27]

Hence, many progressive activists who had originally supported the OPP as the premier anti-base party in Okinawa were overcome by a sense of alienation. They drifted away without a concrete idea of how to form another party that could represent the interests of the workers. This cloudy disillusionment, however, was struck by a "lightning bolt"[28] instance of clarity when students of the University of the Ryukyus set their sights on the sweeping student movements of *Zengakuren* (detailed next) as they surrounded and infiltrated the Japanese Diet with tens of thousands of workers in protest of the U.S.-Japan Security Treaty (herein referred to as "Anpo.")

Demonstrations to oppose the 1960 revision of Anpo are canonized as the most significant moment of mass protest in the history of postwar Japanese political activism. College students emerged as a driving force in the protests. *Zengakuren* (or the *zennichi gakusei jichikai sōrengō*) formed a network of student governances in public and private universities across Japan.[29] It was originally established in 1948 within the JCP, but after years of factionalism from within, *Zengakuren* was taken over by *Bund* (*kyōsanshugidōmei*) leadership in 1958. *Bund* was composed of younger students who clashed with the old guard of the JCP. While the JCP carried out a strongly anti-American platform after 1950 that protested the U.S. military presence in Japan, *Bund* differentiated itself from the JCP by shifting to a critique of the resurgence of Japanese imperialism. It attacked the Stalinism of the JCP[30] as a rigid, narrow-minded, and insular ethno-nationalism that failed to envision world revolution. In this way, the Japanese New Left was born out of *Bund*'s ideological commitments to anti-Stalinism, internationalism, and anti-Japanese imperialism.[31]

Bund splintered into a number of sects after the fanfare of the 1960 Anpo protest settled down. *Maruken* started to interact with *Kakukyōdō* (*Nihon kakumeiteki kyōsanshugisha dōmei*). In 1963, *Kakukyōdō* branched off into *Kakumaruha*[32] and *Chūkakuha*.[33] *Kakumaruha*, in particular, became prominent as many members from *Maruken*, including its leader, Yamazato, joined its sect.[34] These New Left activists persistently inserted a class analysis into the reversion movement while also emphasizing the revolutionary practice of struggle (*jitsuryoku tōsō*) as they routinely took to the streets in protest.[35] For example, Nakaya Kōkichi, who was active in *Kakumaruha*, reversed OPP's emphasis on national struggle manifest in its anti-American rhetoric with an international class analysis. I quote at length here a 1965 article Nakaya published in the *University of the Ryukyus Student Newspaper* that captures the sentiment of *Kakumaruha*.

> . . . as seen in the frequent appearance of tear gas G.I.s throw at civilians, the fights between G.I.s in the bars, their reckless cars, and their bombings of neighborhood shops sensationalized in the daily newspaper, they intentionally commit crimes to get thrown into military prison. These are the G.I.s raging about, who attempt to escape deployment to the battleground (i.e., Vietnam) by intentionally committing crimes in order to get sent to military prison; these are the G.I.s with ghastly and downtrodden expressions as they are taken to Naha military port to be sent off to die in Vietnam. They are an oppressed class used as an instrument of the U.S. imperial war of aggression. Instead of reaching out to these G.I.s to "oppose U.S. imperial war policies and rise up to an anti-war struggle," is it really acceptable to simply yell, "Fucking Americans go home!" or "Yankee go home!," fan hatred toward a foreign race, or [push for] the liberation of the Okinawan people through racial hatred? Is it possible for

this "anti-American racial thought,"[36] which is completely cut off from internationalism, to realize the liberation of humans (i.e., alienated workers or the people)? I will answer [this question] very clearly: No. The reason is that the most fundamental basis of the poverty of the workers is in the "usurpation of profit by Okinawan capitalists in the workplace." This "essential contradiction between capitalists and workers" in the eyes of the class struggle cannot achieve class liberation by asserting "America is the enemy" and subordinating itself to the national activism of "first expel America and then return to Japan."[37]

Nakaya directly opposes the anti-American Japanese ethno-nationalism that informs the reversion movement. Specifically, he attacks the primacy of national over class struggle by criticizing the OPP two-step program to "first expel America and then return to Japan." Instead, he takes the most "sensationalized" fodder for anti-American ideologues—U.S. military crime—and rereads it as a desperate plea for international class liberation. While it is clear that he opposes one kind of internationalism (i.e., the international system of nation-states), his proposal for a different kind of internationalism (i.e., international proletarian revolution) poses some of the same theoretical questions that troubled his ethno-nationalist counterparts. If national unity is a problem for Okinawa, then how about class unity? Or alternatively posited, if Okinawa cannot be represented as a nation, then how can it be represented as a class?

One of the largest complications of a class-based analysis occurred with the conflict between the on-base labor union *Zengunrō* and the off-base workers in the base towns. This labor union, specifically for on-base workers, was originally established in 1961 (under the name *Zengunrōren*, which changed to *Zengunrō* in 1963) and fought for the right to organize without USCAR interference, better wages, better benefits, and better working conditions.[38] Although *Zengunrō* ultimately joined the reversion movement, it was ambivalent on the anti-base issue. By 1968, *Zengunrō* boasted of 20,400 members, making it one of the largest unions in Okinawa with significant political force.[39] *Zengunrō* was able to win concessions from the U.S. military until the 1969 Sato-Nixon Joint Communique in which both states agreed that Okinawa would revert to the Japanese administration.[40] At this point, the United States sought to transfer the economic burden of its military presence in Okinawa to Japan. The process started to unfold in 1969 as the U.S. military trimmed its on-base labor force with 2,826 layoffs.[41] *Zengunrō* responded with two strikes ranging from forty-eight hours to five days in duration. It was during the second

strike in particular that friction between *Zengunrō* and the base town workers reached new heights.

With a tightening of the flow of U.S. dollars, the base town workers—
particularly the debt-stricken women—were the first to feel the devasta-
tion of the change in economic tides. The severity of the situation was
compounded as the U.S. military responded to total paralysis brought on
by the *Zengunrō* strike with its go-to solution: more off-limits orders.
A-sign businesses were forced to close their doors and took to the streets.
Business owners joined forces with the conservative Okinawa Liberal
Democratic Party (*Okinawa Jimintō*, herein referred to as the "Okinawa
LDP"), right-wing organizations, and Okinawan yakuza to launch an
attack on the *Zengunrō* protesters with physical violence, stoning, and arson. Koza was so torn by the conflict that its so-called progressive mayor,
Ōyama Chōjō, was compelled to petition for the strike's cessation.[42] The
following oral history illustrates how the *Zengunrō* strike affected the rest
of Koza.

> . . . As soon as *Zengunrō* engaged in their activism, the neighborhood
> became subject to off-limits orders. Because this foreclosed the ability
> for the Boys of Business Center Street to make a living, they got angry
> and started doing things like punch *Zengunrō* activists. . . .
>
> When we broke through the picket lines of the *Zengunrō* protest-
> ers, the Boys on our street laid in on the union. . . . The Business
> Center Street youth were the right-wingers at the time. They sur-
> rounded *Zengunrō* and created havoc. That time the riot police were
> deployed to protect *Zengunrō*. Usually it is the [riot] police that
> *Zengunrō* fights with, but this time, they were deployed to protect and
> pull them out.[43]

The speaker remembers the incident in terms of an emotional and violent
response to the organized activism of *Zengunrō* picketers who "created
havoc" on the Business Center Street way of life. The "right wingers" are
described here as young and raw. Okinawan New Left activists, however,
characterize the same incident in terms of the organization of a conservative right-wing political force "that parasites" off of the U.S. military.

> "A-sign businesses" are a social stratum[44] that embodies the real
> parasites of the base-dependent Okinawan economy, i.e., existences
> that parasite off the G.I.s. A situation has been created in which
> right-wing forces such as the Okinawa LDP, the anti-reversion
> "Association of Okinawans to Create Okinawa,"[45] and the "Federation
> for Victory over Communism"[46] graft their ideology directly onto the

business owners' concerns for their economic interest and allow
groups of organized violence to forerun attacks on the picketers and
their headquarters. Of course, lingering in the background of such
developments is the U.S. military plot to have "Okinawans fight
amongst themselves."[47]

The business owners here are articulated in terms of a bottom-line "economic interest" that can be harnessed by right-wing political forces. They
are blamed for succumbing to the temptation of economic interest and be-
littled as "parasites" who are not able to realize their potential because
they unproductively depend on the bases for sustenance. The U.S. military is the agent that takes advantage of the situation by orchestrating
right-wing versus left-wing opposition.

Interestingly in this account, it is through the dialectic of force and
counterforce within Okinawa that pushes the politically ambivalent
Zengunrō over to explicitly oppose the U.S. military presence in Okinawa
altogether.

> Through a confrontation with right-wing violence that "opposed
> reversion to the mainland and elimination of bases,"[48] *Zengunrō*
> workers were able to practically[49] realize their struggle as a struggle
> for the "reversion to the mainland and the elimination of bases, i.e.,
> Okinawa's recapture."[50] The self-protection style of [sporting] helmets
> and *gewalt*[51] batons became popular and some even started preparing
> Molotov cocktails.[52]

The jargon of the times here requires explication. The "elimination of
bases" (*kichi tekkyō*) referred to in the passage was a divisive issue within
Zengunrō. In short, by supporting the elimination of bases, these on-base
workers would be effectively advocating the elimination of their employer.
The Okinawa Prefecture Council for Reversion to the Fatherland (*Okinawaken sokoku fukki kyōgikai*) had keenly monitored these deliberations
within *Zengunrō*, as it was eager to gain its endorsement as the largest labor
union in Okinawa. In order to come to a middle ground, members of
Zengunrō split hairs between being "anti-base" (*kichi hantai*) (i.e., in opposition to problems stemming from Okinawa's bases, such as crimes committed by the G.I.s) and being for the "elimination of bases" (i.e., the
eradication of all U.S. military bases from Okinawa).[53] Here, the visceral
confrontation between right-wing Okinawans is what pushed *Zengunrō*
over to the side of supporting the "elimination of bases." This was further
conflated with the New Left slogan "Okinawa's recapture" (*Okinawa dakkan*),

which was a criticism of the bourgeois version of Okinawa's reversion uncritical of the U.S. military and Japanese capitalism. Other Okinawan New Left activists, such as Hateruma Takeshi, similarly described this as a pivotal moment where not only *Zengunrō*, but all involved in the Okinawan struggle (*Okinawa tōsō*) were able to "resolutely fight back" against the "A-sign business owners who attack as an anti-revolutionary group" against the "Okinawan proletariat."[54]

Although New Left thought certainly opened up productive critiques of JCP and OPP ethno-nationalism, Okinawa's on-the-ground historical complexity would soon exhaust the limits of this class-based analysis. As important as it was to question how ethno-nationalism overshadowed class, a small handful of activists, scholars, and poets started to question how a class-based analysis also overlooked its implicit nationalist assumptions. Critics such as Kawata Yō and Matsushima Chōgi problematized the New Left assumption of a "single-state imperialism" and instead linked the regionalism of the Greater East Asia Co-Prosperity Sphere to a renewed postwar regionalism centered on the United States and Japan in the Asia Pacific.

Kawata was a mainland Japanese Marxian activist deeply involved in Okinawan movements of the 1960s and 1970s. In a 1971 essay entitled "Border, State, and the Third Ryukyu Disposition," he argued that the "Japanese proletariat" did not emerge endogenously by overcoming feudal remnants within Japan, but through discrimination toward migrant workers on mainland Japan's workforce. He faulted such assumptions on Eurocentric readings of Marxism. Different from the traditional Leninist model of imperialism defined as the international competition to export finance capital to the colonies, Kawata's understanding was in line with Uno Kōzō's identification of the limitations of single states vis-à-vis the global economy that needed to be overcome by a market-rational regionalism. His contribution to this thread is linking it to what he calls the "transborder domination of labor power."[55] This is the historical context given in the Introduction in which discrimination toward surplus populations from areas such as Korea or Okinawa on the mainland Japanese labor market produced notions of Japaneseness. Kawata called this population the "non-Japan," which is another term for the "world of the industrial reserve army of Japanese capitalism." Class unity could only obtain by "limiting it to a world" constituted as a "Japan within Japan" in which the "existence of a 'non-Japan within Japan' is once again abandoned outside of the concept of 'class.'"[56] Simply put, he inscribed the historicity of Japanese colonialism within the concept of "class." Because Kawata did not see the border as a geopolitical category but as a biopolitical one, he became highly suspicious of the call for international class solidarity framed as a "transborder revolution." Hence, he did not frame imperialism in terms of the logic of invasion and subsequent pillage of a territory, but in terms of a process of discrimination in which the non-Japan within Japan were rendered "outsiders" or "foreigners" to the internal enclosure of "Japan."

Kawata's analyses are complemented by Matsushima's essays published in the years before reversion. Matsushima entered Chuo University to study law in 1966 when he became involved in Okinawan activism on the Japanese mainland before he became active in the New Left movements in Koza.[57] He complements Kawata's critique of single-state imperialism with an analysis of a regional U.S.-Japan imperialism. He writes:

> It must be said that the philosophy of the New Left that preaches reversion to the mainland is very much a single-state theory for revolution. While they carry on about struggle that transcends borders, they are in actuality very much [engaged in] a single-state struggle. Rather, it does little more than play the part of forming the Japanese nation and actualizing power of the Japanese state. . . .
>   . . . The problem is that Okinawa's contradictions do not exist as the contradictions of a single-state Japanese imperialism, but as the contradictions of a U.S.-Japan imperialism.[58]

Matsushima argues that the New Left's transnationalism problematically assumes national unity prior to crossing borders to unite the proletariat. For him, this not only effaces the discrimination toward Korean and Okinawan workers that he witnessed in Tokyo, but it also ignores the heterogeneity of the migrant workforce internal to Okinawa. To the Japanese New Left, *Zengunrō* workers appeared as the proletariat compared to the so-called bourgeois Ryukyu police or A-sign business owners who beat them down.[59] So as to challenge this logic, Matsushima rescues the ethno-linguistic diversity stemming from a "peripheral island–main island–Satsuma domain" geographical triad that preceded the postwar Okinawa-Japan–United States triad.[60] In other words, he points out that the migrant workers carry with them a historical sensibility whereupon the Satsuma domain of the Edo period in present-day Kagoshima Prefecture oppressed the main Okinawan island, which in turn, oppressed the peripheral islands. It is with this historical sensibility that the workers come into contact with the postwar geopolitical triad of the

United States, Japan, and Okinawa. He thereby makes a theoretical intervention by insisting on the inability to sublate the prewar configuration into the postwar.

Instead of positing class as a sublation of difference, Matsushima defines the "Okinawan proletariat" in terms of the *inability to decide* the constitution of a class. He states:

> For example, in the case of the *Zengunrō* struggle, there is a structure in which [some] confront the U.S. military as Miyako islanders or as Yaeyama islanders. It is a question of how to engage that structure and the ability to organize in order to confront power. I think this can only be done by consolidating them into an Okinawan proletariat. In other words, in a structure in which [Okinawans] confront both Japanese state power and also U.S. military power as the Japanese proletariat, [we] *lose sight of the internal axis of unification.* . . . What Okinawa is confused about right now is that even though Okinawans carry on as if they are Japanese, there exists this [non-Japanese] part that gets dissolved.[61]

Here, the consolidation of an "Okinawan proletariat" is not the unification of a class at the expense of eliminating its internal diversity. Quite the opposite, it embraces the "structure in which [some] confront the U.S. military as Miyako islanders or as Yaeyama islanders," or in other words, the failure to unify as "Okinawans" or "Japanese." Hence, the "Okinawan proletariat" is consolidated not as an identity based on ethnicity, language, or even geography, but as an identity based on a fraught relationship with the exclusionary power of sovereignty that unifies heterogeneity. This is what he means by putting "into conversation that" heterogeneous "structure and the ability to organize in order to confront power." What Matsushima proposes is not the end of identity altogether, but rather an identity that forges a different relationship to transcendence implicit in sovereign power.

We will recall from the Introduction that Schmitt's sovereign is a type of God on earth. It is both *of* the law and *above* the law because it has the power to make exceptions to the law in the name of protecting it. In this sense, the sovereign transcends the realm of the law-abiding citizen and justifies his ability to make exceptions to the law by appealing to a holier-than-thou power. It goes without saying that I have been showing over and over throughout the pages of this book that Okinawa is that which is perpetually excepted (excluded) by sovereign power. But here, Matsushima speaks more specifically of a certain type of alegal Okinawan subject—

uprooted migrant laborers, or *ryūmin*, who fail to be constituted as a class. For Matsushima, it misses the point to simply criticize Japan for excepting (excluding) these Okinawans from sovereign power in the constitution of a class because it fails to take hold of the fundamental problem of the relationship to transcendence itself. By reaffirming the act of the exception—even in the guise of criticizing sovereign power for making an unfair or wrong exception—we have done nothing to change our relationship with transcendence. By contrast, Matsushima proposes an Okinawan proletariat that forms through critical vigilance of the "internal axis of unification" whereupon this heterogeneous "element" within Okinawa "gets dissolved." Here, the relationship with transcendence is one in which our eyes are constantly opened up to the act of the exception so as not to be blinded by the phantasmagoria of unity it claims to offer. "[T]his element" is precisely the allegorical rhythm of Okinawa that sovereign power attempts to "dissolve" through transcendence. It is the inability to decide vis-à-vis this sovereign power that defines Okinawa, or as he puts it, Okinawa as an "endless melody" (*mugen senritsu*) of what I have been describing as allegory.[62] Hence, class contradictions for Matsushima, as seen with the clash between *Zengunrō* and the base town workers, are not embarrassments to be glossed over for the sake of power in unity, but a testament to how the colonial condition in Okinawa offers a different method of reading sovereign power.

Can the Subaltern Speak?

Thus far, we have traced the limits of the discourse of national versus class struggle through the lumpenproletariat in the base towns. The former assumes primacy of the state in rectifying class contradictions and the latter fails to see how the biopolitical state is complicit in the constitution of class. Hence, the base town worker fails to be represented by the state and by class. In turning to representations of these women, we may now ask, following the postcolonial feminist scholar Gayatri C. Spivak: Can the subaltern speak?

Spivak famously breaks down the problem of speaking to two forms of representation: *Vertretung* and *Darstellung*. The former is "representation within the state and political economy,"[63] or "proxy,"[64] and the other is "the philosophical concept of representation as staging,"[65] or "portrait."[66] She criticizes Deleuze and Foucault for conflating these two "irreducibly discontinuous"[67] registers of representation. Both make the subaltern speak by assuming her "desire" corresponds to "interest" through a "representationalist realism"[68] that appeals to "what actually happens"[69] on the ground of capitalist exploitation. Spivak instead returns to the well-known passage by Marx in *The Eighteenth Brumaire of Louis Bonaparte* to uncover a more complicated reading of representation.

> [The small peasant proprietors] cannot represent themselves; they must be represented. Their representative must appear simultaneously as their master, as an authority over them, as unrestricted governmental power that protects them from the other classes and sends them rain and sunshine from above.[70]

In his discussion of *ryūmin* (the uprooted migrant worker), Tomiyama reads Spivak's evocation of this passage by Marx in terms of the state of exception. This is the "unrestricted governmental power" (Marx) that, in Tomiyama's words, "represents the externality (*gaibu*) excluded by the linguistic order in one stroke."[71] Although he uses the term "externality," or *gaibu*, here, it is clear that he is talking about the sphere of alegality that is produced as an externality as an effect of the exception. In other words, the sphere of alegality is represented as an externality by virtue of an extralinguistic power (i.e., a governmental power "external to the symbolic order"[72]) that is another name for the state of exception. In sum, Tomiyama reads Spivak as attempting to identify a stratum of existence that constantly fails to be represented by the state. The problem for Spivak is when the "event of representation as *Vertretung* (in the constellation of rhetoric-as-persuasion) behaves like a *Darstellung* (or rhetoric-as-trope), taking its place in the gap between the formation of a (descriptive) class and the nonformation of a (transformative) class." The former, or "rhetoric-as-persuasion," must convince us of the ambition of the state's ability to represent, which all too easily becomes equated with "rhetoric-as-trope," or the symbolic representation of the people in language. For Spivak, "this complicity is precisely what Marxists must expose."[73]

I read Spivak as demanding that the intellectual recognize how she can reproduce the violence of the exception by conflating these two registers of representation, even as she claims to have a progressive ear open to the subaltern's speech. For purposes here, however, I would like to pose the question "Can the subaltern speak?" in the following way. In place of asking how Okinawa, as hermeneutic object, can be translated into a preexisting legal discourse, I reframe the question to ask how it is possible to read the sphere of alegality irreducible to the law. My answer is: Read it allegorically. In this section, I would like to push for an allegorical reading of the base town worker through a reportage text and documentary film from the Japanese New Left.[74]

Ishida Yukio was a Japanese reportage writer who grew critical of the
JCP through anti-base activism on the mainland before he departed to
Okinawa. Through his interaction with activists and poets, he started to
develop a nuanced understanding of Okinawa's class struggle. He published
a number of volumes of reportage, including *Okinawa: Indigeneity and Liberation*, in which he describes a tense collision between *Zengunrō* and an
A-sign madam. I quote at length here because the scene lends itself to a
nuanced account of the various problems of representations of sexual labor.

An A-sign madam emerged alone amongst the picketers in the
demonstration. She started to shoot off at the mouth in dialect. There
was a young *Zentōrō*[75] activist who rushed in from a sugar factory up
north and stood in scrummage formation with me to my right. I asked
him to interpret.

"I came here ten years ago escaping the landslides of the mountain-
ous Kunigami (a valley in the north part of the main Okinawa island).
I've worked hard to make a life here in a corner of Koza, serving G.I.s.
Few can understand how I've been tormented by the U.S. military.
They order renovations whenever the counter isn't high enough or the
stainless sink is starting to rust, and put me in debt. If an Okinawan
client comes in, they threaten to shut the place down. Just as I have
started to see the light at the end of the tunnel of debt, the United
States loses to Vietnam in the war, and the value of the dollar plum-
mets. Then, the Yamato government that killed my parents and older
brother in that war talk about the prospects of Okinawa's return. Will
someone tell me which is more important: prospects for returning my
debt or prospects for returning Okinawa (although I don't know what
Okinawa will be returned to)? When it comes to the anti-war [move-
ment], I'm second to none. I see and hear things about the demonstrations, and I root for them in my heart. There have been times where I
put my hands together to *tōtōtōtōganashi* (word for prayer to the native
god) for them. However, there is nothing as inhumane and lawless as
these picketers. . . . The act of blocking the public street is a transgression against the highway to heaven." A picketer retaliated to her tirade.
"You're the handiwork of the Association to Protect Life.[76] I'll yank out
your tongue for going off as you please."

The woman, flushed with anger, pressed on. "What the hell is wrong
with being the handiwork of the Association to Protect Life? You guys
collide with the U.S. military and my business dries up. I have a life,
too, you *asshole* (this is my translation). Yeah, the bigwigs of the Association to Protect Life tried to organize the bar neighborhood residents

into a counter-demonstration to break up the picketers. I don't join those things. And so, the grand scheme of the bigwigs didn't work. Damn losers. Even I feel like sticking my tongue out at them. I won't come because the bigwigs order me to come, but I got so pissed off that I came out spontaneously on my own to teach you guys a lesson."

One picketer came forward and attacked her by saying "If you keep on with your yapping, I'll rape you." Turning to the man, the woman said, "Come on! Go ahead and try!" and sticking out her crotch, came up against the picketers alone. "I'll take all of you on! My genitals are so strong that they won't flinch even if I take on all of you guys. Guys like you are no big deal. Come on. Hey, rape me. Hey, hey, hey." After all became overwhelmed by her roaring laughter, [the scene] returned to silence. While they were distracted by what was going on, a few cars had rushed into the base. One picketer, half seriously whispered, "She's probably an enemy spy. She's a female ninja who uses enemy tactics to break up the picketers by drawing attention to herself." The picketers broke up and then formed a wide circle around her. A middle-aged, tall *Zengunrō* man resolutely walked away from the picketers, pushed aside the human circle and stood right in front of her. Perhaps it was because she thought the person in charge had come out, she raised her voice even more and said:

"Immediately dissolve this inhuman and lawless picketing. If you don't, then rape me. If you don't follow my order, then I'll twist your necks off between my legs you obstinate pigs. . . ."

Her scream broke off sharply. I flew off to the side. The tall *Zengunrō* man held his hands together behind his back and tilted his head forward. He closed his lips right onto the lips of the woman who, pushing into him with her face up, had just gone off on the rant. He very softly suppressed her speech. It was commendable—the one and only way to shut her up.[77]

Upon my first reading of this passage, my initial thought was: Did this actually happen? Is this what she actually said? Suspicious of yet another Japanese male stepping in to speak on behalf of an Okinawan woman, I succumbed to the seduction of wanting to know the "truth." However, after recognizing this seduction, I returned to examine what Ishida's text is actually doing (form) as a temporarily separate issue of what it is saying (content).

From the beginning, Ishida tries to be transparent about the function of translation in his text. He sees an A-sign madam emerge from the crowd of picketers when she starts to "shoot off at the mouth in dialect." The subaltern is speaking, but he literally fails to understand what she is saying. He documents this failure by introducing the use of an interpreter from a "sugar factory up north." Again, we are given clues to the failure of communication as we think about the ethno-linguistic diversity within Okinawa in this scene. It takes a translator from "up north," the same region as Kunigami where the madam originates, and not just any other Okinawan, to perform the translation. We are left wondering how well the madam is communicating to *Zengunrō* while at the same time we are left wondering what kind of translation the man from "up north" is giving Ishida. Multiple translations abound. Ishida's account is, by no means, definitive; he exposes fissures and fractures of a sovereign translation that attempts to monopolize meaning and instead opens the text up to be claimed by others who come into contact with it.

Not only does the form attempt to undermine sovereign representation, but the content attempts the same. He shows how the ethno-linguistic diversity within Okinawa in the constitution of a class is complicated by gender. According to this passage, the madam resolutely refuses to be organized. She rejects institutional power that hides behind the constitution of class and instead aligns herself with "life" (*seikatsu*). This is seen as she not only clashes with *Zengunrō* on the left, but also as she ridicules the "Association to Protect Life" that attempts to organize the base town workers on the right. Most of the picketers cannot identify her irreducibility to institutional power and instead read her as a "female ninja who uses enemy tactics." The alegality that she embodies is met, yet once again, with gendered violence as a picketer attempts to silence her with threats of rape. This conjures up the not-so-distant memory of state sexual violence committed by the Japanese Imperial Army during the war as well as the U.S. military during the war and postwar. This is a border-inscribing violence that inaugurates sovereignty through the bodies of women at the scene of rape. Yet the madam fires back, "I'll take all of you on!" Ishida suggests, through the reproduction of this scene, that the madam neutralizes the threat of rape integral to sovereign power by purportedly cultivating resilience to sexual transgressions through her experiences in Koza.

At this point in the text the threat of extralinguistic sovereign violence in the form of rape is countered by another extralinguistic act performed by the "tall *Zengunrō* man" who calmly walks over to kiss her. Here, the "tall *Zengunrō* man" has one foot in the movement while at the same time does not forget that he is also more than just a *Zengunrō* member of a class.

It is only through engagement on this level of alegality that he is able to "shut her up." In other words, the subaltern "shoots off at the mouth" precisely at the point where she insists on the impossibility of total representation by institutional power. She is not speaking, but screaming rather confrontationally. Yet no one can hear her in this modality; they instead insist on translating her into a different mode of representation in which all of her actions are channeled into the teleology of state power. It is only when the "tall *Zengunrō* man" recognizes this failure of totalization in representation that he forges the possibility of a different kind of communality with the madam, or what Matsushima might call the "Okinawan proletariat." Here, the subaltern is not silent; she is a loudmouth who is told to shut up. While this is an interesting turn in the text, it also poses limitations. She is shut up by a man so *Zengunrō* can carry on with business as usual. However, the point of an allegorical practice of reading is not to reach a place beyond representation—a place where language is no longer needed—but to keep failing through speech.

While the madam is told to shut up in Ishida's text, we are able to get a glimpse of another woman speaking in the documentary *Motoshinkakarannū: 1969–1971, A Long Okinawan Documentary Film—An Insider Story of Okinawan Eros.*[78] This documentary provides one of the most intimate visual records of sex workers in Okinawa during this time. It was produced by NDU (*Nihon Dokyumentarisuto Yunion*, or Japan Documentarist Union), a Bund-influenced group who departed to Okinawa in 1969.

Producer Nunokawa Tetsurō situates the documentary within the larger picture of New Left movements in Japan. Why 1969? Why Okinawa? NDU members were part of the student movement generation of the late 1960s who participated in *Zenkyōtō*. This was a militant nonsectarian movement centered on the university. It increasingly appealed to spectacular displays of violence by sporting *Gewalt* batons (*gebabō*) or stoning the police.[79] The appeal to violence was part of a larger trend of intra- and intergroup *Gewalt* (violence), or *uchigeba*, that raged throughout the New Left during this time, climaxing in murders. The "practice of struggle" (*jisturyoku tōsō*) was reduced to radical showmanship; those who failed to pick up *Gewalt* batons or boycott classes were attacked as traitors. Participants in the occupation of the University of Tokyo, in particular, engaged in "self-refutation" (*jiko hitei*) in order to correct their class privilege.[80] However, far from succeeding in the actualization of revolution, the intra- and intergroup *Gewalt* catalyzed its decline. This moment in 1969 marked the beginning of the end of the New Left in mainland Japan.

Nunokawa theorizes the impasse through the language of the French philosopher Jean-Paul Sartre in order to foreground his approach to the documentary art form as a practice of decolonization.

> The foray into documentary is for one part of a preexisting social stratification to make a clean break from self-perpetuation (being in-itself), or in other words, the "myth of totality". . . .
>
> The process of filming and producing a documentary is quite naturally to live a process in which the imagination of the object is betrayed and retaliated against before it enters into an actual relationship. This is to, in reverse, move down on the upward ascending process of existence → content → meaning → value → symbol. Further, it is the dissolution of "limited facticity," the bankruptcy of the "practico-inert," and the first encounter that comes after "self-refutation."[81]

From this passage, we get a sense of how intimately Sartre was received by the Japanese New Left. But what was an inside conversation in that circle begs for some unpacking here. In *Critique of Dialectical Reason, Vol. 1*, Sartre writes of the emergence of the group in capitalist society whereupon each individual interiorizes the gaze of an external third. In this process, each individual becomes a third for all the others. Hence, in this triadic structure, there is no longer simple reciprocity between the self and the other, but now a dialectical relationship between the self as an individual vis-à-vis the group and the self that exists as a mediating third for all the others in the group. This had a significant impact on the core tenant of Sartre's existential philosophy—that of the freedom of praxis as it is put in a contradictory relationship with the institution. No longer is freedom the negation of the being in-itself in order to achieve being for-itself, but now the common "pledged inertia" of all individuals to commit to the group. In other words, one can practice his or her freedom only to the extent that it preserves the inertia of the group. What results is the heavy machinery of the "practico-inert" that defines the institution. The institution mediates everyone, and everyone mediates the institution. There is no escape.

It is precisely from within this circularity that Nunokawa positions "self-refutation" as symptomatic of the futile attempt to escape. A refutation of the self does nothing because the self is already mediated by the third. This is why he conflates "self-perpetuation (being in-itself)" with the "myth of totality." Hence, the attempt to refute "self-perpetuation (being in-itself)," as seen in the throes of *Zenkyōtō* activism, becomes a refutation of the group itself. Here we can see why intra- and inter-*Gewalt* do not lurk far behind self-refutation and why this is the place where Sartre situates "*fraternity-terror*," or terrorism, among brothers. It incites a "deep fear of a dissolution of unity" that plagues the group and is displaced onto an imagined "traitor as absolute evil."[82]

It is at this point of arriving at the impasse of the practico-inert that Sartre's theory of language becomes deeply shaken. Here, Nunokawa pulls him close to develop his own approach to the documentary art form. Sartre's interaction with the colonies constantly informed his approach to language. In *What Is Literature?*, first published in 1947, Sartre argues that literature should be "committed," meaning that it should be used as the means to clearly communicate ideas to the people.[83] But as he starts to develop the idea of the practico-inert in *Critique of Dialectical Reason, Vol. 1*, in 1960, communication becomes complicated. Man's ability to freely communicate to another man is problematically mediated by the institution. One cannot speak without speaking the institution. This is why Nunokawa devotes much of his essay to a dismissal of New Left journals such as *Asahi Journal* (*Asahi Jānaru*) or *Modern Eye* (*Gendai no Me*) as inviting narcissistic performances of radical politics through the rote act of reading and paying for one's monthly subscription. No one can communicate anything to get out of the circularity of bourgeois society. Quite the contrary, the act of communicating itself only serves to reinforce it.

So where can one possibly go? Like Sartre, behind the poetry of Léopold Sédar Senghor and Aimé Césaire, Nunokawa follows Okinawa behind the lens of a camera; both embark on a flight that attempts to break the institutional sound barrier of the metropole and voyage into a colonial space they envision as lying beyond. This takes us back to a reworking of Sartre's original philosophy of language. Sartre returns to the opposite of "committed" literature that uses language as a tool to communicate thought: poetry. For Sartre writing *What Is Literature?* in 1947, poetry was overshadowed by prose because the latter could clearly communicate information to incite social change. In contrast to the "language-instrument"[84] of prose, Sartre argued that the poet treats the word like a material object, much like an artist's relation to paint. That is, communicative language can only describe a house through signification, but a material object resembling a house is able to emerge through an artist's use of paint on a canvas. Poetry, for Sartre, was akin to art in that the word conjures up images like a material "*phrase-object*."[85] However, when he writes *Black Orpheus* in 1948, these views undergo a dramatic transformation. For him, "[t]he words of Césaire do not describe negritude" like words signify meaning in prose, and "they do not copy it from outside as a painter does a model" like his previous view of poetry, but "they *make* it."[86] What he means is that "black poetry" already contains within it dialectical movement in which the "Negro," who "is exiled in the midst of the cold buildings of the white culture,"[87] retaliates against and destroys it and, by doing so, is able to "return to the native land" of the "black soul."[88] This, of course, is the "dialectic law of successive transformations"[89] that is merely the "means" that leads the "ultimate goal"[90] of the "black contribution in the evolution of Humanity."[91]

Perhaps because Nunokawa is a producer of documentary films, and not a literary critic, his views are somewhat modified. He retains the visual aspect of Sartre's previous views on poetry by focusing on the materiality of the "image" instead of the "language-instrument" of prose, yet he merges it with Sartre's "dialectic law of successive transformations" because the image of the other is able to retaliate against and destroy the colonizer. In other words, Nunokawa attempts to bypass communication by going directly to the image of the colonial other. But this isn't just any image. He takes the image to an extreme form of materiality; he goes straight to the "flesh" of the colonial other.

Nunokawa quotes the theater critic Kisei Ei to assert that communicative language "homogenizes and reifies the flesh"[92] and seeks to document the "flesh" as something that has an inherent "desire to roam" free from "social constraints."[93] The "flesh" here is precisely that which is antagonistic to the practico-inert, or in his words, that which will lead to its "bankruptcy." Because the "flesh" of the colonial other is supposedly external to both Japanese social relations and language, it has the power to productively betray and retaliate against the symbolic order. In other words, if existence is in a dialectical relationship mediated by the state that is symbolized by the "myth of totality," then he looks for a symbol outside of the semiotic order (i.e., the "flesh" of the colonial other) to forge another possibility for existence. Of course, we know that the roaming flesh he speaks of here is the flesh of the sex worker that belongs to what he calls the "fluid bottom" of the "modern social order"[94]—an existence that is, for him, "closest to revolution."[95]

So, what exactly happens in *Motoshinkakarannū* promising revolution through the "flesh" of the sex worker? The entire script of the documentary, after its immediate release, is published in *Film Critique*.[96] In the original cut, it consists of twenty-three chapters. It haphazardly unfolds by patching each chapter together with interviews of sex workers, an interview with a hand-tattooed elderly woman, a scene depicting women who sell dollars for yen to Japanese tourists on the streets of Naha, interviews with Japanese tourists in Okinawa about their views on prostitution, an interview with members of the Black Panther Party, a scene with Okinawa's yakuza, scenes of the *Zengunrō* strike, scenes of native Okinawan festival dancing and tug-of-war, and scenes from the 1970 Koza Riot. The black and white film is grainy and images fly by with dizzying speed. Integral to the visual and audio effects of the film is the use of a technique called "insert cut" (*insāto katto*). The voice recording is cut and rearranged by the producer. Visual images are then inserted between cuts of the voice recording. This is purportedly to compensate for the interruption of flow between the voice and image. However, in the case of this film, it is often exaggerated to convey an intense suspicion toward the sign in its ability to convey the "truth," which is seen in the interplay between the visual and vocal text.

This tension is most convincing in the chapter on fresh-off-the-boat leftist mainland Japanese labor union members from the General Council of Trade Unions of Japan (*Sōhyō*). After opening with a group of men chanting "return Okinawa," it follows with a series of interviews with men and women on the topic of prostitution in Okinawa. The interviewer is direct and to the point.

Interviewer: Have you ever met a prostitute before?

Man 5: I have. Yesterday, no, the day before yesterday, I met one.

Interviewer: Did you buy her?

Man 5: . . . What the. . . .

Man 6: He asked whether or not you bought her?

Man 5: I bought her.

Interviewer: How much did she cost?

Man 5: . . . This is too difficult. I can't make conversation like this."[97]

The voice is superimposed onto celebratory images of hundreds of Japanese tourists gathering in the streets of Naha to rally for Okinawa's reversion. The infectious feeling of Japanese ethno-nationalism emanating from the fanfare of the mass gathering in the visual text is disturbed by the uncomfortably intimate interview between the men in the vocal text. The documentary shows that this is not merely a case of sexism within the Japanese New Left, but sexism with an added colonial dimension. To the question "Was she a good girl?," we are given an image of men sporting bandanas that say "recapture Okinawa" (*Okinawa dakkan*), suggesting the hypocrisy of the Japanese New Left's desire to recapture Okinawa from the United States as if *she* were an object. Man 5 continues with his fantasy of the Okinawan sex worker.

> Man 5: She was a good girl. . . .

> Man 5: Okinawan women are sort of caring.[98] In that sense, I find them charming. They are nice to anything. And not only that, if you talk to them about anything they can converse in a most carefree manner as if you had been living together for an entire lifetime.[99]

Superimposed onto this statement is the image of a human ocean of hundreds of mainland Japanese demonstrators at an Okinawa Prefecture Council for Reversion to the Fatherland rally. Each respective group within the totality props up a flag representing their originating prefecture. We get a glimpse of the geographical diversity within Japan, only to be reminded that it is a totality separate from Okinawa. The vocal text again does the work of driving home the dissonance between mainland Japan and Okinawa.

> Interviewer: So in other words, your relationship with the woman was a monetary one?

> Man 7: No, that's not the case.

> Man 8: Yeah, we're from Osaka, and with prostitutes in Osaka, it's completely a monetary relationship. People around here aren't concerned with such things. . . . [100]

In Man 8's fantasy world, Okinawan sex workers are not concerned with money like "prostitutes in Osaka." The vocal text is again juxtaposed with actual images of sex workers walking the streets of Koza with G.I.s, lurking in the shadows, and the commodification of the female body seen in shots of mannequins showcasing skimpy lingerie. His fantasy continues by professing firsthand knowledge of the opinions of the sex worker, which mirror his own.

> Man 8: Also, we went to have fun in one of those places. As a . . .
> union . . . official. So, we also went in order to learn. It wasn't of course just to fool around. It was to talk mainly about topics such as Okinawa's return. . . .

> Man 8: Yeah, those people said they want to return [to the mainland Japanese administration]. It's not like we're saying they're at the bottom, but we had an interest in directly asking the prostitutes. Listening to them, they had the same opinions as us.[101]

The hypocrisy of this encounter is ended by the visual images of legions of tourists, picking up their union bags embossed with the words "Abolish the U.S.-Japan Security Treaty," and climbing on board an enormous cruise ship flowing with an entanglement of streamers that the tourists wave as they depart from Okinawa.

In this chapter, the film succeeds in showing the contradictions between Japan and Okinawa by using the sex worker as representative of the "fluid bottom" of the colonial world. However, the documentary meets its limitations when actually turning to the vocal text of the sex worker herself. Certainly, her text presents an example of how "the imagination of the object is betrayed and retaliated against," as hoped for by Nunokawa. But her text betrays expectations in a different way. Far from providing the "flesh" that undermines the symbolic order from the outside, she works clearly within the symbolic order and dismantles Nunokawa's assumptions of transcendence implicit in his theory of the institution and language.

The film opens with an explication of the title by a seventeen-year-old sex worker named Akemi.

> Akemi: "*Motoshinkakarannū, hōremiyachubate?* (You mean someone who lets you do pussy?)[102]

The title of the film "*motoshinkakarannū*" means a business that can be launched without start-up capital in the Okinawan language. Here Akemi understands that NDU is referring to sex work and intuits that the "flesh" Nunokawa has in mind is "pussy." The body part is alienated from its person who "lets" others "do" it. Although the documentary makes this native phrase the title in order to exoticize Okinawa, we learn immediately that this is not a word Akemi uses herself. Rather, she is quick to identify it as language appropriated by mainland Japanese men for their own purposes. She follows:

> Akemi: You guys, when you came from Japan, you went to Yoshiwara huh. Oh my God, you perverts. . . . [103]

Akemi associates the objectification of the *motoshinkakarannū* by the film crew with the commodification of Okinawan bodies in the sex industry. Although it is not evident from the documentary itself, we learn elsewhere that the film crew indeed paid for sex with the women as they interviewed them.[104]

In this scene, Akemi is acutely aware of the various power dynamics in the room. She is surrounded by the NDU film crew and two yakuza named

Asa and Aba in addition to the camera and microphone, although we can hardly see anything but Akemi. The atmosphere is convivial, and they converse in a tone akin to friends reminiscing over drinks. However, the content of the conversation that follows is anything but festive. The tension between form and content here is not given so much with visual over vocal text, but within the visual and vocal text coming from Akemi herself.

> Akemi: I got my cherry popped when I was on my period. So, I don't know if blood came out or not. I was on my period.
>
> Akemi: *Nebā hapun*[105] to a person.
>
> Akemi: I told you. Just now, I told you it hurt!
>
> (Everyone laughs.)
>
> Akemi: Why do you laugh? Stupid assholes.
>
> Akemi: . . . . . .
>
> Aba: . . . . . .
>
> Akemi: *Atarimaeshichi, murumāyamuga!* (Of course, I said it all hurts down there!)
>
> (Aba laughs)
>
> —Akemi, it was like that, wasn't it? You thought of giving yourself, didn't you?
>
> Akemi: No! Rape. It was an outright rape. It was so scary. After it was over, I kept pushing my stomach. Didn't want to get pregnant . . . I was just a *warabā* (child). A seventh grader! *Fakkuyū shārappu!*[106]

The scene comes and goes so quickly that the viewer is left somewhat dumbstruck. Akemi describes a gang rape by the yakuza committed when she was in seventh grade. Thereafter, one yakuza becomes her pimp. Akemi then takes on the pimp's debt and is forced to pay it back through sex work. The pimp is obligated to protect her in the violent world of the sex industry but at the same time poses a threat to Akemi.[107] NDU thereby uncovers the unofficial world of organized violence that parallels the official world of organized state violence.

Although Nunokawa searches for "flesh" outside the linguistic order, in listening to this scene closely we can see that Akemi nonetheless speaks within it. There is not only tension between the joking form and serious content of her speech, but her speech is also linguistically hybrid as she fluidly mixes native Okinawan, Japanese, and English at once to create her own language. Akemi does not just say it like it is, but there is a fundamental tension between what is said and how, or in what language, it is said. It is in this instability, where meaning is never allowed to land on stable ground, that her text opens up to the allegorical. Yet, at the same time, there is something more specific than allegory at play here, namely irony. Allegory, as we will recall, is experienced as the swaying, swinging motion between images without ever being able to fully fixate on one. In this way, we can see that allegory is characterized by a drawn-out temporality of moving through space.[108] Irony, by contrast, collapses temporality into a moment and condenses multiplicity in a single space.[109] As a result, she can only say what she means by showing that she doesn't mean it. She can take possession of the word "outright rape" by laughing it off. Laughter protects her from the gravity of the situation while it also suggests to the men physically surrounding her that she will not challenge them.[110] Her ambivalent relationship to power and language is then captured by the "*Fakkuyū Shārappu!*" (Fuck you, shut up!) that she undoubtedly learned from the only oppressors not present in the room—the men of the U.S. military.

The irony in Akemi's speech suggests a different ontology from Nunokawa's. Whereas Nunokawa searches for something outside of the linguistic order to ground the formation of a new subject, Akemi instead demonstrates a different relationship between the empirical self and language. Her speech exposes language's constant failure to represent the empirical self. It is in this sense that irony is allegory's cousin. In contrast to Nunokawa, who sought to escape representation in language by filming the "flesh" of the colonies, Akemi's life is an existence that is constantly barred from transcendence. She is not far off from Fanon's critique of Sartre here when he writes, "I am overdetermined from without"; "I am locked into the infernal circle"; "I was walled in."[111] Whereas the white man exercises his agency through confrontation with an external object that causes the subject to change through a new dialectical relationship with the object, Fanon's point is that the colonized are afforded no such luxury. The ability to self-determine is already foreclosed by the colonizer who determines colonial existence. Akemi responds to this situation not by appealing to an outside that she is constantly denied, but by attempting to forge a different relationship with transcendence itself.

We get a feeling of being "walled in" when Akemi catches the anger emanating from her own body as it threatens to strike the object and redirects it inward in language.

> Akemi: (Speaking in dialect.) They say they're going to film
> *motoshinkakarannū* right away. Does that mean they're going to
> film me?[112]

At this moment, she realizes that she is being captured both in language
and image by the Japanese film crew. She considers what this means.

> Akemi: (Akemi's speech returns to standard language.) No one knows
> what it means, but they say they're going to make the title
> *motoshinkakarannū*. They come to Okinawa, and go all out like, like
> this to Yoshiwara. They came thinking they're going to film
> *motoshinkakarannū, motoshinkakarannū* in that kind of a place. How
> embarrassing.[113]

At this point, Akemi makes an assessment of the power dynamics in terms
of geopolitics that frames the anger welling up in her soul.

> Akemi: If Okinawa reverts to the mainland, only people in the
> government will get rich. This is the first time that I've spoken to
> Japanese people like this. Even if I argue with you, ah, I mean it's
> not an argument. No matter what kind of dirty words you use, I can't
> get ma . . . ma . . . mad. So, that's why it's worth talking and talking.
> You get it?[114]

Akemi suddenly becomes conscious of her anger but realizes that it will
have no release in communicative language: She cannot directly tell them
"I am mad" and mean it. Instead, her text is again ironic. As if tripping at
this sudden point of transition, she stutters on the word "ma . . . ma . . .
mad" and can only say what she means by saying that she doesn't mean it:
"Even if I argue with you, ah, I mean it's not an argument." Although she
is disgusted with "the dirty words" they use, she nonetheless states that
this is "why it's worth talking."

> Akemi: They say people from the inner territories[115] are nice like this.
> But guys from the inner territories are nice, huh. Just like foreigners.
> —"Are foreigners nice?"
>
> Akemi: Really nice. . . .
>
> Akemi: If I'm going to get mad and speak my mind, then I'll tell a lie.
> My boobs are *nambā wan*.[116] You wanna see? I get compliments from
> everyone.[117]

She gives the camera crew a backhanded compliment by stating that the
"guys from the inner territories are nice . . . [j]ust like foreigners." "Inner

territory" or *naichi* is a term still commonly used in Okinawa to describe mainlanders. It is a relic from imperial Japan as the Japanese termed it the "inner territories" in contrast to the "outer territories" (*gaichi*) of the colonies. Although Okinawa was not an official colony, and was hence technically *naichi* from the perspective of the official *gaichi* of Taiwan or Korea, it nonetheless referred to mainland Japanese as *naichi* people, thereby reflecting consciousness as a colonized people. In her anger toward the colonial violence of the film crew, she could not be more explicit about her irony. "If I'm going to get mad and speak my mind, then I'll tell a lie." She switches from her thoughts to her body, from native Okinawan language to a mixture of Japanese and English. *Nambā wan* (number one) is an English borrow word commonly used in Japanese, but in this context, it conjures up another numerical phrase used by blacks in Okinawa to describe the United States: "number ten." If her "boobs" are the best at number one, then it is because the United States and its mainland Japanese counterpart are the worst at number ten.

The NDU production team was not uniform in thought. Another member, Murase Haruki, published a reportage-style book based on the documentary in 1970 entitled *Does Anyone Know Okinawa?* Unlike Nunokawa, Murase did not emerge from the experience of the documentary immersed in Sartrean existentialism. Rather, he was left "speechless" and turned toward problematizing Japanese society's assumptions about sexuality.[118] Much of his thinking was channeled through his experiences with the Black Panther Party in Okinawa. Three chapters of the original film are dedicated to introducing Black Power in Okinawa. In his book, Murase analyzes the Black Power movement in terms of class. He describes *uchigeba*, or in-fighting, between "cultural nationalists" who rejected white alliances and the Black Panther Party that cultivated a class-based analysis.[119] He spoke with Black Panther Party members critical of Nixon's "black capitalism policy" that sought to "foster a group of puppet nationalist capitalist" in order to integrate African Americans into capitalist society and turn rich African American capitalists against their poorer brethren.[120] He described how members of the Black Panthers in Okinawa lamented how some of their brothers collaborated with "white imperialists" by serving as Green Berets and/or acted as spies for the CIA and CID by sporting ethnic African dress as they infiltrated the communities.[121] Interestingly, however, Murase is pushed outside of his Japanese New Left framework and comes face-to-face with something irreducible to its vocabulary. As if to echo Fanon in *Black Skin, White Masks*—a book he surely read in Japanese translation, as it came out in late 1968—he recognizes a fundamental difference between the position of blacks and himself. He writes:

> They have no other choice but the absolute choice of "being black" in America or Africa where they are ruled by whites. They cannot escape from being "black. . . ."
>
> We "Japanese" who are ruled in "Tokyo" by rulers of the same skin color can make various choices.
>
> We can carefully escape from being "non-nationals,"[122] "rioters," "criminals," and "insane." We can innocently escape from being "aggressors," "oppressors," "discriminating," or even "executioners."[123]

Unlike Nunokawa, who attempts to exercise the freedom of *praxis* through a confrontation with the colonized for the purpose of a dialectical synthesis that results in a renewed humanism, Murase understands that the same "choice" is not available to blacks. While the colonizer produces the colonized through an exclusionary decision—a practice where the colonized is captured as an externality that exists before the colonizer and for the purposes of the colonizer—Murase points to the absence of symmetry in the sovereign decision or "choice." The colonized is not a negation of the colonizer and the colonized is not in possession of reciprocity; the colonized is produced by the colonizer through an exclusionary decision. Hence, having been determined by the colonizer, the colonized cannot simply exercise the "choice" of self-determination as a full realization of his or her humanity. This is because "choice" for the colonized has already been chosen by the colonizer.

Indeed, Sartre's celebration of Fanon's writings on anti-colonial violence articulated in the preface of *The Wretched of the Earth* has been widely criticized as self-congratulatory. Murase himself lived the tension between these two authors in Okinawa in real time. Not long after NDU's arrival in 1969, Murase picked up the hot-off-the-press Japanese translation of this book, which came out in November that year, and read Sartre's preface, quoted here, in the overlapping space of two colonial worlds that existed as the black neighborhood in Okinawa.

> Walking Honmachi Street, I, of course, couldn't discern who was an imperialist and who was a revolutionary amongst the brothers, but all the guys roaming Honmachi Street had an ineffable ghostlike power about them. They perhaps were not into "consciousness[124] [raising]" or "class-based[125] [analysis]," but they had some sort of fundamental dreadfulness about them that was not commensurable with "logic," could not be mediated by "language," and not incapable of rejecting

the formation of "language." Moreover, like Roy and Tom, they were mixed in with experienced veterans who had actually "dirtied their hands" in the Vietnam War and were different from the backup reserves who had graduated from college. Just as Sartre wrote, "no gentleness can efface the marks of violence; only violence itself can destroy them," what "whites" including Sartre feared the most was perhaps the true revolutionary power of "blacks."[126]

The "blacks" that he describes here cannot be constituted as imperialist or revolutionary because they are irreducible to both. Blackness is a fundamental antagonism (i.e., "dreadfulness") that cannot be organized into a "logic," "language," or political party. This is not the "flesh" existing outside of the semiotic order as conceived by Nunokawa, but an "ineffable ghostlike power" irreducible to it as it roams the borderland of Honmachi Street. In the following section, I will turn to a moment where base town workers and African American soldiers come together in a scene of violence irreducible to the state.

The Koza Riot

On December 20, 1970, something remarkable happened. Workers who had just been fraternizing with their clients emerged from Koza's A-sign establishments and took to the streets. They filled up pop bottles with gasoline and started pitching them at U.S. military vehicles. They joined an amorphous crowd of over a thousand Okinawans who pulled G.I.s out of their cars, flipped them over, and set them on fire. The uprising was spontaneous and the word on the street was infectious: Don't touch the black soldiers.

This is the Koza Riot. The historical details that triggered the event itself are rather uneventful. A drunk U.S. soldier hit an Okinawan as he was crossing the street at about 1:00 A.M. As a small crowd gathered around the crash site, they became agitated when the Ryukyu police attempted to turn the car over to the MP. Okinawans knew the routine. Just five weeks earlier a U.S. soldier had hit and killed an Okinawan woman in an Itoman car accident. After the car was turned over to the MP, the soldier was found not guilty. As the fresh memory of this incident cascaded over a continuous flow of memories of countless other rapes and murders committed with impunity by U.S. military soldiers over the years, someone shouted "Try them at a people's court."[127] By 2:00 A.M. the crowd grew to a thousand. Instead of serving the soldiers cocktails in the bars, they were now serving them Molotov cocktails in the street. They identified U.S. military cars by their yellow or F-number license plates, pulled them into the middle of the street, turned them over, and burned them. Approximately five hundred Okinawans penetrated nearly two hundred yards of Kadena Air Base and set fire to the buildings.[128] The MP fired shots into the air. After six hours of violence, no one was killed. Special assistant to the president for Okinawan Affairs attempted to categorize the incident in a report to the president of the United States.

> The Koza riot was not a riot in the usual sense. No damage was done
> to stores or buildings, no one was killed. When an American ser-
> viceman's car was attacked the occupants were pulled from the car
> *before* it was set on fire. (Eighty-three cars were destroyed, so I am
> told.)[129]

The Koza Riot was not an indiscriminate expression of violence. The crowd refrained from killing servicemen, damaging Okinawan property, and as noted elsewhere, they refrained from touching black soldiers or their property.

Yet, at the same time, it was not premeditated either. The report follows, "It seems to have broken out spontaneously."[130] The United States was not gifted with a terrorist group that had planned the violence in advance, nor could they identify a group in the making toward the future. In a confidential Department of Defense Intelligence Information Report, the USAF commander writes: "No information has been developed to date to indicate any group or individual is planning a recurrence of violence. . . . It is impossible to identify when and where it could since the circumstances creating a potential for violence would have to develop first."[131] The mass media as well was denied an object to villainize because of the anonymity of the violence. Although Okinawan politicians paid lip service to the U.S. military by stating the incident was regrettable, they nonetheless sided with the civilians by stating that they understood their actions. Because the Koza Riot belonged to no one, it belonged to everyone.

This odd mixture of organized spontaneous violence deeply troubled the United States. More than simply the cost of property damaged, they sensed a small tear in sovereign power with potentially catastrophic consequences: "The riot, the first to occur on Okinawa, was so serious that it is bound to have important effects upon the relationship between Okinawans and Americans, governmentally, economically, and socially."[132] I read the Koza Riot as a moment of divine, as contrasted to mythic, violence that is inimical to sovereign power. In "Critique of Violence," Benjamin famously uncovered the design of state violence as a teleology in which subjects use violence as a means to a greater end. There he showed how the state allows labor unions the violent means of a strike in order to achieve the end of better working conditions. Although it appears that the state is making concessions to the strikers, what is important is that the strikers remain within the means-end relationship. So long as violence is used as a means to the greater end of challenging the state, the state maintains a monopoly on power. However, real crisis ensues when the means-end relationship is altered.

The significance of the participation of the base town workers in the Koza Riot is that they did so in the absence of mediation by politics or economics. Violence was not used as a means to ask for concessions from sovereign power. They were neither petitioning subjects who worked within the state for better concessions nor were they protesting subjects who came up against the state with the aim of opposing it. This is why base town workers were able to play a central role in the incident despite being labeled as "pro-American." Just as they cannot be reduced to being for the state in their service to the U.S. military, their violence cannot be reduced to being against the state in unleashing their rage toward the U.S. military. More than a terrorist group that plots the downfall of the U.S. military, this violence irreducible to state power posed its greatest threat. A-sign business owner Arakawa Sachio plainly separates doing business from rioting as he recalls the incident.

> During the Koza Riot I was doing business as usual on Business Center Street. Like everyone else, I went to go check out what was going on. That's when I saw that all of the foreigners' cars were set on fire. Poor guys. Woman, child, it didn't matter: Everyone got in on the action of dragging those guys out of their foreign cars from opened doors.
>
> . . . When I witnessed the Koza Riot, I thought it was only natural that the foreigners got what they deserved. . . . Rape someone? Not guilty. Run over and kill someone in a car accident? Not guilty. The civilians were tired of hearing about such incidents as they accumulated year after year. That's why their feelings about "these assholes" suddenly exploded into the riot.
>
> Of course, I was doing business with foreigners during these times when they got off scot-free after committing crime after crime. But business was business and the incident was the incident. They're separate issues. Since I was profiting from their business, I was to a

certain degree appreciative toward the foreigners. But I was also
bullied by them after losing the war.[133]

Arakawa categorically separates profit from emotion, business from violence. He has no trouble expressing sympathy for the "poor guys" while
saying that they "got what they deserved" in the same breath. It was precisely in this separation, in the absence of a telos through which to channel their anger, that the base town workers were able to take pleasure in
the means.

In this moment, roles in Okinawan society were reversed. The base
town workers who were thought to be useless in terms of their ability to
protest U.S. military bases attacked the reversion activists who had prided
themselves in their anti-base politics. Matsushima writes:

> Anyone and everyone who took part in that riot shouted out the word
> *Uchinānchu*. Anyone and everyone agitated the situation with the
> *Uchinānchu* slogan right before they broke into the base. Even the
> A-sign business people who were labeled right-wingers shouted out to
> the civil servant educators,[134] "You guys go on about reversion,
> reversion, but you can't even kill the U.S. military? Quit fucking
> around. Can you still call yourself *Uchinānchu*!!" In that whirlpool [of
> energy], the gawkers could no longer be gawkers, and even the
> educators joined in the fight as *Uchinānchu*. In other words, the
> fundamental characteristic of that riot is that *Uchinānchu* were able to
> express their hatred to the U.S. military as one body.[135]

In this passage, Matsushima defines *Uchinānchu*, or Okinawan identity, as
that which is unintelligible to state power. This is what they chanted before they broke into the base. Liberated from the onus of political goals, it
was this identity that empowered the people thought to be lacking in political life.

When the boundary-inscribing violence of the state started to lose
ground, African American soldiers located the potential to come together
to form a different kind of community. We will recall friction between
African Americans and Okinawans surrounding the economics of the
base town and politics of race managed by state power. Yet there was a
moment of mutual recognition at this point where both gave up on state-
mediated communication that subtends the dream of internationalism. A
bilingual letter written by African American soldiers in Kadena Air Base
starts off with a recognition of communicative failure: "There is a communication barrier between Okinawans and the Black G.I." It continues
by pointing out the in-between position of both groups:

> Black people have fought in wars which they really had nothing to do
> with. Okinawans fought in wars that they had nothing to do with . . .
> . . . This is because Black peopl [sic] have been discriminated against
> for over 400 years, and it hasn't stopped yet. The same with Oki-
> nawans; they've been discriminated against also.[136]

The letter speaks of a parallel minority position that is both used as an instrument of state violence and alienated from it. It was such movements
that pushed activists who lived in Koza, such as Matsushima, to formulate
the Okinawan proletariat in a trans-Pacific context. He writes:

> The relationship between blacks and whites, and the relationship
> between blacks and state power: I think the problem for blacks is that
> they must constantly sublate these two relationships . . . I think that
> question of blackness[137] finds a most similar situation in Okinawa.[138]

Matsushima articulates a moment of connection between subjects who
struggle in their failure to be represented by the state during the tumultu-
ous years of the reversion era. I will return to how it informed his vision
of a global proletariat in the next chapter. But in terms of this moment of
African American–Okinawan solidarity, it was largely unable to grow into
a larger movement.[139] Apprehensive about the Koza Riot and the type of
connections it engendered, the United States became more eager than ever
to transfer Okinawa to the Japanese administration in 1972. The replacement of American dollars with Japanese yen in combination with the ex-
ecution of the Japanese anti-prostitution law meant the formal demise of
the sex industry. The racial politics implied therein faded against yet another attempt to become Japanese as Okinawa was formally integrated into
the Japanese political economy. The following chapter will return to this
moment of failed representation before state power after Okinawa becomes
disillusioned with redemption by the Japanese state and once again
looks beyond in the post-reversion era.

CHAPTER 5

Okinawa, 1972–1995: Life That Matters

Chapters 3 and 4 showed the respective limitations of national and class unity in resisting U.S. military bases in Okinawa alongside the Old and New Japanese Left. Both assumed a single-state logic of imperialism and failed to position Okinawa in terms of a regional form of governance between the United States and Japan. In the post-reversion era, however, the complicit relationship between U.S. militarism and the Japanese political economy became undisguisable, causing much sobering reflection on the past and new ways of thinking about Okinawa's ability to assert its autonomy in a global world where it is not held back by the unfulfilled promises of the Japanese state.

In the effort to think beyond Okinawa's vexed position before Japanese state sovereignty, this chapter reconsiders the logic of bordering based on the philosophical notion of self-determination.[1] In place of the imperative for a unified self and unified nation as the precondition for entry into selfhood and nationhood (i.e., the capacity for "self-determination"), it considers the theoretical implications of Okinawa as a borderland of the Pacific, where bodies and objects circulate. It appeals to Tosaka's critique of static matter wedged in a two-dimensional planar space and his attempt to assign a different kind of agency to morphing matter. In this way, it attempts to think about how Okinawan life, as life that fails to unify before the state, can *matter* or be significant in the quality of its mutability.

This chapter reads the Okinawa failure to achieve self-determination as the potential for developing a different kind of autonomy grounded in the agency of morphing matter through Tanaka Midori's mixed-race memoir *My Distant Specter of a Father*. In it, she fails to become American; she fails to become Japanese. She comes to realize that there is no transcendental power to give meaning to her life. Instead, she grounds the "endeavor to live on" in the uncertainty of her ever-changing self. While she is left bereft of any transcendental truths by which to live, her act, as an unintended consequence, recuperates her life force from the state to ground her ability to continue to live on. For the first time, her life is finally allowed to matter.

The Monotony of the Same

On May 15, 1972, the long-awaited moment had finally arrived: Okinawa fully reverted to the Japanese administration. As the hopes and dreams for a new future were ushered in at the threshold of the Japanese state, a very cold post-reversion morning dawned on the horizon. The threads of the Okinawan dream for liberation had been woven into a different web. Quite cruelly, the more Okinawans resisted, the more they became entangled. Complaints about the U.S. military? Lodge them with *your own* government—the government of Japan that not only welcomes U.S. military bases, but enthusiastically funds them with the might of the yen.

After reversion, the proportion of U.S. military bases on the island increased while it decreased in mainland Japan.[2] This was not because Japan was forced to buckle under the unilateral pressures of the United States; Japan actively opposed a U.S. Department of Defense proposal for withdrawal. As the Vietnam War started to come to a close, the United States was becoming wary of the explosive resentment toward U.S. military bases, as seen in the 1970 Koza Riot. But perhaps more importantly, it could no longer sustain funneling U.S. dollars into military expenditures after an unpopular war. It was in this political climate that Department of Defense analysts concluded it would be "considerably cheaper and probably more effective" to withdraw all marines throughout the Pacific, including Okinawa and Hawai'i, and bring them to Camp Pendleton in San Diego, California.[3] Instead of seeing this as an opportunity for base reduction, Kubo Takaya, head of the Japanese Defense Agency, stated that "Given the need for a mobile force in Asia, the U.S. Marines should be retained."[4] Yara Tomohiro argued that "[h]ad Japan not stopped the process of their withdrawal to the mainland United States it seems most unlikely that the Okinawan base problem would have become such a big political issue."[5]

In 1972, the United States happily turned over its financial responsibilities in Okinawa to Japan. Japan was crowned with the title of the world's second-largest industrial power,[6] and by the reversion year, it was ready to reintegrate Okinawa as its periphery. The government enacted the Special Act on the Promotion and Development of Okinawa (*Okinawa shinkō kaihatsu tokubetsu sochi hō*) ostensibly to close the economic gap with the mainland. This established what Shimabukuro Jun refers to as an "Okinawan promotion and development regime" that operated first through the Okinawa Development Agency until 2011 and now through the Okinawa General Bureau. This means that there is a separate agency within the Cabinet Office of the government of Japan dedicated to collapsing the convoluted political issue of U.S. military bases in Okinawa into the narrow channel of economics. Shimabukuro calls this setup a "dispute canceling device" (*hisōtenka shisutemu*) in which bureaucrats from the Agency for Public Works, Ministry of Finance, or Ministry of Home Affairs occupy the Okinawa General Bureau while those from the Ministry of Foreign Affairs and Ministry of Defense are conspicuously absent.[7] Because Okinawan politics are carried out through the Okinawa General Bureau, it is cut off from the rest of political life in Tokyo and incapable of influencing the ministries where the real politicking happens for the rest of Japan.[8] Moreover, when Okinawa addresses a political issue, it is rechanneled through the Okinawa General Bureau and reconfigured into an economic issue in which the Japanese government doles out money for "promotion and development." The two-way street of negotiation that constitutes political agency for the rest of Japan dissolves into the one-way street of beggary for Okinawa. At first, the "promotion and development regime" was sold to the Okinawan people as a way to close the gap in the standard of living incurred through its painful years of U.S. occupation. However, in the late 1990s, it came to explicitly link reparation with the acceptance of new U.S. military base construction. The quasi-governmental 1996 Shimada Colloquium (*Shimada kondankai*) brazenly mapped out such a carrot and stick approach.[9] Acceptance of new base construction led directly to specific business incentives. Rejection of base construction led to these incentives being taken away. Many later pointed out that the so-called incentives were not as lucrative as what other municipalities in Japan received simply through normal politicking. Nonetheless, since the

Shimada Colloquium, protest against U.S. military bases in Okinawa has been dismissed simply as a way for Okinawans to squeeze more money out of the central government. This is why Kevin Maher, a State Department official in charge of the Japanese affairs office, stated that Okinawans are "masters of manipulation and extortion" when dealing with the central government.[10] It seems that Okinawans had graduated from being petty beggars only to become masterful extortionists.

Yen is not the only problem. Contrary to common belief, dollars flowing out of bases no longer do much for the Okinawan economy. More and more, business leaders in Okinawa are starting to view the bases as unwanted baggage crowding large swaths of the island that could otherwise be used for farming or industry. Military base revenue in 2009 only accounted for 5.2 percent of Okinawa's gross domestic income of nearly $4 billion, down from 15.5 percent in 1972.[11] Tomochi Masaki estimates that the Okinawan gross income would be 1.25 percent greater after the elimination of all U.S. and Japanese Self-Defense Force bases and their accompanying subsidies from the Japanese government.[12]

Finances between the United States and Japan have changed dramatically as well. Japan gives unprecedented financial support to the U.S. military. Per the 1960 Status of Forces Agreement (SOFA), embedded as a subset of articles to the U.S.-Japan Security Treaty, Japan has historically been obligated to provide the land and maintenance costs for the bases free to the United States while the United States pays for the operation of military forces on the bases. However, in 1978, Japan Defense Cabinet Secretary Kanemaru Shin volunteered to go above and beyond this obligation and provide an *omoiyari yosan* (sympathy budget) commonly referred to as "host nation support" that also pays for salaries of Japanese nationals working on the bases and the cost of facility construction.[13] As a result, by 2002, Japan covered 74.5 percent of the operating costs for U.S. military bases there.[14] This means that it is less expensive to maintain forces in Japan than it is in the United States. In the last published figures by the U.S. Department of Defense in 2003, Japan contributed $4.41 billion to U.S. military bases within its borders. This was the largest amongst all U.S. allies: nearly three times Germany's contribution of $1.56 billion and over five times South Korea's $842 million.[15]

Economics came to a head with politics in 1995 whereupon the movement against the U.S. military bases in Okinawa underwent cataclysmic change. This, of course, was the year of the rape of a twelve-year-old Okinawan by three U.S. military personnel. But it was also around the time when the U.S. military started to express a desire to close the dilapidated

Futenma Air Station and build a new U.S. military installation in northern Okinawa. In the space of some thirty years after the reversion era, Okinawans faced the monotony of the same. Instead of scrambling for
American dollars that were soaked up by the Japanese economy during the
reversion era, they now scramble for Japanese yen that is soaked up by the
Japanese economy today. In any case, honing a middle-class Okinawan
work ethic did not correspond to an ability to have their voices heard
through the democratic processes of popular sovereignty. Nor did it afford them equal protection under the Japanese constitution. Their efforts
only led to a reinforced presence of U.S. military bases and marginaliza-
tion within the Japanese economy. Okinawa, hence, continues to be excepted (excluded) from Japanese sovereignty.

Given that Okinawa Prefecture is officially part of the Japanese state,
yet still robbed of decision-making power regarding U.S. military bases
and the economy, what possible recourse does it have for political expression? Understandably, Okinawan scholars of the political economy have
been most conspicuous in arguing for Okinawan autonomy vis-à-vis the
Japanese state. Their proposals have been presented in various forms, including autonomous regional power in place of the centralized Japanese
government, autonomous state within a federalized system, and all-out independence.[16] Furthermore, these proposals are not esoteric discussions
limited to the academic elite; recent opinion polls point to growing popular support. Compared to 61.8 percent in 2011, only 46.1 percent—less than
half—of all respondents in 2016 reported satisfaction with the status quo
of Okinawa as a prefecture within the Japanese state. By contrast,
34.5 percent reported they favored some form of increased local autonomy
with choices ranging from variations of a federal system (with authority
in administrative, economic, and/or diplomatic matters) to all-out independence. This was a marked increase from just 20 percent in 2011.[17] Without belaboring the finer differences of these debates, they indicate a
strong desire for more autonomy within the established system of international law. While I am aligned with the spirit of such debates, my concern here, as it is for this entire book, is to theorize a form of autonomy
irreducible to the law. In the next section, I focus on self-determination
not as a political concept, but as philosophical one, specifically as it relates
to biopolitics and miscegenation. A gap needs to be addressed between the
language of the political economy that expresses the right to "determine
itself" as a unified entity on the stage of international politics and Okinawa's
visceral experience at the crossroads of the Pacific, where bodies and
things (i.e., matter) are in constant motion. Because the Okinawan dream

for autonomy has gotten nowhere by moving forward on the same planar space through *time*, it is time to consider the analytics of *space* where Okinawan lives can finally start to *matter.*

Matter in Motion

Acutely aware of the spatial dynamics in his formulation of biopolitics, Foucault articulated them in terms of circulation in his 1977–1978 lectures at the Collège de France, *Security, Territory, Population*. More than just a discussion on the circulation of bodies and objects, his broader aim was to insert a metaphysics of matter in motion into geopolitics as part of his effort to develop a notion of biopolitics. He writes:

> I mean . . . circulation in the very broad sense of movement, exchange, and contact, as form of dispersion, and also as form of distribution, the problem being: How should things circulate or not circulate? Now it seems to me that . . . we see the emergence of a completely different problem that is no longer that of fixing and demarcating the territory, but of allowing circulations to take place, of controlling them, sifting the good and the bad, ensuring that things are always in movement, constantly moving around, continually going from one point to another, but in such a way that the inherent dangers of this circulation are canceled out.[18]

Foucault points to a shift away from sovereignty defined in terms of the territory and the sovereign's ability to "fix" its borders, to a new form of governmentality concerned with "ensuring that things are always in movement" for the population. Things must move. And the new art of government is contingent on the ability to regulate this imperative for movement.

Matsushima Chōgi paints a vivid picture of what governmentality as the regulation of circulation looked like in U.S. military–occupied Okinawa.

> If you want to see how these [military] roads developed, all you need to do is pick up two Coca-Cola ads. One is from the 1950s and one is from the 1960s. On them you will find Okinawa's roads and bases printed out with Coca-Cola vendors indicated by arrows. On the new map, you can see the expanded bases along with new roads to service them that extend beyond what you see on the first map. If bases are expanded, then roads are elongated. So, if one base was destroyed by something like an explosion, it is designed so that the remaining 99 go unharmed. In this way, the roads that connect independent bases

together are like a nervous system for the entire body called the
"Okinawan base."[19]

Matsushima does not understand sovereign power to be controlled by a
head that commands other parts to move, but as a system that can coun-
teract crisis through its ability to maintain circulation. In this way, he
attempts to give new meaning to the rally to "take to the streets" and
comments how a simple sit-in for ten hours on Highway 1 in 1965 paralyzed base operations for a week at the cost of thirty thousand dollars for
the military.[20] Furthermore, he speaks of the significance of the death of
a Ryukyuan police officer on the same Highway 1 some six years later. The
police officer was used as an instrument of institutional power to maintain circulation that was threatened by a general strike. From the perspective of the U.S. military, his life mattered only to the extent that he could
maintain circulation; from the perspective of the Japanese Left, his life
mattered only to the extent that he could stop it and rally against the bases.
In other words, his life did not really matter for either side outside of its
utility for both. His Okinawan life falls off of a two-dimensional grid of
intelligibility. In this sense, Okinawans did not care if he was for or against
the bases, Matsushima writes, for his life simply mattered as Okinawan.
Matsushima points to a different spatial dimension in which a seemingly
contradictory Okinawan life—as simultaneously instrumental to the U.S.
military and victim to it—refuses to be flattened into mutually exclusive
opposites.[21] This is why he writes, "I want to dwell (*kodawaritai*) upon the
fact of his death just as much as the place where he died."[22]

For both Matsushima and Foucault, circulation is integral to the formation of a spatial order that regulates the intelligibility of life itself. Foucault picks up this thread again in his lectures of the following year, *The
Birth of Biopolitics*, in a more concrete geopolitical configuration through a
discussion of Kant's *Perpetual Peace*. In his reading of this essay, Foucault
notes that states mutually expose themselves to the "unlimited nature of
the external market"[23] (i.e., circulation with the unknown) in order to collapse its infinite expanse into a two-dimensional spatial order. This occurs
when first, the disunity within states is canceled out vis-à-vis economic en-
richment of the "unlimited nature of the external market," and second,
the ability to determine a unified "self" is achieved systematically with
"other" states. In other words, states mutually self-determine vis-à-vis a
potentially self-dissolving encounter and reemerge as a constellation of
states that confront an unknown. The self/other distinction is secured
through the enabling limitation of globalization that reinforces a federa-

tion of free states in pursuit of perpetual peace. Just as the "self" must unify internally in order to express a self-determining will onto the external world, states must unify internally in order to express its ability to self-determine as a state in a system of other nation-states.[24] The irony is that even though the nation-state system is predicated on the synergy of exchange, it is an exchange that does not break down borders, but reinforces them with increasing tenacity. This is a metaphysics of movement in which the agency of its matter in motion is surrendered to the sovereignty of a transcendental power that organizes its intelligibility in terms of a two-dimensional planar space, divided internally between an inside and outside, that is inserted into chronological time. It spatially freezes—or renders static and originary—matter in atomic units as the precondition for its continued systematic movement. A non-idealist conception of movement, however, understands that "matter is *in motion*" and surrenders its agency to this motion.[25]

Chapter 4 attempted to capture the agency of this matter in motion through Matsushima Chōgi's writings on the movement of migrant workers in which he conceptualized the "Okinawan proletariat." This is a class that does not unify internally and therefore fails to self-determine. Matsushima theorized the Okinawan proletariat because he came face-to-face with the contradiction of Okinawans unifying as a Japanese proletariat when they could not even unify as a class of Okinawans. Furthermore, he paralleled this contradiction with the Black Power movement he came into contact with in Koza in which he saw the contradictions of African American soldiers who fight for a state that discriminates against them. Hence, through his contact with the Black Power movement, he was able to see that "Okinawa is not the contradiction of a single state," but that it is the contradiction of something larger that similarly affects others around the world—that is, "the contradiction of capitalism" itself.[26] What he means is that capitalism flattens the world. Okinawa is a contradiction of capitalism insofar as it is wedged as a static entity within a two-dimensional planar space, in which it is supposed to find its place within the inner space of "Japan" so it can gain entry into the outer world of nation-states. His description of Okinawa's "contradiction" resonates with the contradiction of a static materiality within a two-dimensional planar space described by Tosaka. He writes:

> A characteristic of what is called formal logic is that it mediates things
> that fall on two identical planes. Things that move and act within
> these planes are fundamentally contradictory. For example, on one

plane, "A" is α and, at the same time, it is not something else like β. However, on the other plane, "A" could very well be β. (But if so, it is already not α.) And so in the *vertical* relationship between these two planes, the law of contradiction is not played out. On the first plane, the object "A" is α, but if "A" has a *concrete mutability*, on the second plane it is of course not α. (It is β or something else, for example.) Rather than displaying "A's" contradictory nature, this situation demonstrates "A's" materiality. Thus, this so-called formal logic is merely a kind of *three-dimensional logic* of different planes.[27]

What liberates "A's" contradictory nature from a two-dimensional planar space is its materiality described as "*concrete mutability*." It is this mutability that demands a third dimension of matter in motion, and not an "internal axis of unification"[28] as critiqued by Matsushima. The autonomy of this materiality, furthermore, is not surrendered to a sovereign who exists at the limits of a two-dimensional planar space—a demi-god who sutures the space of the inside from the outside through an exceptional decision, but it is retained as motion itself.[29]

When Matsushima argued that the Okinawan proletariat must remain vigilant to the "internal axis of unification," he spoke of a vigilance of sovereign power that unifies according to this two-dimensional plane that has no space for Okinawa's experience of mixing. Hence, different from the mixing of bodies that emerges with configuring nation-states, Matsushima suggests a metaphysics of matter in motion that neutralizes the synergy of the nation-state system.

More contemporary scholars have noted that while mixing has been imposed upon Okinawa, this mixing at the same time does not occur in a way in which Okinawa gains entry into the global world. That is, mixes it does, but self-determines, it does not. For example, Shimabukuro Jun writes:

> . . . it was precisely because assimilation into Japan and exchange with mainland Japan had considerably advanced that Okinawa . . . was able to take notice of the *particularity of a self that cannot easily assimilate.* . . . The postwar Okinawan population included no less than 100,000 members of the U.S. military armed forces and civilian components, and also Indian and Filipino foreign nationals who work in business that service them. . . . This is a condition of being at the crossroads of a plural ethnic mixing. . . . [30]

Shimabukuro points to the experience of mixing, and not a multicultural society subsumed into a globalized Japan whereupon the latter simply needs to learn how to become more tolerant of difference. His writing is mark-edly different, for example, from that of the multicultural advocate Noiri Naomi. Frustrated with the overt racism that mixed-race children encoun-ter, she views Okinawa's *champurū* (mixed) culture as hypocritical and in-stead argues that Okinawans should realize Okinawan AmerAsians receiving a "double" or bilingual education "can be beneficial for all children in our time of globalization."[31] Certainly, Okinawans who dis-criminate against mixed-race children in Okinawa are hypocritical, but the violence is not so much because of lack of a will to embrace the bene-fits of globalization as it is Okinawa's being barred from entry into the global world, as suggested by Shimabukuro. For Okinawa, mixes it does, but self-determines it does not. If this is the case, then what use does Okinawa have for all of those mixed-race children having a run of the islands?

Okinawa's experience of mixing does not lead to a determination of the self as a singular "one" whereupon the mixed-race subject can emerge in either a fraction form of "half" or a multiple form of "double." Such equa-tions are predicated on the stability of a two-dimensional self. There can only be a collapse of a unified self altogether. If the only path to global citi-zenry is to self-determine, then this failure of unification seems to drive Okinawa into a dead end. In the next section, I examine how this failure can be turned into an opportunity for a different sense of autonomy through a close reading of a mixed-race memoir, *My Distant Specter of a Father*.

The Failure of Mixed Race

By the time the reversion year came around in 1972, the first cohort of mixed-raced individuals born in 1946 had turned twenty-six. No longer were they spoken for, but they started to express themselves as embodi-ments of Okinawa's condition of mixing. Koza burst forth with mixed-race rock artists such as Kyan Marie, who sang in Japanese, Okinawan, and En-glish.[32] Suzuki Teruko, a survivor of the 1959 Miyamori Elementary School plane crash by a supersonic fighter jet, published a fictional account of her life entitled *Come Out Kijimuna* in 1990.[33] In 1998, a group of mothers established the AmerAsian School in Okinawa to provide a bilingual edu-cation for their children who were susceptible to bullying in public schools.[34] This gave rise to a short-lived spin-off called the Children of Peace Network in 1999 that was led autonomously by a mixed-race adult, Higa Malia, for the same. As described in the Preface, she helped numer-ous individuals find their long-lost fathers and also problematized their ex-treme alienation from the anti-base movement.[35]

From this experience came widely visible figures such as Fija Byron. He started out as a skilled Okinawan *sanshin* (banjo) musician who released an independent album and soon grew into a leader of the revitalization of endangered Ryukyuan languages. Fija's story resonated with many mixed-race individuals who grew up in Okinawa under Japanese assimilation. Even though he was raised in an Okinawan home and educated in Japanese public schools, his mixed-race identity was met with a "Japanese versus American" binary that sought to pigeonhole him as an English speaker on a daily basis. If he was not interpellated by the obligatory "*Hāfu desuka?*," or "Are you half?"—a question tantamount to asking an Asian in the United States "Where are you *really* from?"—then he was greeted with a "*Harō!*" (the attempt to pronounce "hello" in Japanese), to which he answered "*Haisai!*" (the Okinawan word for the same). He used the Okinawan language as a weapon against racism to show the world that although he may look "American," he is in fact a living embodiment of the unintelligibility of Okinawa itself. This is an unintelligibility so acute that Okinawans can no longer even recognize one of their own (Fija), much less comprehend one speaking their own language.[36]

The extreme alienation that renders mixed-race individuals foreigners in their native islands has driven many to claim an indigenous Okinawan identity irreducible to the U.S.-Japan binary itself as they self-identify as "American-Okinawans."[37] The "American" modifier before the hyphenated "Okinawan" has less to do with their affiliation with the United States than it is a marker of how they have been treated differently in an Okinawan society tenaciously influenced by the myth of Japanese monoethnicity. They came together in 2012 to form an "American-Okinawan Association" and argued for the right to an Okinawan identity in which they can live without the daily harassment of being asked to speak English or answer personal questions about their parentage.[38]

What mixed-race subjects such as Fija demand is not that the true Okinawans accept their racially diluted half-offspring with the arrogance of tolerance disguised as multiculturalism, but that Japanese-assimilated Okinawans realize that their unintelligible offspring are the real Okinawans. What this points to is a different relationship with transcendence in which mixing does not present the self with an opportunity to reinforce its own borders of enclosure; but embracing, instead of excluding, the failure of transcendence as such is the first step in exercising a different kind of autonomy. If the game of international politics is rigged so Okinawans are always destined to lose, then one recourse to autonomy is to embrace this failure—and by extension, others who fail in a similar way and make it work to their advantage.

Next, I would like to turn to the only published American-Okinawan mixed-race memoir, *My Distant Specter of a Father*, written by Tanaka Midori, to think about the possibility of failure. Tanaka is a half-Okinawan, half-white woman, born in Okinawa in 1954, and raised by her mother alongside a non-mixed younger brother and sister. The book is written in first-person narration as a search that she reflects back on, from the end-point of her discovery. Structurally, it unfolds like a detective story: Tanaka is presented with evidence of miscegenation in the form of her own body. This compels her to search for the missing agent of the crime, her "specter of a father," as suggested by the title. She writes:

> I made a new friend in middle school. One day, I went to her house. She lived near the part of town where all the bars were concentrated— so-called A-sign bars. G.I.s abounded. I saw big men up close drunk and shouting rambunctiously for the first time in my life. . . .
>
> The men all looked like big red giants. The women were dirty, vulgar, and always laughing in a lascivious tone.
>
> It didn't take me long to put two and two together. This social landscape overlapped with the face of someone with a "foreign male father and Japanese female mother."
>
> I thought to myself, "Men make women their playthings and fool around with them . . . I wonder if I was also born out of a relationship between such a woman and man."
>
> As a fatherless "*hāfu*," a cloud of doubt always hovered about me: "Was I born to a knocked-up woman?" However, the image was never quite as lucid as what I saw in the bar district. I realized it was those feelings that had prevented me from asking my mother about my father the entire time. This also explains the twisted feelings that are conjured up each time I was called "Amirikā!"[39]

In this passage, Tanaka depicts the American-occupied Okinawan milieu. Japan, one party in the triangular trans-Pacific relationship, comes into relief not as a physically present entity, but as the internalized gaze of an assimilated Okinawan whereupon Tanaka contrasts a "Japanese female mother" (not Okinawan) with a "foreign male father." It is at this point, where bodies racialized and gendered along the lines of state sovereignty circulate, that Tanaka makes a causal connection, putting "two and two together," and asks: "Was I born to a knocked-up woman?" With her American father as the agent, and her mother the victimized medium,

Tanaka is the result of the crime. She is hailed, in native Okinawan pronunciation, *"Amirikā!"* (not the Japanese *"Amerikajin"*), whereupon it becomes clear that the effect (mixed-race child) is substituted for the cause
(American father). Tanaka emerges as her father's creation. Hence, in order to come to terms with her identity, she feels compelled to return to
her purported origins and find her "distant specter of a father."

The smooth surface of the narrative, however, is quickly interrupted by
a split identification. While she feels compelled to recuperate her paternal
lineage, she simultaneously registers her "father's country" as offensive and
alien.

> I thought in the depths of my child-like heart, "What in the world
> is America up to? My father's country that I longed for became
> sullied. . . . The "A" in A-sign bar means the U.S. military sanitation
> office deems it "suitable for entry." Is there anything as insulting to
> the Japanese as this? The arrogance of white people who think that
> they are the only ones who are human is appalling.[40]

And:

> My adverse reaction increased in strength at the sight of G.I.s who
> walk around like they own the place, flaunting the enormous strength
> of the dollar, and the America that brought the crisis of war to
> Okinawa.[41]

How is it possible for Tanaka to be bullied as the evidence of a crime and
feel victimized by the U.S. military like her Okinawan counterparts at the
same time?

Herein lies one of the most vexing moments of mixed-race identity. As
the embodiment of what she perceives is a sexual transgression, Tanaka is
infused with an immense sense of alienation from her own body: "To think
that I was 'a child born to a knocked-up [woman], a child of a disgusting
sin' always caused me sadness and impotent anger."[42] She is disgusted with
both the G.I.s and herself as the product of a "disgusting sin" precisely
because she is also Okinawan. Unable to work out this contradiction, she
is left only with "sadness and impotent anger."

A common response to Tanaka's dilemma is to turn the tragic crime
into a celebrated partnership to rescue mixed individuals from their identity crisis. For example, Takara Kurayoshi, who spearheaded the well-
known Okinawan Initiative in 2000, incorporated mixed-race individuals
and their mothers into a full-scale attack on Okinawa's history of victimization. Instead of the dead-end "victimized view of history" disseminated

by Okinawan intellectuals, Takara asserted that Okinawa should actively draw on its historical heritage not as unfortunate baggage, but as the springboard from which it redefines itself as a cultural leader in Asia. In this way, the military bases are not the festering wounds of colonialism, but "the fermenting agent of postwar Okinawa"[43] worthy of praise that "serves as the fundamental significance linking the U.S.-Japan Alliance together."[44] As an example of the positive products of this fermenting agent, he copiously quoted statements by Okinawan women and their mixed-race children.

> "I got married and bore two kids, but when my G.I. husband said one day he had a drill, I never saw him again," says a woman as if she were talking about someone else. "Before payday, G.I.s are so broke, I don't know how many times I was taken for a free ride," laughs off a former prostitute. One *hāfu* rock musician states, "When I'm on stage, right away I can tell which soldiers are going to Vietnam the next day. When I see guys like that, I get all worked up in my performance and want to send them off to war."[45]

As more mixed individuals such as Tanaka come out with stories of how they were bullied as children by Okinawans imbued with victim consciousness, a theoretical vacuum in Okinawa's politics of resistance is created. It testifies to the ironic consequence that the very individuals used in anti-base protest—and indeed, the very individuals who may bear the most direct consequences of the U.S. military presence—are alienated from the movement. Takara exploited this vulnerability as the opportunity to use mixed Okinawans as a living bridge across cultures so as to seal off this silent gap. The problem, however, is not with determining whether mixed individuals are victims or agents, but rather with determining the relationship between mixed identity and a philosophical notion of causality hinged on the assumption that a "doer" can enact a "deed" in the world by virtue of his or her sheer free will.[46]

If she is the effect, then Tanaka is determined to know the cause: the doer behind the deed, or her specter of a father. She starts by asking her mother about her paternity and is shocked by the ease and glibness with which she speaks. She learns that her father was the branch manager of American Express Bank on Camp Zukeran. Her mother worked as his maid in a mansion for foreigners where the two became romantically involved. When her mother became pregnant, she quit her job and gave birth to the baby alone. Her father repeatedly asked her mother for her hand in marriage and pleaded with her to join him in America. He even followed her

in a "sparkling foreign car" from which she resolutely walked away without ever looking back.[47]

The journey progresses as Tanaka leaves for the United States, with the
help of a church friend, to search for her father. She finds his name in a
phone book from Florida and agrees to meet him over the Christmas hol-
iday. The reunion is cinematic—literally, as a popular media outlet from
Japan covers the entire event by camera. She dives into her father's arms
and weeps like a child. After the reunion, she learns that he never had any
other children and attempted to look for her in Okinawa, only to be refused multiple times by her mother. At first, when Tanaka's intense desire
to know her origins is satisfied through the discovery of her father, she feels
complete.

> . . . New blood started to flow through my veins. The black "blood"
> that I imagined stagnating through my veins turned into fresh blood
> and started pulsing vivaciously. . . . I decided to live my life very, very
> preciously. This decision filled my body to the point where I became
> feverish. In this way, . . . I searched and found the "evidence of my
> blood" that had always hovered fearfully in my spirit. In this way,
> I have now "resolved" everything. There is nothing to be afraid of
> anymore.[48]

However, even though her mother encourages her beforehand to take U.S.
citizenship and undergo adoption procedures by her father, Tanaka hesi-
tates when the prospect materializes into a reality. Instead, she decides she
is neither Japanese nor American, but in a state of exile.

> There was another article that caught my attention and shook me to
> the depths of my heart. The article was to the effect of an Okinawan
> woman who married a G.I., lived in America, got a divorce after
> four-and-a-half years, and returned to Okinawa. Her young daughter
> was ridiculed for being a "Jap" in preschool.
>   Mixed-race children are discriminated as "Amirikā" in Okinawa, and
> despised as "Jap" when they cross over to America. No matter where
> mixed-race children go, they will always have to live as a "people in
> exile." This article overlapped with the issue of me becoming an
> adoptive daughter to my father, and taking on U.S. citizenship.[49]

When the prospect of fulfilling her dream comes within arm's reach,
Tanaka does not simply switch over, but takes a step back. Instead of fulfilling her destiny, dictated by the causal chain by becoming the American
father's daughter she often fantasized about in the midst of intense suffering,

she problematizes it altogether. Here, Tanaka resists clinging to either polar opposite, and the mythic rhythm of her text starts to dabble in the divine.

The very force that attempts to galvanize mixed Okinawans into oppositional categories mythologizes their origins in terms of a pure singularity and gains inertia by neutralizing their excess. They are neither the evidence of Okinawa's victimization nor the promise of the U.S.-Japan relationship. The compulsion to lock them into one extreme says less about what they really are, and more about how their rich ambiguity is secured as a site of mythic violence that seeks to submit everything to the logic of the law. It is through this mythology that we again and again locate the mixed-race subject as a tragedy of bilateral state violence that is redeemed through a rebirth into a biological bridge across cultures.

What is crucial in experiencing Tanaka's memoir is not adjudicating whether her decisions are right or wrong, whether she is American or Japanese. Rather, it is crucial to take stock of the various decisions she made in her journey so as to undermine the field of representation that constantly seeks to exclude her contradictions, inconsistencies, and ambiguities. By laying bare the rich ambiguity of Tanaka's journey, the goal here is not to delineate a victim or agent, but to reveal a constant thirst to search for meaning in life. This laying bare inherently antagonizes the field of representation that both produces mixed people and simultaneously erases them.

Yet, at the same time, to merely suggest that the alegal is precisely that which is in excess of the law and representation only gestures to the existence of a truth beyond human grasp that we can never know. Upon coming up against the crisis of indecision—of not being able to decide on the meaning of her life—Tanaka certainly appeals to the power of God to fill this void in meaning.

> . . . then one day, I began to pray.
> On that day, I became liberated from the utter hopelessness, and my heart became peaceful. Sadness and hatred vanished, and I began to firmly believe that my birth was "desired by God who endowed me with life on this earth."[50]

Although her faith in God, in certain instances, answers her prayers (such as saving her sister from death in the hospital), I would like to focus on a different moment in her faith. God delivers her to the cold reality of meaninglessness whereupon she is empowered to survive as an individual who embodies Okinawa's condition of uncertainty. This is not self-determination that emerges triumphantly from a space completely lacking in sovereignty.

Rather, just as Benjamin answers Schmitt's trap of sovereignty with allegory defined as "the non-existence of what it presents,"[51] it is that unname-
able thing which is not outside of sovereignty, but what must be *assumed* as
a fixity in order for sovereignty to establish itself; it is the value x in an
equation that defines a system of sovereignty. But it is precisely the ambivalence, liminality, and inconsistency of the un-namable that undermines
this assumption and becomes a nullifying force that denies the sovereign's
ecstatic flight to transcendence; that is to say, in this case, it refuses to wait
for salvation from a superhuman force that we can never know. It is this
great ambivalence of constantly living as a member of a "people in exile"
that leaves her with the resolution to write in classical Japanese, "I must
nevertheless endeavor to live on (*iza ikimeyamo*)." Here, the text does not
present us with the truth that the truth is inaccessible to humans and only
lies beyond, in the transcendental realm of God. Rather, the text appeals to a God who says very little and only imparts an endeavor to live
on; it turns not away from representation as a failed means to deliver
the truth, but rather toward this failure as a different means—pure
means—to a different end. That is, by embracing this failure, it can
now be that which disarms the fantasy of accessing truth in the dialectical rhythm of myth. This is precisely what Benjamin suggested with
divine violence.

The failure of the memoir lies in the ambivalent first-person narration
itself. At first, Tanaka's text seems to offer what Okinawa, in its seventy
years of American-Okinawan miscegenation, has not been able to achieve
because of the plethora of media representations on mixed individuals: a
full-length memoir published by a mixed Okinawan herself. All ears are
open to hear the subaltern speak. Yet, upon closer inspection, it becomes
clear that it is precisely this media that not only invited the manuscript,
but aided Tanaka in her journey to find her father with documentation at
every step. She writes:

> One day, by way of an introduction from a cameraman who had been
> following Okinawa's mixed-race children, I met Nakamura Sumiko
> from the *Woman*[52] magazine. Even though Ms. Nakamura wanted to
> meet me outside of work, simply hearing *Woman* evoked an adverse
> reaction [within me]. Even if she said it was outside of work, I had the
> uneasy feeling that it would ultimately be turned into an article.
> Furthermore, at the risk of sounding rude, I had the feeling that it
> would be an article that caters to the sensational curiosities of its
> readership.

By that point, I had already been covered in a series of articles in *Yomiuri Shimbun*, *Asahi Shimbun*, and the *Ryukyu Shimpo*, and I was accustomed to being interviewed. Nonetheless, I had a fear of this weekly women's magazine.

However, after meeting Ms. Nakamura a number of times, my fears seemed to fade away. Actually, she started to come across as a maternal figure.[53]

What is missing from the deliberate documentation of the role the media played in forming her memoir is the degree to which Nakamura had shepherded or perhaps even wrote part of it herself. Yet it is precisely this failure to deliver a memoir written without mediation from the Japanese media that makes it a success.

The Decision to "Nevertheless Endeavor to Live On"

Although it may be difficult to identify who wrote which part, it is clear that Tanaka at least has attempted to write the memoir herself. This, in itself, shows that her relationship to representation, particularly in its written form, is markedly different from her mother's. Tanaka learned the details of her parents' romance narrated by her mother for the first time in a weekly magazine. She is alarmed that her mother divulged such intimate information to the media, yet left her own daughter starving for clues to her identity growing up as a child. "If only my mother would have rehearsed to me—[a child] who was in despair about my birth—the details of that story over and over again like a lullaby. . . ." When her mother tells her that her father was an important person for her, Tanaka casually responds, "That kind of story is too much for the written text." Her mother then responds, "Midori, not at all. A person's life and death cannot be expressed in the written text. It was more than that."[54] Tanaka's mother, from the beginning, only tells the media what it wants to hear while always knowing that it constantly fails to capture her experience.[55] By doing so, she points to something ineffable, beyond representation.

Tanaka, by contrast, does not give up on representation, but rather dives into it, not as a means to access the truth, but to ironically undermine its own promise to deliver the truth. Hence, she does not look to the sovereign or to God to rescue her from the crisis of meaning. Rather, it is the perpetual state of exile that deflates hope of deliverance from such a crisis in the first place. In this way, she turns away from the symbolic that promises access to transcendence and turns toward allegory that comes crashing down to the living with the force of a "cataract."[56] Her appeal to God gives her hope not to defer the decision to attribute meaning to her life to a higher power, but to decide to "nevertheless endeavor to live on." In desolation, her life starts to matter. She reclaims her own life force from the biopolitical state that attempts to monopolize it. Instead of looking to the promise of transcendental power to deliver her from her troubles, she dives into the morass of failures, contradictions, and inconsistencies, where the responsibility to decide falls upon herself. This is precisely why Benjamin contrasted "the modern concept of sovereignty" that "amounts to a supreme executive power on the part of the prince" with "the baroque concept . . . of the state of emergency" in which "the most important function of the prince [is] to avert this."[57] This inability to decide is not a curse, but hope for a different sense of autonomy that refuses to surrender to the translating force of the sovereign authority. It struggles, it contradicts, it fails. But for the first time, the failure is finally one's own.

Conclusion

Today the Okinawa prefectural government is engaged in an all-out political battle with the Japanese government's determination to build a new base in Henoko, despite overwhelming opposition. The "right versus left" bipartisanship of political life in Okinawa that undergirds the ideology of a democratic state has largely melted away. "Conservative" business leaders have joined hands with "radical" anti-base activists where now 76 percent of the people and all elected leaders oppose construction of this new military base.[1] Riot police are recruited from mainland Japan to reinforce the local Okinawan police force thought to be "too soft" on protecting the construction sites from its own people. Although the Japanese government technically needs local compliance for base construction, it continues to make exceptions to the law in order to push through with brute force.

Okinawa, with exponentially accumulating force, is being propelled into a space where the seduction of sovereignty is quickly losing its charm. Public opinion is edging for more autonomy in various forms, and an all-out independence movement is on the horizon. In my discussion on self-determination in Chapter 5, I reframed the problem of determining a single "self" by capturing the motion of in-betweenness of multiple "selves"

embodied by mixed-race subjects. This is the motion of multiple character changes within the same actor and actress on the stage of Chinen's "The
Human Pavilion"[2] that captivates the audience more than it would if the
stage were simply populated with multiple actors and actresses who represent singular characters.[3] To self-determine is to excise the motion of in-
betweeness and instead set into motion a constellation of enclosed unities
that self-determine. By contrast, I argue for a form of mixing that attempts
to generate a different kind of inertia by disengaging sovereignty with the
failure to determine a unified self. In place of a constellation set into motion by the magnetic force of unities against an externality beyond its limits, I propose developing a different relationship with the alegal as not an
externality, but as a rhythm felt immanently throughout. The self does not
enclose with static boundaries, but is constantly engaged in the kaleidoscopic movement of overlapping in motion. The brilliance is in the motion where a singular space is enhanced, not contaminated, by multiples.
Borders and difference do not dissolve, but they simply develop a different
relationship to the process of enclosure in which they continue to *matter.*

On a similar point, Ariko Ikehara writes, "some of us Okinawans de-
ploy the expression, Okinawan Lives Matter, resonating in relational si-
militude with the concept, Black Lives Matter, overlaying the history of
African Americans onto the Okinawan con/text."[4] Here, difference is not
locked into a binary where it matters as a "fact" in the way that Fanon problematized the "fact of blackness." Nor does it cease to matter because it
was exposed as a fiction. Rather, the "mixed-multiplying" effect of
"champurū f/actors" allows it to matter in a different way. Ikehara, in this
way, opens up a powerful path to Okinawan autonomy—one that she shows
us has been there all along in plain sight.

"Champurū," as she explains, is an Okinawan word for mixing and "often refers to the Okinawan way of blending cultures including culinary
ones."[5] Champurū f/actors are those "who neither reject nor accept their
lives, but cope with and negotiate the mundane in making life possible for
everyone by those who suffered and sacrifice for others to live."[6] By focusing
on the mundane, she deals a double rejection. First, she rejects traditional
notions of free will, as they "neither reject nor accept their lives." Second,
she rejects the dialectical oscillation of myth that locks miscegenation
into a binary of tragedy or triumph. Instead, she traces their ability to
"cope" under the conditions of colonialism. This coping cultivates a
know-how in which champurū f/actors not only learn how to survive, but
they cultivate a way of living in which they come to thrive. In her reading
of Nakada Tsuyoshi's *Black District Red Telephone Booth*, both set in and

written by an author from the Teruya district in Koza, she writes of one such character, "Eri."

> There is a specter of tragedy in Eri's story, as we learn that she grew up without her parents, being called "blackie" by the neighborhood kids. But the story exceeds the trope by giving her a "normal" Okinawan life of challenge and chance because of her grandmother's attitude and action that defuses the stigma of Eri's "blackness" and/or "mixed-ness" in the Okinawan context. Eri is raised like a common Okinawan child without silencing the fact of life/blackness that, in fact, makes her Okinawan-ness come alive as a child of Okinawa. Eri defies both the narrative and character of black-Okinawan female by not only surviving in the story, but also thriving as one who holds the key to the future of Teruya and Koza, both places predetermined as fixed and past in the story and in real life.[7]

I bring this book to a close by reengaging the words of the "father of Okinawan studies," Ifa Fuyū, some seventy years ago with Ikehara's quotation above. If Okinawa is, like many others, at the forefront of a new sense of the global, it is because of the historical experience of mixed-race subjects who were born under conditions in which, as Ifa wrote, Okinawans knew that they were "not in a position to determine their own fate amidst the whirlwind of current world affairs. . . ."[8] This man who devoted his life to the desperate attempt to eke out even a modest form of Okinawan autonomy under Japanese colonialism, died in desolation as he caught a glimpse of the formation of a new postwar empire. As Okinawa's figurative "father," he was bereft of the power to even "command [his] descendants to be in possession" of the ability to "determine their own fate." Hence, he concluded that "[t]he only choice Okinawans have is to throw themselves before the will of their descendants after them."[9] Not then, and not now, have Okinawans been able to self-determine.

Precisely because this is the case, it is time to look to how Okinawa's descendants have not only learned to survive, but thrive in a vacuum of sovereignty. I read an answer to Ifa's last will and testament in the quotation shown earlier from Ikehara. Eri is raised as a "common Okinawan child," but this does not mean that she is forced the impossible, that is, to become a global citizen in a world of enclosures from which Okinawa is barred from entry. Rather, she becomes Okinawa's possibility. By not "silencing the fact of life/blackness," the grandmother "in fact" enables Eri's "Okinawan-ness come alive as a child of Okinawa." She embodies the kaleidoscopic movement of Koza at the crossroads of the Asia Pacific whereupon Okinawa's brilliance is finally able to shine upon the brilliance of others.

In this passage, the grandmother, who would have been a contemporary of Ifa, did for her daughter as a proxy for what her own daughter could not do for Eri. She exercised autonomy in perhaps the most intimate and powerful way possible by claiming her own descendant as one of her own. That she was black did not matter in the sense that the decision was not surrendered to the logic of a patriarchal monoethnic form of Japanese state sovereignty. Rather, it mattered for her as an Okinawan woman who was empowered to make a decision without relying on a transcendental power to reaffirm whether or not it was the right one. And without hesitation, she reclaimed Okinawan life for her descendants after her.

ACKNOWLEDGMENTS

Nearly fifteen years ago, a friend and I dreamed of what it would be like to publish a book. We both registered anxiety about a most peculiar part: the acknowledgments. We noticed how some Okinawan authors hardly acknowledged anyone. Was it that these authors were ungrateful? In retrospect, I realize what we were discussing was Okinawa's fraught relationship with representation. What of the people who helped not because they envisioned some form of recognition by proxy of this book, but because they wanted to form a social possibility outside of public recognition? What of the people whose influence is all the more pervasive precisely because it goes undetected? It is these people who breathe life into this book, and to whom I am most grateful.

But as readers of these pages have seen, this book is not about the power of Okinawa's back channels per se, but about rethinking the ways it comes into contact with institutional power. The production of this very book itself has been made possible with the help of countless individuals who gave me a part of their lives in institutional settings. Ueno Chizuko was a tough yet loving Ph.D. advisor at the University of Tokyo who suggested the topic of this book to me many years ago. Kang Sang Jung's seminars helped me put it into the context of postcolonial Japanese studies. Brett de Bary and Naoki Sakai gave me an intellectual home at Cornell University that was nothing short of magical. Together, they give students just the right amount of space to roam free and dream of a new world while being there to offer guidance when needed. Satya Mohanty and Derek Chang allowed me to explore identity politics and trans-Pacific studies in unconventional ways. Learning the continental tradition from the backdoor of feminist theory with Paula Moya at Stanford University was the best way to bring everything home—literally in the Bay Area, where I was able to engage in trans-Pacific grassroots community building. My colleagues in the Department of East Asian Studies at New York University provided me the most precious gift of departmental support

147

and stability: Eliot Borenstein, Laurence Coderre, Ethan Harkness, Tom Looser, Yoon Jeong Oh, Moss Roberts, Robert Stoltz, and Xudong Zhang. That a department can reach consensus through hearty discussion without resorting to a vote restores my faith in a government. I am also thankful to the faculty in Japanese language, who open up their classrooms to me and put on events loved by my family: Yukiko Hanawa, Kazue Kurokawa, Mayumi Matsumoto, Kayo Nonaka, and Tsumugi Yamamoto. Alejandra Beltran, Candace Laning, and Stacy Sakane are lifesavers who keep me on track. Beth Katzoff, NYU's East Asian Studies librarian, ordered essential texts for this book with much-appreciated speed. I am indebted to the participants of the NYU Humanities First Book Colloquium Program held in July 2017 who gave essential feedback for this manuscript: Rebecca Karl, Tom Looser, Fabian Schäfer, and Travis Workman. Tom Lay of Fordham University Press, I thank you for introducing me to historic Italian cafés, telling me that you "got it," and all the encouragement along the way.

Finally, a word of thanks for the cover image that stands as the only photograph used in this book. Too often is Okinawa, particularly at the site of miscegenation, visually given to capture the fascination of the world at large when the impacted individuals are never able to see themselves as such. Not sure what to do, I turned to the photographer and scholar Arakaki Makoto. He took the cover image for me on February 4, 2018, the day Nago City citizens elected a mayor who supposedly "consents" (*yōnin*) to building a new base in Henoko. That a people who never once asked for the U.S. military to come to their islands have come to be read as offering their "consent" to new base construction is a testament to the twisted nature of liberal democracy. Sometimes when language becomes exhausting, images such as these can be enigmatically beautiful. The U.S. military fence looks down on Okinawans who *nonetheless endeavor to live on* as they comingle with the dead incapable of transcendence to the other world. Thank you, Makoto.

1. "Tomiyama" was her family name when she was involved in the Children of Peace Network, and "Hirano" after she moved to mainland Japan. She now goes by "Higa."

2. Noiri Naomi, Seiyā Midori, Terumoto Hirotaka, and Yonamine Masae, *Amerajian sukūru: kyōsei no chihei o Okinawa kara* (Tokyo: Fukinotō Shobō, 2001), 98–99.

3. Tomiyama Malia, "Yūki," *Buraku kaihō* 477 (November 2000): 11. For more on this network in the context of mixed-race Okinawan history, see Ōshiro Yasutaka, "Kokusaiji ni kansuru mondai to taiou no jidai kubun shian," *Okinawa chiiki fukushi kenkyū: Nihon shakai fukushi gakkai dai 49 kai zenkoku taikai kaisai kinen gō* (October 20, 2001): 3–29.

4. Norma Field provides a well-known account of the sexual implications of mixed-race in U.S. military–occupied Japan from personal experience. Reading the following passage, one can get a sense of why mixed-race individuals might avoid each other under these circumstances. She writes: "The subtle shame that clung like an odor to those years of American male presence in the form of military occupation marked Okinawa as a place I would unintentionally avoid. There, the ubiquity and the seeming sempiternity of American bases made the shame more palpable than on the mainland. Seventeen years after Okinawa's reversion to Japan, I find myself recounting my first, recent visit there to a friend from a classical literature research group. We are drinking. He is surprised: I hadn't been there as a child? I am not sure what I am being asked. Whether, after all, I was illegitimate? Or more simply, being a half-breed of my generation, I must surely have been there where my kind are concentrated? Many years into my growing up, I thought I had understood the awkward piquancy of biracial children with the formulation, they are nothing if not the embodiment of sex itself; now, I modify it to, the biracial offspring of war are at once more offensive and intriguing because they bear the imprint of sex as domination." Norma Field, *In the Realm of a Dying Emperor: Japan at a Century's End* (New York: Vintage Books, 1991), 39.

5. *Hāfu* refers to an individual with half-Japanese and half-foreign ancestry. For a thorough genealogy of this term, see Hyoue Okamura, "The Language of 'Racial Mixture': How Ainoko Became Haafu, and the Haafu-gao Makeup Fad," *Asia Pacific Perspectives* 14 (Spring 2017), https://www.usfca.edu/center-asia-pacific/perspectives/v14n2/okamura. Okamura conjectures that *hāfu* probably came from the introduction of the terms "half-caste" and "half-breed" into the Japanese lexicon. Although *hāfu* appeared in the 1930s, he shows how it became circulated in the realm of popular culture starting from the 1960s. He writes, "[b]y the 1980s, though, *haafu* had become the most fashionable racialist label for mixed-blood people in Japan."

6. Tomiyama Malia, "Amerajian o ikiru," *Akemodoro*, no. 19 (2000): 23.

7. The following articles were published in 2012 by Hirano Malia in the "Ochibo" series of *Okinawa taimusu*: "Amerajian," July 2; "Yankī gō hōmu," July 16; "Mori no naka no ki," July 30; "Nayamashii Eikaiwa kyōshitsu," August 11; "Watashi no naka no Taiheiyō sensō," August 25; "Icharibachōdē," September 7; "*Uchinānchu*," September 20; "Motomerareru baransu," October 3; "Meimei," October 17; "Ryōshin to watashi," October 31; "Tattoi tsunagari," November 12; "Oya e no tegami," November 26; "Yume no keikaku," December 8; and "Aruga mama ni," December 24.

8. Tomiyama Malia, "Beigun kichi," Facebook, July 19, 2013, https://www.facebook.com/photo.php?fbid=481134368644277&set=a.117687014989016.24618.100002431539882&type=3&theater.

9. *kichi no otoshigo*

10. "*Amejo*" is short for "*Amerikā jōgū*" and means someone with an affinity for America. "*Ame*" comes from the English "America" and "*jo*" comes from the Okinawan "*jōgū*," as in "*saki jōgū*," or someone who savors alcohol. It is likely that mainland Japanese who do not understand the Okinawan language interpreted the "jo" to mean "woman," as it has come to mean "woman of the Americans." Fluent in the Okinawan language, Higa understands the nuances of this term that conveys discrimination toward women mediated by a mainland Japanese gaze.

11. Naoki Sakai and Hyon Joo Yoo, eds., *The Trans-Pacific Imagination: Rethinking Boundary, Culture, and Society* (Singapore: World Scientific Publishing Company, 2012), 11.

12. Sakai and Yoo, *Trans-Pacific Imagination*, 8, 9, 12.

INTRODUCTION

1. "Extralegal" strictly means that which is outside of the legal order and can be used in two ways. First, as problematized here, it describes subjects who are assumed to be excluded from the protections of a preexist-

ing law such as prisoners at Guantánamo Bay. However, there is a second usage not adopted in this book that describes sovereign power that exists outside of the law. For example, in the United States, this might refer to police violence against African Americans, or in Okinawa, U.S. military violence against Okinawans. In either case, police officers or military personnel exercise violence as if they were a god-like sovereign power above the law. I do not use the word in this sense because, as we shall see in the pages to come, although the sovereign may be "god-like," it is not a god. That is, the sovereign may suspend the law and is therefore, in that sense, above the law, but the suspension is only validated to the extent that it can restore normativity to the legal order. And normativity, in turn, requires on-the-ground people who subscribe to norms. Hence, the sovereign is a liminal power that is both above and part of the legal order and, in this sense, can be more accurately described as "quasi-extralegal." Theoretically, what is at stake here is whether or not the sovereign can make a clean break from a preexisting legal order. Carl Schmitt addressed this question in *Dictatorship* in terms of the difference between commissary and sovereign dictatorship. He writes, "despite all its extra-legal authorization," the commissary dictator nonetheless "remains within the prescriptions of a constitutional order." Here, as suggested by use of the word "despite," the sovereign is clearly quasi-extralegal. By contrast, a sovereign dictatorship exists when "the whole existing legal order is rendered obsolete and a completely new order is intended." By introducing a new legal order without reference to the previous one, Schmitt tries to present a case in which the sovereign dictator is a purely originary creator above the law and, therefore, extralegal. Carl Schmitt, *Dictatorship: From the Origin of the Modern Concept of Sovereignty to Proletarian Class Struggle* (Cambridge: Polity Press, 2014), xxiv.

2. Carl Schmitt, *Political Theology: Four Chapters on the Concept of Sovereignty*, trans. George Schwab (Cambridge: MIT Press, 1985), 5.

3. Jacques Derrida, "Force of Law: The 'Mystical Foundation of Authority,'" in *Deconstruction and the Possibility of Justice*, ed. David Carlson, Drucilla Cornell, and Michel Rosenfeld (New York: Routledge, 1992).

4. According to Department of Defense reports, the majority of U.S. military bases abroad are located in Germany, Japan, and South Korea. In terms of all metrics, except for surface area, Japan is more densely concentrated with U.S. military bases when compared to Germany. The surface area of U.S. military bases in Germany is 137,360 acres to Japan's 126,146 acres. The number of active service members in Japan is 48,485 to Germany's 39,408. The plant replacement value of Japan's U.S. military bases is valued at $61.9 billion to Germany's $40.5 billion. Since U.S. military base acreage

in Germany has steadily decreased over the years in contrast to Japan, which has steadily increased, it is projected that Japan will soon come to surpass Germany in terms of this metric as well. Department of Defense, "Base Structure Report: Fiscal Year 2015 Baseline," http://www.acq.osd.mil/eie /Downloads/BSI/Base%20Structure%20Report%20FY15.pdf. For an analysis based on fiscal year 2010 data, see Hayashi Hirofumi, *Beigun kichi no rekishi: sekai nettowāku no keisei to tenkai* (Tokyo: Yoshikawa Kōbunkan, 2012), 1–5.

These metrics show how Japan is recorded as one of the most densely concentrated countries in the world, but when broken down to U.S. military base installation proportions within the Japanese state, it becomes clear that it is in fact Okinawa Prefecture that is the most densely concentrated region in the world. Until recently, Okinawa Prefecture housed 74 percent of all U.S. military bases in the Japanese state, even though it only makes up 0.6 percent of total state territory. With the recent return of areas in northern Okinawa in 2016, it now houses 70 percent of all U.S. military bases in the state of Japan. "Beigun hokubu kunrenjyō 4 senha henkan Okinawa e no shūchū 74% → 70% ni," *Okinawa taimusu*, December 22, 2016. According to *Ryukyu Shimpo* newspaper calculations, Okinawa hosts 17.99 U.S. military personnel to Japan's 0.086 per 1,000 people in the population. This concentration is 209 times that of Japan's. "Okinawa no futando, hondo no 209 bai fukki 45 nen, kichinaki shima tōku," *Ryukyu shinpō*, May 14, 2017.

5. Department of Defense, *Military and Civilian Personnel by Service/ Agency by State/Country: December 2016*, https://www.dmdc.osd.mil/appj/dwp /dwp_reports.jsp.

6. Statistics of Japan, *Heisei 27 nen kokusei chōsa: jinkō sokuhō shūkei kekka*, February 26, 2016, http://www.stat.go.jp/data/kokusei/2015/kekka /pdf/gaiyou.pdf.

7. Department of Defense, *Active Duty Military Personnel by Service Rank/Grade: December 2016*, https://www.dmdc.osd.mil/appj/dwp/dwp _reports.jsp.

8. As Peggy Pascoe explains, the term "miscegenation" first appeared during the U.S. presidential election of 1864 to replace the term "amalgamation." It combined *miscere* (mix) and *genus* (race) to refer to the "mixture of two or more races." Peggy Pascoe, *What Comes Naturally: Miscegenation Law and the Making of Race in America* (New York: Oxford University Press, 2009), 2.

9. Miscegenation and its relation to heteronormativity requires careful examination that I unfortunately could not address within the scope of this book. For new interventions in this area, see Ikuo Shinjou, "The Political

Formation of the Homoerotics and the Cold War: The Battle of Gazes at and from Okinawa," in *The Trans-Pacific Imagination: Rethinking Boundary, Culture, and Society*, ed. Naoki Sakai and Hyon Joo Yoo (Singapore: World Scientific Publishing Company, 2012), 97–105.

10. Nihon Kokkai Gijiroku, *Kanpō gōgai: dai 13 kai Kokkai Sangiin, dai 24 gō kaigiroku, dai 24 gō*, March 25, 1952, no. 24:5.

11. Christopher T. Sandars, *America's Overseas Garrisons: The Leasehold Empire* (New York: Oxford University Press, 2000), 7.

12. I have shown elsewhere how Schmitt detected the role of the U.S. military in the formation of a new regional economic spatial order that superseded the territorial spatial order of the *jus publicum Europaeum*. Schmitt based his analysis on the Monroe Doctrine, which asserted the basic principle of nonintervention in the political affairs of the Americas while simultaneously encouraging free trade. In this new spatial order, the United States avoided intervening in the public institutions of the state while it sought to maintain invisible economic influence in the private sphere. This new *nomos* opened up the possibility for the emergence of the U.S. military basing project as the United States justified its "right of garrison" in these territories by making "guarantees of the controlling power's economic *Großraum*." In other words, the "controlled state's territorial sovereignty remains inviolate" while it is effectively absorbed into the "spatial sovereignty" of the controlling state's economic bloc, whereupon the United States justifies its military intervention and occupation. Carl Schmitt, *The Nomos of the Earth in the International Law of the Jus Publicum Europaeum*, trans. G. L. Ulmen (New York: Telos Press, 2003), 252. In this way, Schmitt was one of the first to identify an American imperialism without colonies, but with client states that house military bases. Annmaria Shimabuku, "Schmitt and Foucault on the Question of Sovereignty under Military Occupation," *Política Común* 5 (2014), http://dx.doi.org/10.3998/pc.12322227.0005.007.

13. Oguma Eiji, *A Genealogy of 'Japanese' Self-Images*, trans. David Askew (Melbourne: Trans Pacific Press, 2002), 298–320.

14. This is exactly how Kanō Mikiyo linked two seemingly historically disparate outsiders to the postwar Japanese state—Koreans who remained in Japan after liberation and mixed-race subjects who were being born into this in-between world. In other words, Koreans, as living specters of the colonial past, and mixed-race subjects, as the progeny that must be prevented from being born into the postwar future, were both figures in need of erasure in order to erect the fantasy of a monoethnic Japanese state. Kanō Mikiyo, "'Konketsuji' mondai to tan'itsuminzoku shinwa no seisei," in *Senryō to sei: seisaku jittai hyōshō*, ed. Keisen Jogakuen Daigaku Heiwa Bunka Kenkyūjo (Tokyo: Inpakuto Shuppankai, 2007), 213–260.

15. Gabe Masaaki, *Okinawa henkan to wa nan datta no ka: Nichi-Bei sengo kōshō shi no naka de* (Tokyo: Nihon Hōsō Shuppankyōkai, 2000), 51.

16. Nihon Kokkai Gijiroku, *Kanpō gōgai*, 5.

17. According to the Japanese Welfare Ministry, 244, or 21.7 percent of the 1,127 of marriages registered in Japan with a Japanese national bride and U.S. citizen groom came from Okinawa Prefecture in 2015. Furthermore, 267, or 18 percent of the 1,480 children registered in Japan who were born to a U.S. citizen father and Japanese national mother came from Okinawa Prefecture that same year. Director-General for Statistics and Information Policy, Ministry of Health, Labour, and Welfare, ed., *Vital Statistics of Japan 2015*, vol. 1 (Tokyo: Kō seishō Daijin Kambō Tōkei Jōhōbu, 2015).

18. For excellent studies on assimilation (*dōka*) and imperialization (*kōminka*) in Japanese empire, see Leo T. S. Ching, *Becoming "Japanese": Colonial Taiwan and the Politics of Identity Formation* (Berkeley and Los Angeles: University of California Press, 2001) and Tomiyama Ichirō, *Kindai Nihon shakai to "Okinawajin": "Nihonjin" ni naru to iu koto* (Tokyo: Nihon Keizai Hyōronsha, 1990).

19. For more on this historical context, see Ken C. Kawashima, *The Proletarian Gamble: Korean Workers in Interwar Japan* (Durham, N.C.: Duke University Press, 2009), 134.

20. *Zaibatsu* were "privately owned industrial empires" that were often family led and had substantial ties with the state. Chalmers A. Johnson, *MITI and the Japanese Miracle: The Growth of Industrial Policy, 1925–1975* (Stanford: Stanford University Press, 2012), 23.

21. Uno Kōzō, "Shihonshugi no sōshikika to minshushugi," in *Uno Kōzō chosakushū*, vol. 8 (Tokyo: Iwanami Shoten, 1974), 283.

22. Uno, "Shihonshugi no sōshikika to minshushugi," 284.

23. Ibid., 293.

24. Gavin Walker, *The Sublime Perversion of Capital: Marxist Theory and the Politics of History in Modern Japan* (Durham, N.C.: Duke University Press, 2016), 189. Walker's book provides an excellent discussion on Uno's writings on this "impossibility" (*muri*).

25. For more on the emergence of "social policy" in the context of the formation of a Japanese biopolitical state in interwar Japan, see Katsuhiko Endo, "The Science of Capital: The Uses and Abuses of Social Sciences in Interwar Japan" (Ph.D. diss., New York University, 2004). On social policy in relation to Uno in particular, Endo writes: "Based on this primary theory, called *keizai genron* or *genriron* (theory of economic principles), he also theorized, as *keizai seisakuron* (theory of economic policy) (or, more commonly, *dankairon* [stage theory]), the way finance capital distorts economic law, and also how the distortion creates 'social problems' and necessitates

shakai seisaku (social policy) (hence, biopolitics . . .)." Katsuhiko Endo, "A Secret History: Tosaka Jun and the Kyoto Schools," in *Confronting Capital and Empire: Rethinking Kyoto School Philosophy*, ed. Viren Murthy, Fabian Schäfer, and Max Ward (Leiden: Brill, 2017), 358.

26. Foucault quotes François Bilger to define an "institutional framework" as ". . . the specific domain of the state, the public domain, in which it can fully exercise its 'organizing *(ordonnatrice)*' function. It contains all that does not arise spontaneously in economic life. . . ." Michel Foucault, *The Birth of Biopolitics: Lectures at the Collège de France, 1978–1979*, ed. Michel Senellart, trans. Graham Burchell (New York: Palgrave Macmillan, 2008), 154 n. 40.

27. The full passage reads:

For capitalist entrepreneurs, according to the law of population particular to the capitalist method of production, the worker responds to need and is absorbed into the factory or is rendered susceptible to layoffs. Unemployment caused by economic depression or recession is therefore not thought to be a burden that the capitalist shoulders. The worker, just like any other capitalist commodity, is thought to have fallen into a condition where its labor-power commodity is unsellable. This phenomenon is common to both the capitalist and the worker as a seller of commodities. In reality, this is the cruel mechanism of the commodity economy. However, alongside the transition to large-scale capitalist enterprises, the large enterprises themselves find organization by economic depression increasingly difficult on the one hand, but it cannot entrust the vastly increasing number of unemployed workers to the pure commodity economy on the other. Naturally, the state must intervene to some extent. On this point as well, so-called liberalism must already be witness to its end. At first, a resolution was sought by so-called social policy from a position of neutrality. However, it could not provide a fundamental solution to the problem and could not escape the numerous obstacles in a mere makeshift fashion. At least the major countries around the world during the depression of the 1930s already could not provide a solution to this. In actuality, the depression of these times did not just call for measures for the unemployed, but it transpired as a problem of the industrial mechanisms of a single state. Uno, "Shihonshugi no sōshikika to minshushugi," 283–284.

28. Tomiyama, *Kindai Nihon shakai to "Okinawajin,"* 100–101.

29. Katsuhiko Endo, "The Multitude and the Holy Family: Empire, Fascism, and the War Machine," in *Tosaka Jun: A Critical Reader*, ed. Ken C. Kawashima, Fabian Schäfer, and Robert Stolz (Ithaca, N.Y.: Cornell East Asia Series, 2013), 284.

30. Uno, "Shihonshugi no sōshikika to minshushugi," 284.

31. Ibid., 284.

32. Endo, "Science of Capital," 299.

33. Ibid., 217. As Endo notes, this usage of "socialist state" comes from Uno.

34. Michel Foucault, *Security, Territory, Population: Lectures at the Collège de France, 1977–1978*, ed. Michel Senellart, trans. Graham Burchell (New York: Palgrave Macmillan, 2007), 326–327.

35. Italics in original. Tosaka Jun, "The Police Function," trans. Ken C. Kawashima, in *Tosaka Jun: A Critical Reader*, ed. Ken C. Kawashima, Fabian Schäfer, and Robert Stolz (Ithaca, N.Y.: Cornell East Asia Series, 2013), 102.

36. Ken C. Kawashima, "Notes toward a Critical Analysis of Chronic Recession and Ideology: Tosaka Jun on the Police Function," in *Tosaka Jun: A Critical Reader*, ed. Ken C. Kawashima, Fabian Schäfer, and Robert Stolz (Ithaca, N.Y.: Cornell East Asia Series, 2013), 264.

37. Kawashima, "Critical Analysis," 270.

38. Endo, "Science of Capital," 228. As Endo notes, "community of the same" comes from his reading of William Haver, *The Body of This Death: Historicity and Sociality in the Time of AIDS* (Stanford: Stanford University Press, 1996).

39. Tosaka Jun, "The Fate of Japanism: From Fascism to Emperorism," trans. John Person, in *Tosaka Jun: A Critical Reader*, ed. Ken C. Kawashima, Fabian Schäfer, and Robert Stolz (Ithaca, N.Y.: Cornell East Asia Series, 2013), 60.

40. Tosaka, "Fate of Japanism," 63–65.

41. The full quotation reads: "Agamben tempered Schmitt's emphasis on decisionism with Walter Benjamin's insistence that the exception can become the norm, and thus extend beyond the adjudication of a single sovereign authority to become the prerogative of the swarming sovereigns within the population. This forces us to think of exceptionalism alongside the governmentalities that exert power through everyday rationalities of conduct." Stephen Legg, *Prostitution and the Ends of Empire: Scale, Governmentalities, and Interwar India* (Durham, N.C.: Duke University Press, 2014), 49.

42. Eiji Takemae, *Inside GHQ: The Allied Occupation of Japan and Its Legacy*, trans. Robert Ricketts and Sebastian Swann (New York: Continuum, 2002), 173.

43. Takemae, *Inside GHQ*, 142.

44. Uno, "Shihonshugi no sōshikika to minshushugi," 282.

45. Ibid., 290. In Endo's provocative reading, Uno was not so much opposed to the biopolitical configuration of the middle class in service to the state as he was concerned with the form of autonomy that the middle class could retain its mediatory function between the state and finance capital. Quoting Uno, he provides a sketch of Uno's vision of a true "democracy of

the middle class" in which the "workers' autonomously organized criticism" would not be "eliminated" in order to "leave room for finance capital to act" without limit. However, tracing Uno's postwar thought to 1957, he shows how he became increasingly skeptical of a "middle-class movement" that "revolts" against finance capital to the extent that it pursues "excessive profit" but nonetheless believes that "finance capital represents the interests of the entire nation." Endo's reading is cutting edge and requires more discussion that goes beyond the scope of this book. Endo, "Secret History," 358.

46. The term "developmental state," which has become used by scholars of the international political economy, was originally conceptualized by Johnson in his impressive study on the formation of Japan's Ministry of International Trade and Industry (MITI). He argued that in contrast to "regulatory states" such as the United States that monitor the autonomy of the economy through regulatory agencies, "developmental states" intervene more directly into the economy to shape industrial policies. Developmental states are different from states with planned economies because the former is keyed to the rationality of economic growth, whereas the latter is keyed to the rationality of state control. Hence, even though the state interventionist policies of Japan were akin to socialism, Japan should not be confused for state-controlled economies of the Soviet Union. Rather, Japanese socialism was comfortably at home with capitalism; the relationship of the state in service of capitalism was structurally the same as that found in the United States, even though the particular expression may have differed. Johnson, *MITI and the Japanese Miracle*, 11.

47. Ibid., 19.

48. Bruce Cumings, "The Origins and Development of the Northeast Asian Political Economy: Industrial Sectors, Product Cycles, and Political Consequences," *International Organization* 38, no. 1 (Winter 1984): 9

49. Ariko Ikehara, "Champurū Text: Decolonial Okinawan Writing," in *Rethinking Postwar Okinawa: Beyond American Occupation*, ed. Pedro Iocabelli and Hiroko Matsuda (Lanham, Md.: Lexington Books, 2017), 141.

50. For more on the performance of the everyday in Okinawa, see Christopher Nelson, *Dancing with the Dead: Memory, Performance, and Everyday Life in Postwar Okinawa* (Durham, N.C.: Duke University Press: 2008).

1. JAPAN IN THE 1950S: SYMBOLIC VICTIMS

1. Kanzaki Kiyoshi, *Baishun: Ketteiban/Kanzaki repōto* (Tokyo: Gendaishi Shuppankai, 1974), 129.

2. Kanzaki, *Baishun*, 128.

3. Ibid., 133.

4. Ōmori Minoru, *Sengo hishi 6: kinjirareta seiji* (Tokyo: Kōdansha, 1976), 149.

5. Duus Masayo, *Haisha no okurimono: kokusaku ianfu o meguru senryōka hishi* (Tokyo: Kōdansha, 1979), 41.

6. For more on the continuity of the *kōshō seido*, starting with prewar Japanese empire to its postcolonial aftermath of Allied occupation, see Suzuki Yūko, "Karayukisan—'jūgunianfu'—senryōgun 'ianfu,'" in *Iwanami kōza kindai Nihon to shokuminchi: bōchosuru teikoku no jinryū*, ed. Asada Kyōji, Mitani Taichirō, and Ōe Shinobu, vol. 5 (Tokyo: Iwanami Shoten, 1992), 223–250. Also, for a detailed account of the establishment of *kōshō seido*, see Fujime Yuki, *Sei no rekishigaku: kōshō seido, dataizai taisei kara baishun bōshihō, yūsei hogohō taisei e* (Tokyo: Fuji Shuppan, 1997).

7. Kanzaki, *Baishun*, 129–130.

8. Michiko Takeuchi, "'Pan-Pan Girls' Performing and Resisting Neocolonialism(s) in the Pacific Theater: U.S. Military Prostitution in Occupied Japan, 1945–1952," in *Over There: Living with the U.S. Military Empire from World War Two to the Present*, ed. Maria Höhn and Seungsook Moon (Durham, N.C.: Duke University Press, 2010), 81–82.

9. John W. Dower, *Embracing Defeat: Japan in the Wake of World War II* (New York: W.W. Norton, 1999), 46–47.

10. Ichikawa Fusae, ed., *Nihon fujin mondai shiryō shūsei: jinken*, vol. 1 (Tokyo: Domesu Shuppan, 1976), 536.

11. Kanzaki, *Baishun*, 4.

12. Ozawa Nobuo, "Panpan" in *Onna no sengoshi: Shōwa 20 nendai*, ed. Asahi Jānaru, vol. 1 (Tokyo: Asahi Shinbunsha, 1984), 22.

13. Quoted in Sarah Kovner, *Occupying Power: Sex Workers and Servicemen in Postwar Japan* (Stanford: Stanford University Press, 2012), 30. The original document can be found in Ichikawa, *Nihon fujin mondai shiryō shūsei*, 550.

14. Ozawa, "Panpan," 22.

15. Yoneyama's pathbreaking study positions trans-Pacific sexual politics amidst a strongly U.S.-driven reconstitution of international law in the post–World War II era. Reading Carl Schmitt closely, she points to America's disarticulation of the old *nomos* of the *jus publicum Europaeum* through the illegalization of war. This became a central Cold War strategy in which the United States sought to monopolize the power of "abstracting an absolute evil" in the name of its civilizing mission. Lisa Yoneyama, *Cold War Ruins: Transpacific Critique of American Justice and Japanese War Crimes* (Durham, N.C.: Duke University Press, 2016), 34.

16. Takeuchi, "'Pan-Pan Girls,'" 93–95.

17. John Lie, "The State as Pimp: Prostitution and the Patriarchal State in Japan in the 1940s," *The Sociological Quarterly* 38, no. 2 (Spring 1997): 258.

18. Fujino Yutaka, *Sei no kokka kanri: baibaishun no kingendaishi* (Tokyo: Fuji Shuppan, 2001), 178.

19. Kovner, *Occupying Power*, 153.

20. Takenaka Katsuo, *Gaishō: jittai to sono shuki* (Tokyo: Yūkōsha, 1949), 141.

21. Holly V. Sanders, "Prostitution in Postwar Japan: Debt and Labor" (Ph.D. diss., Princeton University, 2005), 85–86.

22. Robert Kramm, *Sanitized Sex: Regulating Prostitution, Venereal Disease, and Intimacy in Occupied Japan, 1945–1952* (Berkeley and Los Angeles: University of California Press, 2017), 2. Kanzaki Kiyoshi estimated approximately fifty thousand throughout Japan by 1953. Kanzaki Kiyoshi, "Gaishōron," in *Kichi Nihon*, ed. Inomata Kōzō, Kimura Kihachirō, and Shimizu Ikutarō (Tokyo: Wakōsha, 1953), 341.

23. Along these lines, Kramm also argues that regulating prostitution in the interwar period became an "integral part of the modern health and education regime" designed to protect the "'wise mother and good housewife' that defined middle-class domesticity." Kramm, *Sanitized Sex*, 42.

24. Tosaka Jun, "Fukko genshō no bunseki," in *Tosaka Jun zenshū*, vol. 2 (Tokyo: Keisō shobō, 1966), 310.

25. Tosaka, "Fukko genshō no bunseki," 310.

26. Ibid., 310–311.

27. Ibid., 315.

28. Ibid., 310.

29. Ibid., 314.

30. Carl Schmitt, *Political Theology: Four Chapters on the Concept of Sovereignty*, trans. George Schwab (Cambridge: MIT Press, 1985), 5.

31. Lutz P. Koepnick, "Allegory and Power: Walter Benjamin and the Politics of Representation," *Soundings: An Interdisciplinary Journal* 79, no. 2 (Spring/Summer 1 1996): 64.

32. Koepnick, "Allegory and Power," 69.

33. Stephen Legg, *Prostitution and the Ends of Empire: Scale, Governmentalities, and Interwar India* (Durham, N.C.: Duke University Press, 2014), 49.

34. Tosaka, "Fukko genshō no bunseki," 309.

35. Ibid., 311.

36. Ibid., 315.

37. Ibid., 314.

38. Ibid., 314.

39. Ibid., 313.

40. Chalmers Johnson, *MITI and the Japanese Miracle: The Growth of Industrial Policy, 1925–1975* (Stanford: Stanford University Press, 2012), 307.

41. "U.S. Criticized in Japanese Publications," *Washington Post*, May 16, 1952. Also, see "Anti-American Feeling Is Seething in Japan," *Washington Post*, October 12, 1952. According to this article, "The United States today is being blamed by many Japanese for an assortment of national ills, real and imaginary, ranging from 'Occupation babies' and 'Caucasian' crime waves to the lack of trade with Communist China."

42. Toba Kōji, *1950 nendai: "kiroku" no jidai* (Tokyo: Kawade Shobō Shinsha, 2010), 8–18.

43. Toba, *1950 nendai*, 115–144.

44. Kanzaki Kiyoshi, *Musume o uru machi: Kanzaki repōto* (Tokyo: Shinkō Shuppansha, 1952), 1.

45. Miyahara Seiichi, Shimizu Ikutarō, and Ueda Shōzaburō, eds., *Kichi no ko: kono jijitsu o dō kangaetara yoika* (Tokyo: Kōbunsha, 1953), 4.

46. In 1951, the JCP declared that first, Japan was a "colony/dependent state" *(shokuminchi/jūzokukoku)* to the United States, and second, the Yoshida cabinet represents the "interests of anti-revolutionary forces" including the "emperor, former militarists, elite bureaucrats, parasitic landlords, and monopoly capitalists." In order to break free from this oppression, it prescribed a postwar version of its two-stage program: U.S. imperialism that serves the interests of anti-revolutionary forces must be resisted in order to achieve "national independence" *(minzoku dokuritsu)*. The JCP once again based its program on the assumption of a top-down power that stunts Japan's indigenous progress toward revolution. Kojima Tsunehisa, *Nihon shihonshugi ronsōshi* (Tokyo: Ariesu Shobō, 1976), 57.

47. General Headquarters, Far East Command, "Administrative Agreement under Article III of the Security Treaty Between the United States and Japan," February 28, 1952, https://www.olpl.org/documents/Administrative Agreement.pdf.

48. Quoted in Howard B. Schonberger, *Aftermath of War: Americans and the Remaking of Japan, 1945–1952* (Kent, Ohio: Kent State University Press, 1989), 247.

49. Maedomari Hiromori, *Hontō wa kenpō yori taisetsuna "Nichi-Bei chii kyōtei nyūmon,"* (Osaka: Sōgenha, 2013), 54–55.

50. Inomata, Kimura, and Shimizu, *Kichi Nihon*, 227.

51. Ibid., 244.

52. Ibid., 246, 248.

53. Ibid., 246.

54. Ibid., 262.

55. Ibid., 256.

56. Ibid., 250.

57. Ibid., 220.

58. Ibid., 199.
59. Ibid., 198.
60. Miyahara, Shimizu, and Ueda, *Kichi no ko*, 1.
61. Inomata, Kimura, and Shimizu, *Kichi Nihon*, 94.
62. Ibid., 95.
63. Miyahara, Shimizu, and Ueda, *Kichi no ko*, 155.
64. Ibid., 175.
65. Ibid., 170.
66. Kovner, *Occupying Power*, 154.
67. Miyahara, Shimizu, and Ueda, *Kichi no ko*, 199.
68. Ibid., 210.
69. Ibid., 213.
70. Ibid., 218.
71. For a short survey of miscegenation in Japanese fiction, see Hyoue Okamura, "The Language of 'Racial Mixture': How Ainoko Became Haafu, and the Haafu-gao Makeup Fad," *Asia Pacific Perspectives* 14 (Spring 2017), https://www.usfca.edu/center-asia-pacific/perspectives/v14n2/okamura.
72. Kurahara Korehito, "Geijutsuteki hōhō ni tsuite no kansō (kōhen)," in *Kurahara Korehito hyōronshū*, vol. 2 (Tokyo: Shin Nihon Shuppansha, 1980), 251. For more on Kurahara, see Mats Karlsson, "Kurahara Korehito's Road to Proletarian Realism," *Japan Review* 20 (2008): 231–273.
73. Aono Suekichi, *"Puroretaria riarizumu no jissen ni tsuite,"* in *Undō kaika no jidai: senki sōkan kara bunka renmei kessei made*, ed. Noma Hiroshi (Tokyo: San'ichi Shobō, 1955), 241. For more on Kurahara, Aono, and proletarian literature, see Heather Bowen-Struyk and Norma Field, eds., *For Dignity, Justice, and Revolution: An Anthology of Japanese Proletarian Literature* (Chicago: University of Chicago Press, 2016).
74. Aono Suekichi, "Shizen seichō to mokuteki ishiki" *Hirabayashi Hatsuno-suke, Aono Suekichi, Kurahara Korehito, Nakano Shigeharu shū*, ed. Aono Suekichi, et al. (Tokyo: Chikuma Shobō, 1957), 78.
75. Aono, "Shizen seichō to mokuteki ishiki," 207.
76. Georg Lukács, "Class Consciousness," in *History and Class Consciousness: Studies in Marxist Dialectics*, trans. Rodney Livingstone (Cambridge: MIT Press, 1971), 76.
77. Lukács, "Class Consciousness," 169.
78. Georg Lukács, "Reportage or Portrayal?," in *Essays on Realism*, ed. Rodney Livingstone, trans. David Fernbach (Cambridge: MIT Press, 1981), 49. Italics are mine.
79. Ibid., 49.
80. Ibid., 50.
81. Ibid., 52.

82. Kurahara, "Geijutsuteki hōhō ni tsuite no kansō (kōhen)," 252.
83. Ibid., 255.
84. Ibid., 258.
85. Lukács, "Reportage or Portrayal?," 54. As Fabian Schäfer notes, the leading member of the JCP, Fukumoto Kazuo, who had done much of the work of introducing Lukács's thought into Japan, similarly conceptualized a party that included the *"lumpen"* as "disastrous." Fabian Schäfer, *Public Opinion, Propaganda, Ideology: Theories on the Press and Its Social Function in Interwar Japan, 1918–1937* (Leiden: Brill, 2012), 104.
86. Sakai and Yoo's description of how the United States and Japan cofigure in the formation of a "global sovereign state" resonates closely with this point. They write:

> Of decisive importance in this regard is the sort of nationalism one witnesses in Japan in which the hubris of imperial nationalism remains unchallenged in symbiosis with the victim consciousness of anti-Americanism. One of the sources for inspiration in Japanese nationalism has been a victim fantasy. . . . The sense of victimhood is an essential moment of their "nationality" and has become a sort of keynote for public discourse on Japanese politics since the 1950s.
> Naoki Sakai and Hyon Joo Yoo, eds. *The Trans-Pacific Imagination: Rethinking Boundary, Culture, and Society* (Singapore: World Scientific Publishing Company, 2012), 8–9.

87. Michel Foucault, *The Birth of Biopolitics: Lectures at the Collège de France, 1978–1979*, ed. Michel Senellart, trans. Graham Burchell (New York: Palgrave Macmillan, 2008), 282.
88. He defines the client state as "a state that enjoys the formal trappings of Westphalian sovereignty and independence, and is therefore neither a colony nor a puppet state, but which has internalised the requirement to give preference to 'other' interests over its own." He continues, the "puzzling but crucial fact is that submission is not forced but chosen." In very simple terms, a client state retains its territorial sovereignty but submits to a stronger state of its own accord. Gavan McCormack, "Japan's Client State (Zokkoku) Problem," *The Asia-Pacific Journal* 11, no. 25:2 (June 23, 2013), http://apjjf.org/2013/11/25/Gavan-McCormack/3961/article.html.
89. McCormack, "Japan's Client State."
90. Kōya Nomura, "Undying Colonialism: A Case Study of the Japanese Colonizer," trans. Annmaria Shimabuku, *CR: The New Centennial Review* 12, no. 1 (2012): 94.
91. "The contest over the Marine Corps base at Futenma and the plan to replace it . . . is therefore much more. It pits the Okinawan community

against the nation-states of both Japan and the United States. . . . [W]e believe that Okinawa as of 2012, fiercely insisting on the constitutional principle of popular sovereignty (*shuken zaimin*), astonishingly holds the advantage." Gavan McCormack and Satoko Oka Norimatsu, *Resistant Islands: Okinawa Confronts Japan and the United States* (Lanham, Md.: Rowman and Littlefield Publishers, Inc., 2012), 10.

92. In an NHK survey conducted in 2010, on the fiftieth anniversary of the 1960 revision of the original U.S.-Japan Security Treaty, 42 percent answered that the treaty should be kept in place as is, and 29 percent answered that it should be reinforced. Only 14 percent answered that its powers should be weakened, and just 7 percent answered that it should be abolished altogether. Of the combined 21 percent that answered weakened or abolished, only 27 percent answered that their criticism of the treaty rested on the burden of U.S. military bases. In other words, only an extremely minor segment of people considered U.S. military bases a burden to Japan. Sekitani Michiō, "NichiBei anpō no ima: anzen hoshō ni kansuru denwa chōsa kara," *Hōsō Kenkyū to Chōsa*, (March 2011), https://www.nhk.or.jp/bunken/summary/research/report/2011_03/110302.pdf.

93. For example, see the following script of the improvisational play first performed in October 1999: Kokoro ni Todoke Onnatachi no Koe Nettowāku, "Kichi no tarai mawashi wa yameteyo!" *Kēshi kaji* 26 (March 2000): 29–37. Also, see chinin ushii, *ushii ga yuku: shokuminchi shugi o tanken shi watakushi o sagasu tabi* (Naha: Okinawa Taimususha, 2010); and chinin ushii, *Shiranfūnā no bōryoku: chinin ushii seiji hatsugenshū* (Tokyo: Miraisha, 2013).

94. After Liberal Democratic Party (LDP) Prime Minister Koizumi Junichirō left office in 2006, the aftermath of his neoliberal policies deepened the economic gap between the rich and poor and generated widespread social unrest. His LDP successors attempted to make amends, but after a series of mishaps, the strongly pro-American party that enjoyed a nearly continuous grip on Japanese politics since 1955 lost popular support. In this political climate, the opposing Democratic Party of Japan (DPJ) won a historic majority in the Diet in September 2009. Recognizing this political alignment of the stars, Hatoyama put emphasis on the *kengai isetsu* argument as a way to win votes in the Okinawan voting district and emerge victorious in his historic DPJ bid for prime minister. Annmaria Shimabuku, "Who Should Bear the Burden of U.S. Bases? Governor Nakaima's Plea for a 'Relocation Site Outside of Okinawa Prefecture, but within Japan,'" *The Asia-Pacific Journal* 9, no. 45:1 (November 16, 2011), http://www.japanfocus.org/-Annmaria-Shimabuku/3641. There is evidence to suggest, however, that Hatoyama's deployment of *kengai isetsu* was not just an empty campaign promise, as he had already gone on record with the argument as early as

1998. "Futenma kichi no hondo isetsu shiji: Hatoyama Minshutō kanjichō dairi," *Okinawa taimusu*, November 7, 1998.

95. Hayashi Hirofumi, *Beigun kichi no rekishi: sekai nettowāku no keisei to tenkai* (Tokyo: Yoshikawa Kōbunkan, 2012), 92.

96. Hayashi, *Beigun kichi no rekishi*, 93.

97. According to the monumental 1959 ruling by a Tokyo court, the protesters were innocent because the U.S.-Japan Security Treaty was in violation of the Article 9 "no war" clause of the Japanese Constitution. However, this decision was reversed in December, the same year when the Japanese Supreme Court ruled that it was not within its jurisdiction to make decisions about the validity of the treaty based on the constitution. This set the precedent of the judiciary abstaining from questions of legitimacy of the treaty that once again prevailed over Japanese law. Yara Tomohiro, *Sajō no dōmei: Beigun saihen ga akasu uso* (Naha: Okinawa Taimususha, 2009), 95.

98. "Nihon no nayami: kichi mondai," *Asahi shinbun*, September 15, 1953, 1.

99. Oguma Eiji, *Shimizu Ikutarō: aru sengo chishikijin no kiseki* (Tokyo: Ochanomizu Shobō, 2003), 49; Shimizu Ikutarō, *Waga jinsei no danpen* (Tokyo: Bungei Shunjū, 1975), 50.

100. Yara, *Sajō no dōmei*, 96.

101. "Nihon no nayami," 1.

102. "Sabireta 'kichi' sakkon," *Asahi shinbun*, November 23, 1956, 3.

103. Yara Tomohiro, *Gokai darake no Okinawa/Beigun kichi* (Tokyo: Junpōsha, 2012), 58.

104. Nihon Kokkai Gijiroku, *Kanpō gōgai: dai 19 kai Kokkai Shūgiin kaigiroku, dai 7 gō*, January 29, 1954, no. 7:3. This is the same prime minister who went on to assert Japan's superiority as a "homogeneous" "Yamato race" over the United States with its "many Blacks, Puerto Ricans, and Mexicans." Gavan McCormack, "Introduction," in *Multicultural Japan: Palaeolithic to Postmodern*, ed. Donald Denoon et al., (Cambridge: Cambridge University Press, 1996), 1.

105. Hayashi, *Beigun kichi no rekishi*, 100.

106. "Hondo no hanpatsu uke kaiheitai o Okinawa e: daitōryō, Kishi seiken ni hairyo," *Okinawa taimusu*, May 14, 2015.

107. Ibid., 107.

108. Mitsuo Saito, *The Japanese Economy* (Singapore: World Scientific Publishing, 2000), 221.

109. Mixed-race Koreans born to fathers from the U.S. military were the first adoptees out of South Korea's massive adoption enterprise. Grace M. Cho and Hosu Kim write that these children became "perhaps the first major biopolitical project for the budding South Korean nation" in which the "U.S. is framed as the only nation that has the capacity to care for this

population." Grace M. Cho and Hosu Kim, "The Kinship of Violence," *Journal of Korean Adoption Studies* 1, no. 3 (2012): 11, 12. As the "living proof of South Korea's compromised sovereignty for having established itself as a dependent of the U.S. military," they were deemed unsuitable for life in their native motherland, and were selectively targeted for elimination from the social landscape. Quoting from SooJin Pate, they estimate that between 1955 and 1957, 90 percent of Korean adoptees were of mixed race, despite the fact that they made up less than 1 percent of the entire war orphan population. Cho and Kim, "The Kinship of Violence," 13.

On Japan, Yukiko Koshiro writes that the American Joint Committee spearheaded the endeavor to adopt mixed-race Japanese children to the United States. By 1955, only 15 had been adopted under the 1953 Refugee Relief Act; other private bills put forth by Congressman Francis Walter had admitted about 350 Japanese orphans by 1956 who were both mixed and non-mixed. By 1956, there were about 1,280 mixed-race children enrolled in Japanese schools nationwide. Yukiko Koshiro, *Trans-Pacific Racisms and the U.S. Occupation of Japan* (New York: Columbia University Press, 1999), 199.

South Korea also started adopting to the United States under the 1953 Refugee Relief Act, but transnational adoption did not start to take off until the Orphan Eligibility Clause of the Immigration and Nationality Act permanently guaranteed visas for transnational adoptees to enter the United States in 1961. Kim Park Nelson, *Invisible Asians: Korean American Adoptees, Asian American Experiences, and Racial Exceptionalism* (New Brunswick, N.J.: Rutgers University Press, 2016), 52.

110. Koshiro, *Trans-Pacific Racisms*, 162.

2. OKINAWA, 1945–1952: ALLEGORIES OF BECOMING

1. This is not to suggest that an allegorical reading of the cultural texts of postwar Japan and symbolic reading of the cultural texts of postwar Okinawa is impossible. Benjamin's resurrection of baroque allegory to read the commodity form in Baudelaire's Paris certainly lends itself to unlocking the phantasmagoria of consumer culture in postwar Japan. See Walter Benjamin, *The Writer of Modern Life: Essays on Charles Baudelaire*, ed. Michael W. Jennings, trans. Howard Eiland et al. (Cambridge: The Belknap Press of Harvard University Press, 2006). Conversely, slippage into symbolic notions of community in Okinawa are examined in Chapter 3.

2. Katsuhiko Endo, "A Unique Tradition of Materialism in Japan: Osugi Sakae, Tosaka Jun, and Uno Kozo," *Positions: East Asian Cultures Critique* 20, vol. 4 (Fall 2012): 1017.

3. Tomiyama Ichirō, *Ryūchaku no shisō: "Okinawa mondai" no keifugaku* (Tokyo: Inpakuto Shuppankai, 2013), 191–195.

4. Uno Kōzō, "Tōgyō yori mitaru kōiki keizai no kenkyū joron/ketsugo," in *Uno Kōzō chosakushū*, vol. 8 (Tokyo: Iwanami Shoten, 1974): 401.

5. Wendy Matsumura, *The Limits of Okinawa: Japanese Capitalism, Living Labor, and Theorizations of Community* (Durham, N.C.: Duke University Press, 2015), 153.

6. Tomiyama, *Ryūchaku no shisō*, 186.

7. Tomiyama Ichirō, *Kindai Nihon shakai to "Okinawajin": "Nihonjin" ni naru to iu koto* (Tokyo: Nihon Keizai Hyōronsha, 1990), 101.

8. Tomiyama, *Kindai Nihon shakai to "Okinawajin,"* 278.

9. Ibid., 4.

10. Tomiyama Ichirō, *Senjō no kioku* (Tokyo: Nihon Keizai Hyōronsha, 1995), 42.

11. Stephen Legg, *Prostitution and the Ends of Empire: Scale, Governmentalities, and Interwar India* (Durham, N.C.: Duke University Press, 2014), 49.

12. Tomiyama, *Ryūchaku no shisō*, 41–49.

13. Matsumura gives an excellent account of cultural representations of the Sago Palm Hell (*sotetsu jigoku*), or economic crisis that ensued after the collapse of the sugar industry. She shows how the reportage that described Okinawa's destitute conditions to mainland Japan "blamed the laziness and backwardness of the people for the prefecture's financial collapse." Matsumura, *Limits of Okinawa*, 151.

14. *seikatsu dekiru*

15. Quoted in Tomiyama, *Senjō no kioku*, 8.

16. Naoki Sakai, "Two Negations: The Fear of Being Excluded and the Logic of Self-Esteem," in *Contemporary Japanese Thought*, ed. Richard F. Calichman (New York: Columbia University Press, 2005), 159–191.

17. Walter Benjamin, *The Origin of German Tragic Drama*, trans. John Osborne (London: Verso, 1998), 176. Hereafter, I refer to this text by its original German title, the *Trauerspiel*.

18. For a nuanced exposition on the formation of allegory from Greek antiquity, through baroque theological discourse, to twentieth-century commodity culture, see Susan Buck-Morss, *The Dialectics of Seeing: Walter Benjamin and the Arcades Project* (Cambridge: MIT Press, 1991).

19. Benjamin, *Origin of German Tragic Drama*, 232.

20. Carl Schmitt, *The Concept of the Political*, trans. George Schwab (Chicago: University of Chicago Press, 1996), 32–33.

21. Kabira Nario, *Okinawa: kūhaku no ichinen, 1945–1946* (Tokyo: Yoshikawa Kōbunkan, 2011), 3.

22. Hong Yunshin, *Okinawa senjō no kioku to "ianjo"* (Tokyo: Inpakuto Shuppankai, 2016), 23. Also see Yunshin Hong, *"Comfort Stations" as Remembered by Okinawans During World War II*, trans. Robert Ricketts (Leiden: Brill, forthcoming).

23. For my own discussion on Foucault's race war, see "Petitioning Subjects: Miscegenation in Okinawa from 1945 to 1952 and the Crisis of Sovereignty," *Inter-Asia Cultural Studies* 11, no. 3 (2010): 356–359.

24. Hong, *Okinawa senjō no kioku to "ianjo,"* 9–10.

25. Ibid., 9.

26. Ibid., 12.

27. Carl Schmitt, *Political Theology: Four Chapters on the Concept of Sovereignty*, trans. George Schwab (Cambridge: MIT Press, 1985), 5.

28. My reading here that questions the assumed purity of the community and stability of the norm is informed by Nahum D. Chandler, *X: The Problem of the Negro as a Problem for Thought* (New York: Fordham University Press, 2014). He argues against the assumption of a "putative pure position of origination" that founds a legal order. For him, hierarchy and origination "acquire their form in, by way of, and from this relation," and not prior to it. Chandler, *X*, 152. Instead, following W. E. B. Du Bois, he traces the "movement of between" that is the movement of double consciousness. Accordingly, double consciousness is not simply two ways of seeing the world, but it is resistance toward the attempt to monopolize consciousness itself by purporting its originating universality.

29. Hong, *Okinawa senjō no kioku to "ianjo,"* 357.

30. After completion of the *Trauerspiel*, Benjamin sent Schmitt a copy appended with a letter that stated he received a "confirmation of my modes of research in the philosophy of art from yours in the philosophy of the state." For the full text of the letter, see Samuel Weber, "Taking Exception to Decision: Walter Benjamin and Carl Schmitt," *Diacritics* 22, nos. 3/4 (1993): 5.

31. Weber, "Taking Exception to Decision," 10.

32. Feminists such as Takazato Suzuyo have not forgotten that Okinawans were guilty of hailing racist epithets at the women and generally came to accept the so-called comfort stations as there for their benefit. See Takazato Suzuyo, "Kyōsei jūgun 'ianfu,'" in *Naha/onna no ashiato: Naha joseishi (kindaihen)*, ed. Nahashi Sōmubu Joseishitsu (Tokyo: Domesu Shuppan, 1998), 453, 456.

33. Walter Benjamin, "Critique of Violence," in *Reflections: Essays, Aphorisms, Autobiographical Writings*, ed. Peter Demetz, trans. Edmund Jephcott (New York: Schocken Books, 1978), 281. The translation here is "outside the law," but given the context, it is clear that Benjamin is pointing to the "alegal," or what is irreducible to the law.

34. Benjamin, *Origin of German Tragic Drama*, 66.

35. Hong, *Okinawa senjō no kioku to "ianjo,"* 23–24.

36. Ibid., 270.

37. Gekkan Okinawa Sha, ed., *Laws and Regulations During the U.S. Administration of Okinawa, 1945–1972*, vol. 1 (Naha, Ikemiya Shokai & Co., 1983), 38.

38. Arnold G. Fisch, Jr., *Military Government in the Ryukyu Islands, 1945–1950* (Washington: Center of Military History, U.S. Army, 1988), 20.

39. Civil affairs personnel were instructed to avoid using the term "concentration centers" and were advised that descriptions of the deplorable conditions of camp life would be censored from letters home. Fisch, *Military Government*, 49. There were sixteen camps throughout the Okinawa mainland. Okinawans were forbidden to leave, despite insufficient food rations. Okinawa Jinmintōshi Henshū Kankō Iinkai, ed., *Okinawa jinmintō no rekishi* (Naha: Okinawa Jinmintōshi Henshū Kankō Iinkai, 1985), 51.

40. Kabira, *Okinawa*, 65.

41. Fisch, *Military Government*, 20.

42. Miyagi Harumi, "Okinawa no Amerika gunkichi to seibōryoku: Amerikagun jōriku kara kōwajōyaku hakkō mae no seihanzai no jittai o tōshite," in *Okinawa no senryō to Nihon no fukkō: shokuminchishugi wa ikani keizoku shika ka*, ed. Nakano Tshio, Namihira Tsuneo, Yakabi Osamu, and Yi Hyodŏk (Tokyo: Seikyūsha, 2006), 47.

43. Kabira, *Okinawa*, 65.

44. Okinawaken Bunka Shinkōkai Kōbunshokan Kanribu Shiryōhenshūshitsu, ed., *Military Government Activities Reports* (Naha: Okinawaken Kyōiku Iinkai, 2000), 58.

45. *Activities Reports*, 62.

46. Ibid., 58.

47. Ibid., 62.

48. "Potsdam Declaration," July 26, 1945, full document given in James M. Vardaman, Jr., *"Hiroshima,"* in *Encyclopedia of Leadership*, ed. George R. Goethals, Georgia J. Sorenson, and James MacGregor Burns (Thousand Oaks: Sage Publications, Inc., 2004), 662, http://dx.doi.org/10.4135/9781412952392.n149, http://www.atomicarchive.com/Docs/Hiroshima/Potsdam.shtml.

49. Eleanor Lattimore, "Pacific Ocean or American Lake?," *Far Eastern Survey* 14, no. 22 (1945): 313.

50. Atlantic Charter, August 14, 1941, http://avalon.law.yale.edu/wwii/atlantic.asp.

51. Cairo Conference, December 1, 1943, http://avalon.law.yale.edu/wwii/cairo.asp.

52. Miyazato Seigen, *Sengo Okinawa no seiji to hō: 1945–72 nen* (Tokyo: Tokyo Daigaku Shuppankai, 1975), 5.

53. Frank Gibney, "Okinawa: Forgotten Island," *Time* 54, no. 22, 26; Mikio Higa, *Politics and Parties in Postwar Okinawa* (Vancouver: Publications Centre, University of British Columbia, 1963), 7–8.

54. Ikemiyagi Shūi, *Okinawa no Amerikajin: Okinawa jānarisuto no kiroku "Okinawa ni ikite" dai sanbu* (Tokyo: Saimaru Shuppankai, 1971), 11.

55. Fisch, *Military Government*, 82.

56. Gene Weltfish, "American Racisms: Japan's Secret Weapon," *Far Eastern Survey* 14, no. 17 (1945): 236. For more on the fear of a "global alliance of color," see Takashi Fujitani's pathbreaking trans-Pacific study, *Race for Empire: Koreans as Japanese and Japanese as Americans During World War II* (Berkeley and Los Angeles: University of California Press), 83–96.

57. Fisch, *Military Government*, 83. For more on the 24th Infantry, see William T. Bowers, William M. Hammond, and George L. MacGarrigle, *Black Soldier, White Army: The 24th Infantry Regiment in Korea* (Washington: Center of Military History, U.S. Army, 1996).

58. Fisch, *Military Government*, 83.

59. "Sayonara!! Kokujin butai Nihon e shinchū," *Uruma shinpō*, February 7, 1947. The assigned strength of the 24th Infantry as of February 1947 was 102 officers, 2 warrant officers, and 3,263 enlisted men. Yasuhiro Okada, "Race, Masculinity, and Military Occupation: African American Soldiers' Encounters with the Japanese at Camp Gifu, 1947–1951," *The Journal of African American History* 96, no. 2 (Spring 2011), 182.

60. Nicholas E. Sarantakes, *Keystone: The American Occupation of Okinawa and U.S.-Japanese Relations* (College Station: Texas A & M University, 2001), 38.

61. "Hitōjin butai: Okinawa shubi sanka," *Uruma shinpō*, February 7, 1947.

62. Fisch, *Military Government*, 86.

63. Ikemiyagi Shūi, *Okinawa ni ikite* (Tokyo: Saimaru Shuppankai, 1970), 270.

64. M. D. Morris, *Okinawa: A Tiger by the Tail* (New York: Hawthorn Books, 1968), 84.

65. Shima Masu, *Shima Masu no ganbari jinsei: kichi no machi no fukushi ni ikite* (Okinawa: Shima Masu Sensei Kaisōroku Henshū Iinkai, 1986), 89.

66. Okinawa Kokusai Daigaku Bungakubu Shakaigakka Ishihara Zemināru ed., *Sengo Koza ni okeru minshū seikatsu to ongaku bunka* (Ginowan: Ryokurindō Shoten, 1994), 93.

67. Takushi Etsuko, *Okinawa umi o wattata Amerikahei hanayometachi* (Tokyo: Kōbunken, 2000), 114. This volume has recently been translated into English as Etsuko Takushi Crissey, *Okinawa's G.I. Brides: Their Lives in America*, trans. Steve Rabson (Honolulu: University of Hawai'i Press, 2017);

Miyazato Etsu, ed., *Okinawa, onnatachi no sengo: shōdo kara no shuppatsu* (Naha: Hirugisha, 1986), 19.

68. Miyagi, "Okinawa no Amerika gunkichi to seibōryoku," 49.

69. According to a national survey published in 1952, 21 percent of the female population over the age of fifteen were war widows in Okinawa. Nakandakari Asami, "Arakaki Mitoko 'mibōjin'ron: 1950 nen Okinawa no shinbun ni okeru 'sensō mibōjin' hyōshō o meguru kōsō," *Ryukyu Ajia shakai bunka kenkyū* 14 (October 2011): 45.

70. Morris, *Okinawa*, 60.

71. Teruya Zensuke, "Kōshū eisei gyōsei: yūsenteki jōkenka de dassoku," *Okinawa genkōhōshi* 3, no. 3 (March 1979), 24.

72. Gibney, "Forgotten Island," 26.

73. Memorandum from W. J. Sebald to General MacArthur, Supreme Commander of the Allied Powers, September 20, 1947, General Records of the Department of State, Central File, 1945–49, box 7180, folder 1, record no. 0000017550 Okinawa Prefectural Archives.

74. Foreign Relations of the United States, 1948, Vol. VI, The Far East and Australasia (Washington: United States Government Printing Office, 1974), 692.

75. Ibid., 699–700.

76. Ibid., 709. Italics in original.

77. Kokuba Kōtarō, "Okinawa to Amerika teikokushugi: keizai seisaku o chūshin ni" *Keizai hyōron* 1 (1962): 113.

78. Kokuba, "Okinawa to Amerika teikokushugi," 114.

79. Ibid., 113.

80. Ryūkyū Ginkō Chōsabu, ed., *Sengo Okinawa keizaishi* (Naha: Ryūkyū Ginkō, 1984), 85–86.

81. Kokuba, "Okinawa to Amerika teikokushugi," 112.

82. Onga Takashi, "Koza no jidai o kangaeru: taifū ni yotte tsukurareta machi," in *Koza Bunka Box* 1, vol. 1, ed. Okinawashi Sōmubu Sōmuka Shishi (Okinawa: Okinawa Shiyakusho, 1998), 27.

83. Maehara Hozumi, *Kenshō Okinawa no rōdō undo: Okinawa sengoshi no nagare no naka de* (Naha: Okinawaken Rōdōsha Gakushū Kyōkai, 2000), 18–19.

84. Onga, "Koza no jidai o kangaeru," 26–27.

85. Yonakuni Noboru, *Sengo Okinawa no shakai hendō to kindaika: Beigun shihai to taishū undō no dainamizumu* (Naha: Okinawa Taimususha, 2001), 76.

86. Fisch, *Military Government*, 127.

87. From September 1945 to March 1946, Okinawa was divided into sixteen voting districts under the Okinawa Advisory Council, one of which was named "Koza City" (故差市). When it was replaced by the Okinawa Civilian Administration in April 1946, "Koza City" reverted back to the

more commonly used prewar name "Goyeku Village"(越来村). So as to complicate matters further, the U.S. military confused the name of a central part of the village, "Goya" (故屋), for "Koza" (故差), and called it "Camp Koza" (キャンプ・コザ). Tasato Yūtetsu, *Ronshū: Okinawa no shūraku kenkyū* (Naha: Riuchūsha, 1983), 199–201. Then in 1956, by popular support, the name "Goyeku Village" was changed to "Koza City" (コザ市) in *katakana* (the phonetic syllabary used for writing foreign words) since the received name was already the result of a U.S. military mistake. Ibid., 217. Even though Ōyama Chōjō petitioned the U.S. military to correct the mistake later in his capacity as Koza City mayor, he was told that "revisions are done in Washington, D.C." Koza City stood as the only city in the entire Japanese state that was written in *katakana*. Finally in 1974, Koza City merged with Misato Village and was renamed "Okinawa City" (沖縄市). Ōyama Chōjō, *Okinawa dokuritsu sengen: Yamato wa kaerubeki "sokoku" dewa nakatta* (Tokyo: Gendai Shorin, 1997), 133.

    88. Onga, "Koza no jidai o kangaeru," 27.

    89. Fisch, *Military Government*, 169.

    90. Toriyama Atsushi, *Okinawa: Kichi shakai no kigen to sōkoku* (Tokyo: Keisō Shobō, 2013), 159–160.

    91. Okinawa Kokusai Daigaku Bungakubu Shakaigakka Ishihara Zemināru, *Sengo Koza ni okeru minshū seikatsu to ongaku bunka*, 92–94; Kikuchi Natsuno, *Posutokoroniarizumu to jendā* (Tokyo: Seikyūsha, 2010), 113.

    92. Shiroma Seizen, "Shiroma Seizen," in *Watakushi no sengoshi*, vol. 6 (Naha: Okinawa Taimususha, 1982), 289. Since the term *"kokujinhei"* or black soldier can be singular or plural, it is unlear how many Shiroma had in mind. However, he continues with a description of "their" (*karera*) hatred, indicating more than one. Shiroma, "Shiroma Seizen," 290.

    93. Ibid., 289.

    94. Ibid., 290.

    95. Amongst Shiroma's prewar students are luminaries such as Ōshiro Tatsuhiro, who won the Akutagawa Prize for *Cocktail Party* in 1967 that dealt extensively with the question of translation and occupation. Ibid., 276. Shiroma credits himself for convincing the U.S. military to substitute the terms "gooks" and "native" for "inhabitants" in 1945. Ibid., 282–283. More importantly, he requested that the *rippō kikan* of the indigenous Ryukyu government be translated as "legislature" instead of "assembly," thereby ensuring its lawmaking function. Ibid., 296.

    Shiroma translated alongside Nisei (second-generation) U.S. military soldiers, giving him insight into racial politics within the U.S. military. He also understood Okinawa to be ethno-linguistically diverse, as he writes that there was so much "diversity in dialect and accent" that "it was easier to translate what the people of Okinawa spoke into English" versus translating it into Japanese. Ibid., 284.

96. Ikemiyagi writes that Sheetz wanted to (1) promote friendship between the people of the United States and the Ryukyus, (2) give the people of Okinawa an opportunity to earn dollars, (3) prevent American soldiers from entering villages, (4) establish souvenir and art shops, and (5) establish recreation halls. Ikemiyagi, *Okinawa no Amerikajin*, 45.

97. Shiroma, "Shiroma Seizen," 292.

98. "Bijinesu sentā: Beijin to Okinawajin no akarui gorakujo," *Uruma shinpō*, December 9, 1949.

99. Ikemiyagi was not sure if Sheetz was feigning ignorance or simply naïve. He writes:

> Major General Sheetz forgot that the soldiers were young men. He seemed to be under the "misunderstanding" that they would embrace these youthful "good women" in their arms as they danced, and then just return to the barracks of their respective units. Or perhaps the major general was convinced the soldiers of the U.S. military were all Puritans like himself who would never embrace a sullied prostitute. Ikemiyagi, *Okinawa no Amerikajin*, 45.

100. Shiroma, "Shiroma Seizen," 293.

101. "Bijinesu sentā."

102. *goraku*

103. *kanrakugai*

104. It is reasonable to assume that this "individual" is a reference to Senaga Kamejirō, discussed in this chapter.

105. *tsuji yūkaku*

106. "Bijinesu sentā."

107. "Toriharawareta kinshi kuiki," *Okinawa taimusu*, January 13, 1950.

108. Ikemiyagi, *Okinawa no Amerikajin*, 43.

109. Katō Masahiro, "Bijinesu sentā kōsō to 'Yaejima,'" in *Koza Bunka Box*, vol. 8, ed. Okinawashi Sōmubu Sōmuka Shihi (Okinawa: Okinawa Shiyakusho, 2012), 40–53.

110. Kincaid

111. *tokushu fujin*, or the term used for "prostitute"

112. Hokama Yoneko, "Kutsujoku to eikō karano shuppatsu," in *Okinawa, onnatachi no sengo: shōdo ka a no shuppatsu*, ed. Miyazato Etsu (Naha: Hirugisha, 1986), 47.

113. Okinawa Kokusai Daigaku Bungakubu Shakaigakka Ishihara Zemināru, *Sengo Koza ni okeru minshū seikatsu to ongaku bunka*, 94; Hokama, "Kutsujoku to eikō karano shuppatsu," 44.

114. "Hayame ni secchi: Gorakuchitai," *Uruma shinpō*, August 30, 1949.

115. "Kanrakugai 5 kasho ni secchi: Keisatsubu ga gutaian teishutsu," *Okinawa taimusu*, September 22, 1949, quoted in Katō Masahiro, "Bijinesu sentā kōsō to 'Yaejima,'" 43.

116. "'Gorakugai' ōyure: risō to genjitsu no ronsō," *Uruma shinpō*, October 4, 1949.

117. Okinawa Jinmintōshi Henshū Kankō Iinkai, ed., *Okinawa jinmintō no rekishi*, 59. The party platform moved to "represent the interests of the working masses . . . and fight against all feudalistic conservative reactionary forces." Maehara, *Kenshō Okinawa no rōdō undō*, 17.

118. Maehara, *Kenshō Okinawa no rōdō undō*, 17.

119. Miyazato Seigen, *Amerika no Okinawa tōchi* (Tokyo: Iwanami Shoten, 1966), 17–18.

120. "'Gorakugai' ōyure."

121. Shima, *Shima Masu no ganbari jinsei*, 91.

122. "'Gorakugai' ōyure."

123. Inafuku Seiki, *Okinawa no shippeishi* (Tokyo: Daiichi Shobō, 1995), 399.

124. Inafuku Seiki, *Okinawa no igaku: igaku, hoken tōkei shiryō hen* (Naha: Kōbundō, 1979), 159.

125. Yamazaki Takashi, "USCAR bunshō kara mita A sain seido to baishun/seibyō kisei: 1970 nen zengo no Beigun fūki torishimari iinkai gijiroku no kentō kara," *Okinawa kōbun shokan kenkyū kiyō* 10 (March 2008): 40.

126. Kayō Yoshiharu, "Shinbun kiji o chūshin ni miru tokuingai e no ofu rimittsu hatsurei (1951–52 nen)," in *Koza Bunka Box*, vol. 3, ed. Okinawashi Sōmubu Sōmuka Shishi (Okinawa: Okinawa Shiyakusho, 2007), 51.

127. Kayō, "Shinbun kiji o chūshin ni miru tokuingai," 51.

128. Colonel Crawford Sams, the chief of the Public Health and Welfare Section of SCAP, suggested Okinawa set up these health centers when he visited Okinawa on December 10, 1949. Starting 1951, these health centers were established throughout Okinawa. Okinawaken Kankyō Hokenbu Yobōka, *Okinawa sengo no hokenjo no ayumi: hokenjo 30 shūnen kinenshi* (unknown: Okinawaken Kankyō Hokenbu Yobōka, 1981), 19. From December of that year, they started to offer free VD exams.

129. Morris, *Okinawa*, 84.

130. Okinawashi, Urasoeshi, Ginowanshi, Gushikawashi, Ishikawashi oyobi Nakagamigun Rōjin Fukushi Sentā Un'ei Kyōgikai, eds., *Chūbu chiku shakai fukushi no kiseki: sōron*, vol. 1 (Okinawa: Okinawashi, Urasoeshi, Ginowanshi, Gushikawashi, Ishikawashi oyobi Nakagamigun Rōjin Fukushi Sentā Un'ei Kyōgikai, 1986), 65–66.

131. Tomiyama Ichirō, *Bōryoku no yokan: Ifa Fuyū ni okeru kiki no mondai* (Tokyo: Iwanami Shoten, 2002), 283–289.

132. "Yabui no mon tataku datai," *Okinawa taimusu*, August 13, 1948.

133. As was the case in Japan, international marriage was not initially allowed in Okinawa. On August 1, 1947, *Uruma Shimpo* reported the first marriage between a twenty-three-year-old Okinawan woman named Higa Hatsuko and a Ryukyus Command (RYCOM) engineer from Ohio named Frank Anderson. Although the couple had already registered their marriage in Ginowan City where the bride was from, a public liaison officer explained that there was no U.S. order formally permitting the marriage between a U.S. citizen and Japanese national. This prompted them to visit Okinawa Civilian Administration Governor Shikiya Kōshin to request a marriage certificate. The marriage was ultimately annulled and the couple was forced to separate. Takushi, *Okinawa umi o wattata Amerikahei hanayometachi*, 116.

Because of anti-miscegenation laws and Asian discrimination in the United States, Nisei (second-generation) Japanese-American soldiers, many of whom were of Okinawan descent, clamored for the right to bring home their foreign brides. This was also the case in Allied occupied Japan. Mike Masaoka of the Japanese American Citizens League took this up as a Japanese-American issue and lobbied President Harry S. Truman to sign Public Law 213 that allowed for a one-month window for soldiers to bring their brides home. This was later revised as Public Law 717 in 1950 to extend for additional marriages. Okada, "Race, Masculinity, and Military Occupation," 192. During this period, 63 marriages were recognized in Okinawa: 53 with Nisei grooms, 8 with white grooms, 1 between a Nisei groom and bride, and 1 with a black groom. The breakdown in Japan consisted of 825 total marriages, 397 with a Nisei groom, 211 with a white groom, and 15 with a black groom. The remaining 202 are not mentioned. "Kokujin mo tōjō," *Uruma shinpō*, September 5, 1947. According to the April 1, 1948, Special Proclamation 28, "Marriage between Ryukyuan Civilians and Occupying Soldiers," any intention to marry was deemed illegal. Nakano Yoshio, ed., *Sengo shiryō Okinawa* (Tokyo: Nihon Hyōronsha, 1969), 10–11. This would not fundamentally change until the 1952 McCarran-Walter Act, which kept discriminatory immigration quotas vis-à-vis Asia as seen in the 1924 Immigration Act in place, but made allowances for war brides and their children to immigrate and acquire U.S. citizenship.

134. From the Meiji era, nationality in Japan was transferred through the patrilineal line. The foreign wife of a Japanese husband was to take the nationality of her Japanese husband while the Japanese wife of a foreign husband was to take the nationality of her foreign husband. Furthermore, a Japanese mother could not confer nationality to her child. This discriminatory nationality law was revised in 1985 because of the large number of

stateless children in Okinawa born to local women and American fathers. Kinjō Kiyoko, *Hō joseigaku no susume: josei kara no hōritsu e no toikake* (Tokyo: Yūhikaku, 1992), 82–97.

135. "Yabui no mon tataku datai," *Okinawa taimusu*, August 13, 1948.

136. A September 22, 1949, *Okinawa Times* article provides a different breakdown of mixed-race children from the Naha Police Department covering only Naha (39), Mawashi (21), Oroku (20), and Minato (14) children in those districts. Of these children, half-Filipino children (53) were the most numerous, followed by half-white children (21), half-black children (17), and half-Nisei children (3). There were 52 mothers between ages seventeen and twenty-three, 27 mothers between ages twenty-four and twenty-seven, and 15 mothers above twenty-seven. Only 2 mothers were married under Naha City jurisdiction, 1 woman in her forties was a victim of sexual assault, and 28 fathers of the children had already repatriated to their respective countries. "Umareta konketsuji 94 nin: danzen hitōkei ga ooi," *Okinawa taimusu*, September 22, 1949.

137. Ifa Fuyū, *Okinawa rekishi monogatari: Nihon no shukuzu* (Tokyo: Heibonsha, 1998), 194.

138. Ifa, *Okinawa rekishi monogatari*, 194.

139. Sakiyama Tami, *Kotoba no umareru basho* (Tokyo: Sunagoya Shobō, 2004), 18.

3. OKINAWA, 1952–1958: SOLIDARITY UNDER THE COVER OF DARKNESS

1. Kokuba Kōtarō, "Okinawa to Amerika teikokushugi: keizai seisaku o chūshin ni," *Keizai hyōron* 1 (1962): 115.

2. The Amami population peaked at about 230,000 people in 1949 after the resettlement of 46,000 returnees from abroad. By the end of 1953, however, about 35,000 emigrated to the Okinawan mainland in search of work. Mori Yoshio, *Tsuchi no naka no kakumei: Okinawa sengoshi ni okeru sonzai no kaihō* (Tokyo: Gendai Kikakushitsu, 2010), 265–266.

3. Mori, *Tsuchi no naka no kakumei*, 272.

4. Maehara Hozumi, *Kenshō Okinawa no rōdō undō: Okinawa sengoshi no nagare no naka de* (Naha: Okinawaken Rōdōsha Gakushū Kyōkai, 2000), 26.

5. Mori, *Tsuchi no naka no kakumei*, 273.

6. Maehara, *Kenshō Okinawa no rōdō undō*, 27.

7. "Treaty of Peace with Japan," *United Nations Treaty Series*, 136, 50.

8. Miyazato, *Sengo Okinawa no seiji to hō: 1945–72 nen* (Tokyo: Tokyo Daigaku Shuppankai, 1975), 143–144.

9. Taira Yoshitoshi, *Sengo Okinawa to Beigun kichi: "juyō" to "kyozetsu" no hazama de, 1945–1972 nen* (Tokyo: Hōsei Daigaku Shuppankyoku, 2012), 87.

10. Taira, *Sengo Okinawa to Beigun kichi*, 44.

11. Ibid., 44.

12. Ryukyu Ginkō Chōsabu, ed., *Sengo Okinawa keizaishi* (Naha: Ryukyu Ginkō, 1984), 436.

13. Taira, *Sengo Okinawa to Beigun kichi*, 77.

14. Miyazato, *Sengo Okinawa no seiji to hō*, 144.

15. Arasaki Moriteru, *Sengo Okinawashi* (Tokyo: Nihon Hyōronsha, 1976), 131.

16. Miyazato, *Amerika no Okinawa tōchi* (Tokyo: Iwanami Shoten, 1966), 43–46.

17. Senaga Kamejirō, *Minzoku no higeki: Okinawa kenmin no teikō* (Tokyo: Shin Nihon Shuppansha, 1971), 68.

18. Miyazato, *Sengo Okinawa no seiji to hō*, 139–140.

19. Miyazato, *Amerika no Okinawa tōchi*, 62.

20. Toriyama Atsushi, *Okinawa: kichi shakai no kigen to sōkoku* (Tokyo: Keisō Shobō, 2013), 191.

21. *seikatsu*

22. "Ofu rimitsu to chūbu senkyo," *Ryukyu shinpō*, April 10, 1953.

23. Karl Marx, *Capital*, vol. 1, trans. Ben Fowkes (London: Penguin Classics, 1990), 797.

24. Ernesto Laclau, *On Populist Reason* (London: Verso, 2005), 146.

25. Laclau, *On Populist Reason*, 147.

26. Ibid., 147.

27. Marx, *Capital*, 797.

28. Tomiyama Ichirō, *Ryūchaku no shisō: "Okinawa mondai" no keifugaku* (Tokyo: Inpakuto Shuppankai, 2013), 213.

29. Tomiyama, *Ryūchaku no shisō*, 213.

30. Ibid., 216.

31. Miyazato, *Amerika no Okinawa tōchi*, 79.

32. Arasaki Moriteru, ed., *Dokyumento Okinawa tōsō*, (Tokyo: Aki Shobō, 1969), 106.

33. Miyazato, *Sengo Okinawa no seiji to hō*, 144–146.

34. Ibid., 143.

35. Arasaki, *Sengo Okinawashi*, 96.

36. In this context, "*higōhō*" is usually translated as "illegal" in English. For example, in "Legality and Illegality," Lukács cautions against valorizing the "romanticism of illegality" in the communist party because it risks unwittingly legitimizing the bourgeois state as the ultimate object of struggle instead of exposing "the system of law as the brutal power instrument of capitalist oppression." Georg Lukács, "Legality and Illegality," in *History and Class Consciousness: Studies in Marxist Dialectics*, trans. Rodney

Livingstone (Cambridge: MIT Press, 1979), 256, 265. Here, Lukács under-stands illegality in terms of a "theory of force," or the force of law within capitalism. Lukács, "Legality and Illegality," 257. This is why he argues for the deployment of "illegality," not as in opposition to the law—an act that implicitly pays it the compliment of recognition—but as the "simultane-ous and alternating use of both legal and illegal methods" that serves to disarticulate the validity of the law from within. Ibid., 265. In this sense, the Japanese "*higōhō*," literally meaning "that which does not accord with the law," describes this method more accurately than the Japanese term for illegal, "*fuhō*."

37. Kokuba Kōtarō, "Sekai Okinawa/1950 nendai no Beigun gunsei ni kō suru," *Sekai* 9 (2005): 98.

38. Mori, *Tsuchi no naka no kakumei*, 276.

39. Kokuba, "Sekai Okinawa," 224.

40. Ibid., 101.

41. Ibid., 101; Mori Yoshio and Toriyama Atsushi, eds., *"Shimagurumi tōsō" wa dō junbi sareta ka: Okinawa ga mezasu "amayū" e no michi* (Tokyo: Fuji Shuppan, 2013), 51.

42. "Kodomo o sodateru tameni tochi wa mamoranebanaranu," *Minzoku no jiyū to dokuritsu no tameni*, February 18, 1954, reprinted in Katō Tetsurō and Kokuba Kōtarō, eds., *Sengo shoki Okinawa kaihō undo shiryōshū*, vol. 2 (Tokyo: Fuji Shuppan, 2004), 304.

43. Mori and Toriyama, *"Shimagurumi tōsō" wa dō junbi sareta ka*, 65.

44. The full text of the letter can be found in Ahagon Shōkō, *Ningen no sundeiru shima: shashin kiroku* (unknown: Erio Shashin Shuppan, 1988), 78–79.

45. Ahagon Shōkō, *Beigun to nōmin* (Tokyo: Iwanami Shoten, 1980), 95.

46. Ahagon, *Beigun to nōmin*, 127.

47. Ibid., 132.

48. Mori and Toriyama, *"Shimagurumi tōsō" wa dō junbi sareta ka*, 75.

49. Mori, *Tsuchi no naka no kakumei*.

50. James R. Martel, *The One and Only Law: Walter Benjamin and the Second Commandment* (Ann Arbor: University of Michigan Press, 2014), 169.

51. Ahagon, *Beigun to nōmin*, 8.

52. Mori and Toriyama, *"Shimagurumi tōsō" wa dō junbi sareta ka*, 77.

53. Kinjo in particular discusses the use of violence in the literature of Medoruma Shun. He writes, "Could it be . . . what the law fears the most is the carnivalesque taking up of violence by the people themselves whereas it is usually only privy to the state?" Masaki Kinjo, "Internal Revolution: The Postwar Okinawan Literature of Kiyota Masanobu and Medoruma Shun" (Ph.D. diss., Cornell University, 2017), 81.

54. Kokuba Kōtaro and Mori Yoshio, *Sengo shoki Okinawa kaihō undo shiryōshū*, vol. 3 (Tokyo: Fuji Shuppan, 2005), 71.

55. Kokuba and Mori, *Sengo shoki Okinawa kaihō undo shiryōshū*, 71–72.

56. In fact, Kokuba's cover was only blown after he predictably visited Senaga, who was hospitalized for an illness. He was captured on August 13, 1955, and tortured for days. CIC stripped him down naked and interrogated him without food, water, or sleep. He found his experiences in Okinawa eerily similar to reports of torture in Abu Ghraib in 2003. Kokuba, "Sekai Okinawa," 103.

57. For example, a headline from a November 21, 1952, *Akahata* article reads "Owareru nōmin itamashi 13 sai no panpan." A reprint of the article can be found in Kokuba and Mori, *Sengo shoki Okinawa kaihō undo shiryōshū*, vol. 3, 222.

58. For a reprint of *Minzoku no jiyū to dokuritsu no tameni* from December 15, 1954, to May 5, 1955, see Katō and Kokuba, eds., *Sengo shoki Okinawa kaihō undō shiryōshū*, vol. 2, 269–344.

59. Taira Yoshitoshi, *Sengo Okinawa to Beigun kichi*, 121.

60. *shichōson jūmin taikai*

61. *minshū*

62. Arasaki, *Sengo Okinawashi*, 146.

63. Arasaki, *Dokyumento Okinawa tōsō*, 107.

64. Ibid., 110–111.

65. Miyazato, *Sengo Okinawa no seiji to hō*, 135.

66. *nashonarizumu.*

67. Kokuba and Mori, *Sengo shoki Okinawa kaihō undo shiryōshū*, 24.

68. Ryukyu Ginkō Chōsabu, *Sengo Okinawa keizaishi*, 480.

69. Report and Petition from Seiji Oshiro, President of the Okinawa Federation Night Clubs Associations, to Brigadier General Vonna F. Burger, Civil Administrator of USCAR, August 13, 1956, General Correspondence ("Decimal") Files, 1954–1956, record no. 0000000780, Okinawa Prefectural Archives.

70. Senaga Kamejirō, *Okinawa kara no hōkoku* (Tokyo: Iwanami Shoten, 1959), 191.

71. *seikatsu*

72. Senaga, *Okinawa kara no hōkoku*, 191–192.

73. Ibid., 201.

74. Ibid., 197.

75. Ibid., 314.

76. Kokuba, "Okinawa no Nihon fukki undō to kakushin seitō: minzoku ishiki keisei no mondai ni yosete," *Shisō* 2, no. 452 (1962): 91.

77. Higashionna Kanjun, "Konketsuji," in *Higashionna Kanjun zenshū*, vol. 5. (Tokyo: Daiichi Shobō, 1978), 388.

78. Higashionna, "Konketsuji," 388.

79. *seikatsu*

80. Higashionna, "Konketsuji," 387–388.

81. Kojō Yoshiko, "Nichibei anpo taisei to doru bōei seisaku: Bōeihi futan yōkyū no rekishi kōzu," *Kokusai seiji* 115 (1997): 95; Kokuba, "Okinawa to Amerika teikokushugi," 123.

82. Iwata Hiroshi, *Gekikasuru sekai kiki to gendai kakumei: Marukusushugi no konnichiteki kadai* (Tokyo: Ryōjisha, 1969), 66.

83. Kojō, "Nichibei anpo taisei to doru bōei seisaku," 94–109.

84. Arasaki, *Sengo Okinawashi*, 187.

85. *kaisō*

86. Kokuba, "Okinawa to Amerika teikokushugi," 121.

87. USCAR rendered GRI Order 35 "Law Concerning the Punishment of Individuals Who Prostitute Women" insufficient. Yamazaki Takashi, "USCAR bunsho kara mita A sain seido to ofu rimittsu," in *Koza Bunka Box* 4, ed. Okinawashi Sōmubu Sōmuka Shishi (Okinawa: Okinawa Shiyakusho, 2009), 37.

88. Yamazaki, "USCAR bunsho kara mita A sain seido to ofu rimittsu," 37.

89. Mori, *Tsuchi no naka no kakumei*, 238.

90. The Japan-Ryukyu Trade Memorandum was also known as the "*Hondo to Nansei Shotō tono aida no bōeki oyobi shiharai ni kansuru oboegaki.*" Ryukyu Ginkō Chōsabu, *Sengo Okinawa keizaishi*, 290–291; 1183–1184. After sugar, Okinawa's main export was scrap metal scattered around the islands from the aftermath of the Okinawan War. The export of scrap metal peaked in 1956, making up 58 percent of Okinawa's exports compared to 32.7 percent from sugar, and tapered off thereafter as it was a naturally unreplenashable resource. Ibid., 290–291.

91. Kokuba Kōtarō, "Okinawa no Nihon fukki undo to kakushin seitō, 90.

92. The economist Miyada Hiroshi has developed a more recent analysis on the "colander economy" and argues that the Japanese government's economic policy in Okinawa is structurally similar to Japan's Official Development Assistant (ODA) programs in developing countries. In other words, the assistance that pours into Okinawa does not contribute to structuring an autonomous Okinawan economy, but rather provides work for Japanese industries in Okinawa with the capital always flowing back to Japan. Miyada Hiroshi, "Okinawa keizai no tokuisei wa dōshite tsukurareta ka," in *Okinawa "jiritsu" e no michi o motomete: kichi keizai jichi no shiten kara*, ed. Masaaki Gabe, Miyazato Seigen, Arasaki Moriteru, and Ōshiro Hajime (Tokyo: Kōbunken, 2009), 112–125.

93. Takazato Suzuyo, *Okinawa no onnatachi: josei no jinken to kichi, guntai* (Tokyo: Akashi Shoten, 1996), 98–99.
94. Ryukyu Ginkō Chōsabu, *Sengo Okinawa keizaishi*, 588.
95. Ibid., 591–592.
96. Ibid., 596–597.
97. Kokuba, "Okinawa to Amerika teikokushugi," 126.
98. Ibid., 126.
99. Specifically, the amount of exports to imports expressed in millions of U.S. dollars are: 16.4 to 99.1 in 1958, 21.2 to 112.1 in 1959, 29.1 to 133.4 in 1960, 33.7 to 148.2 in 1961, 48.6 to 179.9 in 1962, 70.5 to 194.9 in 1963, 67.7 to 195.6 in 1964, 84.2 to 234.8 in 1965, 76 to 308.4 in 1966, 78.3 to 363.2 in 1967, 89.4 to 369.8 in 1968, 95.5 to 420.8 in 1969, 104.1 to 497.5 in 1970, and 138.9 to 637.8 in 1971, the year before the reversion to the Japanese administration. Ryukyu Ginkō Chōsabu, *Sengo Okinawa keizaishi*, 1081.
100. Ibid., 126–127. Specifically, the percentage of income from generated by the base presence versus income from exports was 59.7 percent versus 21.1 percent in 1959, 59.7 percent versus 22.6 percent in 1960, 57.6 percent versus 21.5 in 1961, 54.1 percent versus 26.6 percent in 1962, 41.7 percent versus 32.7 percent in 1963, 51.4 percent versus 26.8 percent in 1964, 43.5 percent versus 34 percent in 1965, 39.3 percent versus 26 percent in 1966, 56.6 percent versus 22 percent in 1967, 50.5 percent versus 23.1 percent in 1968, 51.6 percent versus 22.4 percent in 1969, 53.2 percent versus 18.5 percent in 1970, and 50 percent versus 16.7 percent in 1971, the year before the reversion to the Japanese administration. Ryukyu Ginkō Chōsabu, *Sengo Okinawa keizaishi*, 1084.
101. Makino Hirotaka, *Saikō: Okinawa keizai* (Naha: Okinawa Taimususha, 1997), 35; Ryukyu Ginkō Chōsabu, *Sengo Okinawa keizaishi*, 609.
102. Kokuba, "Okinawa to Amerika teikokushugi," 126.
103. Public Law 86–629, "An Act to Provide for Promotion of Economic and Social Development in the Ryukyu Islands," July 12, 1960, https://www.gpo.gov/fdsys/pkg/STATUTE-74/pdf/STATUTE-74-Pg461.pdf.
104. Ryukyu Ginkō Chōsabu, *Sengo Okinawa keizaishi*, 657.
105. Aid from the Japanese government started at $55,000 in 1962 and ended at $68.3 million in 1971 to America's $5.2 million and $13.2 million for the same years. Ryukyu Ginkō Chōsabu, *Sengo Okinawa keizaishi*, 682.
106. Ryukyu Ginkō Chōsabu, *Sengo Okinawa keizaishi*, 622.
107. Kokuba, "Okinawa no Nihon fukki undō to kakushin seitō," 227.

4. OKINAWA, 1958–1972: THE SUBALTERN SPEAKS

1. Endonym for "the peoples of Okinawa."
2. Okinawan term for "mixed."

3. Okinawa Kokusai Daigaku Bungakubu Shakaigakka Ishihara Zemināru, ed., *Sengo Koza ni okeru minshū seikatsu to ongaku bunka*, 156.

4. Okinawa Kokusai Daigaku Bungakubu Shakaigakka Ishihara Zemināru, ed., *Sengo Koza*, 99–100. According to Hiroyama Yōichi, segregation was already firmly in place by late 1950, as the Misato Village "Back Street" was dedicated to black soldiers. After the imposition of off-limits orders, businesses went under, and the black soldiers started to frequent the livelier Teruya. Hiroyama Yōichi, "Koza Jūjiro ni okeru kuro no machi to shiro no machi," in *Koza Bunka Box* 3, ed. Okinawashi Sōmubu Sōmuka Shishi (Okinawa: Okinawa Shiyakusho, 2007), 62.

5. Takamine Tomokazu, *Shirarezaru Okinawa no Beihei: Beigun kichi 15 nen no shuzai memo kara* (Tokyo: Kōbunken, 1984), 203.

6. Tōma Kensuke, "Okinawa no kuroi chikara: Burakku pawā," *Dassōhei tsushin* 4, October 7, 1969.

7. Okinawa Kokusai Daigaku Bungakubu Shakaigakka Ishihara Zemināru, *Sengo Koza ni okeru minshū seikatsu to ongaku bunka*, 126.

8. Ibid., 275–276.

9. Ibid., 282.

10. Ōta Masahide, "Nokosareta mondai," *Ushio* (June 1972), 109.

11. In a study conducted in 1965 by the Legal Affairs Bureau (*Hōmukyoku*), the average age of the sex workers was twenty-six. Between 30 percent and 50 percent of the women were mothers and 60 percent were widowers. Furthermore, most of the women had only compulsory education through middle school. Okinawaken Sokoku Fukki Tōsōshi Hensan Iinkai, ed., *Okinawaken sokoku fukki tōsōshi* (Naha: Okinawa Jiji Shuppan, 1982), 1212; Sugaya Naoko, "Okinawa no baishun mondai: fukki ni ka getsu mae," *Fujin mondai kondankai kaihō* 16, (June 1972): 10.

12. Shimabukuro Hiroshi, "Okinawa saidai no sangyō 'sekkusu keizai' no jittai," *Ushio* (June 1972): 124.

13. Ōta, "Nokosareta mondai," 109.

14. Hokama Yoneko, "Kikikaki: Okinawa no baishun mondai to Nihon fukki," in *Zenkyōtō kara ribu e: jūgoshi nōto sengohen*, ed. Onnatachi no Ima o Tōkai (Tokyo: Inpakuto Shuppankai, 1997), 378.

15. Okinawaken Josei Dantai Renraku Kyōgikai, ed., *Heiwa/byōdō/hatten o tomoshitsuzukete shiryōhen* (Okinawa: Ryukyu Shuppansha, 2003), 82.

16. Okinawaken Sokoku Fukki Tōsōshi Hensan Iinkai, ed., *Okinawaken sokoku fukki tōsōshi*, 1207.

17. Ibid., 1206.

18. Hokama Yoneko, "Kichi/guntai/baishun: baishun mondai ni shoten o atete," *Okinawa keiken* 1, no. 2 (1971): 42.

19. Shimabukuro, "Okinawa saidai no sangyō," 120.

182

Notes to pages 93–94

20. Gushiken Sōsei, ed., *Okinawa no shakai fukushi 25 nen: Okisha kyōsōritsu 20 shūnen kinenshi* (Naha: Okinawa Shakai Fukushi Kyōgikai, 1971), 304. This figure is consistent with reversion year estimates of 7,400 although it was suspected that the number was actually greater than 10,000. Proportionately the number was equivalent to 2.2 percent of the female population over the age of fifteen, or more than five times that of the suspected female prostitute population in mainland Japan (0.4 percent) the year its anti-prostitution law came into effect. Sugaya, "Okinawa no baishun mondai," 7–8.

21. Takazato Suzuyo, "The Past and Future of Unai, Sisters in Okinawa," *AMPO Japan-Asia Quarterly Review* 25, no. 4 (1995): 76.

22. Okinawaken Sokoku Fukki Tōsōshi Hensan Iinkai, ed., *Okinawaken sokoku fukki tōsōshi*, 1210.

23. Both Tomiyama Ichirō and Mori Yoshio have recently revisited this archive through contemporary debates on postcolonialism, sovereignty, and Marxism. Tomiyama Ichirō, *Ryūchaku no shisō:"Okinawa mondai" no keifugaku* (Tokyo: Inpakuto Shuppankai, 2013) and Mori Yoshio, *Tsuchi no naka no kakumei: Okinawa sengoshi ni okeru sonzai no kaihō* (Tokyo: Gendai Kikakushitsu, 2010).

24. Matsushima writes:

In the base [island of] Okinawa, U.S. military dollars are channeled into the "prostitute." For example, if the U.S. military issues a roadblock on the northern island for the purposes of managing the G.I.s, all metropolitan life north of Koza is brought to a near standstill. The northern village leaders then go so far as to submit a written report entitled "For U.S.-Ryukyuan Friendship" that outlines the prostitution district establishments. In this way, it is possible to say that the "prosperity" of Okinawan areas have been secured through the centrality of "woman." Therefore, Okinawa's men of influence (*yūryokusha*) and the intelligentsia were able to emerge out of a power elite by tending to prostitution.

Matsushima Chōgi, "Okinawa kaihō to *Uchinānchu*: 'Henkan funsuika' 'kyōtei funsui' ka" *Jōkyō* (December 1971), 98.

25. Yamazato Akira, *Gyakuryū ni kōshite: Okinawa gakusei undōshi* (Tokyo: Okinawa Mondai Kenkyūkai, 1967), 8–9.

26. Kokuba, "Okinawa to Amerika teikokushugi: keizai seisaku o chūshin ni," *Keizai hyōron* 1 (1962): 110–129, 127.

27. Kokuba, "Okinawa to Amerika teikokushugi," 127.

28. Yamazato, *Gyakuryū ni kōshite*, 10.

29. Nagasaki Hiroshi, *Hanran no 60 nendai: Anpo tōsō to Zenkyōtō undō* (Tokyo: Ronsōsha, 2010), 43.

30. This is in line with the global emergence of the New Left that disassociated itself from the Soviet Union. When the Soviet military intervened in the Hungarian revolution of 1956 by killing citizens who protested Soviet-imposed policies, the cruel political repression sent shivers throughout the global Left and prompted the emergence of the New Left. Takemasa Ando, *Japan's New Left Movements: Legacies for Civil Society* (London: Routledge, 2014), 6.

31. Oguma Eiji, *1968*, vol. 1 (Tokyo: Shin'yōsha, 2009), 179; Wesley M. Sasaki-Uemura, *Organizing the Spontaneous: Citizen Protest in Postwar Japan* (Honolulu: University of Hawai'i Press, 2001), 35–36.

32. Okinawaken Hansen Seinen Iinkai, ed., *Zengunrō hansenha* (Tokyo: San'ichi Shobō, 1970), 18.

33. Takeda Makoto, *Okinawa kaikyū tōsō: Zengunrō sutoraiki (1972) to Beigun Kisenbaru enshū jitsuryoku soshi tōsō (1974–77)* (Nagoya: Gendai Bunka Kenkyūsha, 2001), 49.

34. Arasaki, *Sengo Okinawashi* (Tokyo: Nihon Hyōronsha, 1976), 278–279.

35. Takeda, *Okinawa kaikyū tōsō*, 233.

36. *hanbei minzoku shisō*

37. Nakaya Kōkichi, *Namae yo tatte aruke: Okinawa sengo sedai no kiseki Nakaya Kōkichi ikōshū* (Tokyo: San'ichi Shobō, 1972), 264.

38. Maehara Hozumi, *Kenshō Okinawa no rōdō undo: Okinawa sengoshi no nagare no naka de* (Naha: Okinawaken Rōdōsha Gakushū Kyōkai, 2000), 73.

39. Taira Yoshitoshi, *Sengo Okinawa to Beigun kichi: "Juyō" to "kyozetsu" no hazama de, 1945–1972 nen* (Tokyo: Hōsei Daigaku Shuppankyoku, 2012), 228. In 1966, the Okinawan population was 944,000 and the working labor force was 412,000. This latter number included 198,000 wage laborers, of which 54,000 were employed by the U.S. military. This means about 13 percent of the entire Okinawan labor force comprised U.S. military base employees. Okinawaken Hansen Seinen Iinkai, *Zengunrō hansenha*, 33.

40. For an incisive comparison between postwar labor unions in mainland Japan and Okinawa, see Kawata Yō "Shinsayoku undō to Okinawa tōsō: Zengunrō daisanha no 'ryūzan' to 4.28 tōsō" *Jōkyō* (June 1970): 5–25. He argues that the Japanese proletariat too easily fled to Okinawa without thoroughly theorizing their defeat and instead pinned their hopes onto an idealized Okinawan proletariat. For him, this was not an "alliance *(rentai)*" that sought to clarify the complex relationship between the United States, Japan, Okinawa, and the rest of the Asia Pacific, but the use of Okinawa as a "crutch *(motarekakari)*" to prop up its crippling defeat that obscured it.

41. As many have pointed out, a smaller labor force did not entail a smaller U.S. military presence, but merely its institutional rationalization.

42. Okinawa Kenkyūkai, ed., *Okinawa kaihō e no shikaku*, 90.

43. Okinawa Kokusai Daigaku Bungakubu Shakaigakka Ishihara Zemināru, *Sengo Koza ni okeru minshū seikatsu to ongaku bunka*, 246.

44. *sō*

45. *Okinawajin no Okinawa o tsukurukai*

46. *katsukyōgō*

47. Okinawaken Hansen Seinen Iinkai, *Zengunrō hansenha*, 47.

48. *kichi tekkyō*

49. *jissennteki*

50. *Okinawa dakkan*

51. violence

52. Okinawaken Hansen Seinen Iinkai, *Zengunrō hansenha*, 48.

53. Taira, *Sengo Okinawa to Beigun kichi*, 231–234.

54. Okinawa Kenkyūkai, *Okinawa kaihō e no shikaku*, 91.

55. Kawata Yō, "Kokkyō/kokka/daisanji Ryukyu shobun," *Jōkyō* (April 1971), 82.

56. Kawata, "Kokkyō/kokka/daisanji Ryukyu shobun," 82.

57. Mori Yoshio, Tobe Hideaki, and Tomiyama Ichirō, eds., *Amayu e: Okinawa sengoshi no jiritsu ni mukete* (Tokyo: Hōsei Daigaku Shuppankyoku, 2017), 84.

58. Matsushima Chōgi, "Naze Kaunaānchu ka," *Kōzō* (June 1971), 139.

59. Matsushima writes that "there is no proletariat in Okinawa" in the sense of the word assumed by the New Left because first and foremost, "there are no factories in Okinawa." Matsushima, "Okinawa kaihō to Uchinānchu," 93. Hence, in a powerful essay on the death of a Ryukyuan police officer on a general strike that took place on November 10, 1971, he writes that Okinawans were unable to process it as the death of a bourgeois instrument of state power and instead took it as the murder of a fellow Okinawan. Some even spread rumors that it was a Japanese from the mainland who killed him. Ibid., 91–92.

60. The Ryukyu Kingdom was made a vassal state by the invading Satsuma domain in 1609 before it was incorporated into the Japanese state in 1879. While the Ryukyus/Okinawa existed in a subordinate position vis-à-vis its northern overlords, the main island (particularly the capital in Shuri where the aristocracy resided) discriminated against the peripheral islands.

61. Italics are mine. Matsushima Chōgi and Tanigawa Ken'ichi, "Okinawa=kokka o koeru mugen senritsu," *Jōkyō* (March 1971), 223.

62. Matsushima and Tanigawa, "Okinawa=kokka o koeru mugen senritsu," 223.

63. Gayatri C. Spivak, "Can the Subaltern Speak?," in *Marxism and the Interpretation of Culture*, ed. Lawrence Grossberg and Cary Nelson (Urbana: University of Illinois Press, 1988), 275.

64. Spivak, "Can the Subaltern Speak?," 276.

65. Ibid., 278.

66. Ibid., 276.

67. Ibid., 275.

68. Ibid., 274.

69. Spivak is quoting the words of Deleuze here in his conversation with Foucault. Ibid., 275. For the original script, see Michel Foucault, "Intellectuals and Power," in *Language, Counter-Memory, Practice: Selected Essays and Interviews*, ed. Donald F. Bouchard, trans. Donald F. Bouchard and Sherry Simon (Ithaca, N.Y.: Cornell University Press, 1977), 205–217.

70. Quoted in Spivak, "Can the Subaltern Speak?," 276–277.

71. Tomiyama, *Ryūchaku no shisō*, 96.

72. Ibid., 97.

73. Spivak, "Can the Subaltern Speak?," 277.

74. For more contemporary readings on Okinawan female agency, see Linda Isako Angst, "Loudmouth Feminists and Unchaste Prostitutes: 'Bad Girls' Misbehaving in Postwar Okinawa," *U.S.-Japan Women's Journal* 36 (2009), 117–141.

75. All-sugar labor union.

76. *seikatsu o mamorukai*

77. Ishida Ikuo, *Okinawa/dochaku to kaihō* (Tokyo: Gōdō Shuppan, 1969), 54–56.

78. I am grateful to film critic Nakazato Isao, who generously lent me this hard-to-acquire film from his private collection in Okinawa.

79. Oguma, *1968*, 878.

80. Ibid., 877.

81. Nunokawa Tetsurō, "Dokyumentarī e no shuttastu: 'Motoshinkakarannūtachi' ga kaishi suru mono," *Eiga hihyō* 2 (October 1971): 52.

82. Jean-Paul Sartre, *Critique of Dialectical Reason*, vol. 1, trans. Alan Sheridan-Smith (London: Verso, 2004), 582.

83. Jean-Paul Sartre, *What Is Literature?*, trans. Bernard Frechtman (London: Methuen and Co. Ltd., 1950), 13.

84. Sartre, *What Is Literature?*, 5.

85. Ibid., 8. Italics in original.

86. Jean-Paul Sartre, *Black Orpheus*, trans. S. W. Allen (Paris: Présence Africaine, 1976), 39.

87. Sartre, *Black Orpheus*, 19.

88. Ibid., 20–21.

89. Ibid., 31.

90. Ibid., 60.

91. Ibid., 57.

92. Nunokawa, "Dokyumentarī e no shuttatsu," 57.

93. Ibid., 57.

94. Ibid., 55.

95. Ibid., 55.

96. I base my translations of the documentary on this published script. Nihon Dokyumentarisuto Yunion, "Shinario 'Motoshinkakarannū': '69–'71 Okinawa chōpen kiroku eiga—Okinawa erosu gaiden," *Eiga hihyō* 2 (October 1971): 58–77. It was reproduced in 1987 as *Takkurusē: kokutai kaitai no tame no purorōgu* by replacing scenes from the original with new scenes from the post-1972 reversion era.

97. Nihon Dokyumentarisuto Yunion, "Shinario 'Motoshinkakarannū,'" 62–63.

98. *ninjō bukai*

99. Nihon Dokyumentarisuto Yunion, "Shinario 'Motoshinkakarannū,'" 63.

100. Ibid., 63.

101. Ibid., 63.

102. Ibid., 58.

103. Ibid., 58.

104. Murase Haruki, *Dare ka Okinawa o shiranai ka* (Tokyo: San'ichi Shobō Murase, 1970), 152.

105. never happen

106. Nihon Dokyumentarisuto Yunion, "Shinario 'Motoshinkakarannū,'" 58–59.

107. Murase, *Dare ka Okinawa o shiranai ka*, 182–183.

108. Benjamin describes allegory as "panoramic," or a "chronological progression in spatial terms." Walter Benjamin, *The Origin of German Tragic Drama*, trans. John Osborne (London: Verso, 1998), 92, 94.

109. I am informed here by Paul de Man's description of the kinship between allegory and irony. He writes: ". . . irony comes closer to the pattern of factual experience and recaptures some of the factitiousness of human existence as a succession of isolated moments lived by a divided self. Essentially the mode of the present, it knows neither memory nor prefigurative duration, whereas allegory exists entirely within an ideal time that is never here and now but always a past or an endless future. Irony is a synchronic structure, while allegory appears as a successive mode capable of engendering duration as the illusion of a continuity that it knows to be illusionary. Yet the two modes, for all their profound distinctions in mood and structure, are the two faces of the same fundamental experience of time." Paul De Man, *Blindness and Insight: Essays in the Rhetoric of Contemporary Criticism*, trans. Wlad Godzich (Minneapolis: University of Minnesota Press, 2006), 226.

110. Ariko Ikehara's work on trans-linguistic border crossing in her study of Okinawan comedy informed my understanding of irony here. Ariko Ikehara, "A Third as Decolonial Con/Text: Okinawa's American Champurū," *Journal of Transnational Asian Studies* 1, 1:1 (December 2016), http://transnationalasia.rice.edu/Content.aspx?id=105.

111. Frantz Fanon, *Black Skin, White Masks*, trans. Charles Lam Markmann (New York: Grove Press, 1967), 116–117. Fanon is useful here in thinking about the relationship between the left-wing colonizer and colonized as he critiques Sartre. However, limitations to a parallel analysis here are worth noting. The white man Fanon speaks of here includes the Jew. He argues that, different from the Jew, the Negro is "overdetermined from without" by virtue of his skin color. Although the ethnic difference between mainland Japanese and Okinawans has been the object of anthropological research since the late nineteenth century, the disparate epidermal-historical racial schemata beg for further theorization.

112. Nihon Dokyumentarisuto Yunion, "Shinario 'Motoshinkakarannū,'"75.

113. Ibid., 75.

114. Ibid., 75–76.

115. *naichi*, or mainland Japan

116. number one

117. Nihon Dokyumentarisuto Yunion, "Shinario 'Motoshinkakarannū,'"76.

118. Murase, *Dare ka Okinawa o shiranai ka*, 230.

119. Ibid., 57.

120. Ibid., 55.

121. Ibid., 54–55.

122. *hikokumin*

123. Ibid., 59.

124. *ishikiteki*

125. *kaikyūteki*

126. Ibid., 56.

127. Okinawashi Kikakubu Heiwa Bunka Shinkōka, ed., *Beikoku ga mita Koza bōdō: Beikoku kōbunsho Ei-Wa taiyaku* (Okinawa: Yui Shuppan, 1999), 36.

128. Ibid., 100.

129. Ibid., 270.

130. Ibid., 270.

131. Ibid., 104.

132. Ibid., 268.

133. Okinawa Kokusai Daigaku Bungakubu Shakaigakka Ishihara Zemināru, *Sengo Koza ni okeru minshū seikatsu to ongaku bunka*, 415.

134. *kyōshokuin*, or civil servant public school teachers, were some of the most adamant pro-reversion supporters. Not only did they inherit the historical tradition of imperialized Japanese education (*kōminka kyōiku*), but they also looked forward to wage increases after Okinawa was brought up to Japanese standards through reversion to the Japanese administration.

135. Matsushima, "Okinawa kaihō to *Uchinānchu*," 97.

136. Okinawashi Heiwa Bunka Shinkōkai, ed., *Koza hito/machi/koto: shashin ga toraeta 1970 nen zengo anata ga rekishi no mokugekisha* (Okinawa: Naha Shuppansha, 1997), 66.

137. *kokujin mondai*

138. Matsushima and Tanigawa, "Okinawa=kokka o koeru mugen senritsu," 223–224.

139. This is not to say that these connections did not continue to form, but only that they were not formed so openly to the public eye. How to properly bring together these connections requires more discussion at the crossroads of African American studies and postcolonial Japanese studies and goes beyond the scope of this book. In other words, I would be remiss to offer a comprehensive interpretation to this history now, as it begs for the formation of a community of interlocutors who could breathe new life into it and make it meaningful. I can, however, mark important studies that have started the conversation. Yuichiro Onishi, *Transpacific Antiracism: Afro-Asian Solidarity in Twentieth-Century Black America, Japan, and Okinawa* (New York: New York University Press, 2013) for an American studies perspective. Wesley Ueunten has been instrumental in bridging these two communities through his work in the Bay Area. Wesley Ueunten, "Ikari no umi kara no funki: Amerika gunsenryōka no Okinawa ni okeru Koza sōdo," trans. Makoto Arakaki, in *Gendai Okinawa no rekishi keiken: kibō, aruiwa mikessei ni tsuite*, ed. Mori Yoshio and Tomiyama Ichirō (Tokyo: Seikyusha, 2010), 359–381. Mitzi Uehara Carter is an important example of the kind of community formation I have in mind here. She understands the fraught relationship racialized communities have with modes of speech aligned with the state and hence reconsiders an ethnographic method that allows for them to come together to unravel these convoluted and complex entanglements. See Mitzi Uehara Carter, "Nappy Roots and Tangled Tales: Critical Ethnography in a Militarised Okinawa," in *Under Occupation: Resistance and Struggle in a Militarised Asia-Pacific*, ed. Daniel Broudy, Peter Simpson, and Makoto Arakaki (Newcastle upon Tyne: Cambridge Scholars Publication, 2013), 2–22; and "Mixed Race Okinawans and Their Obscure In-Betweeness," *Journal of Intercultural Studies* 35, no. 6: 646–661, http://dx.doi.org/10.1080/07256868.2014.963531. Also, Ariko Ikehara, in "Third Space as Decolonial Con/Text: Okinawa's American Champurū" and "Champurū Text: Decolo-

nial Okinawan Writing," reads Japanese-language Okinawan texts on black-Okinawan mixing through the lens of a Chicana feminist theory of language with breathtaking results. Ueunten, Ikehara, and Uehara Carter all take community building as central praxis of their scholarship and forge these connections as they excavate them.

5. OKINAWA, 1972–1995: LIFE THAT MATTERS

1. My discussion of self-determination here should be read as a philosophical examination and not a political criticism of the actual movements for and around self-determination in Okinawa. Although I choose not to use this term, it does not take away from the meaningful content of these real-life movements.

2. Arasaki Moriteru, *Okinawa Gendaishi* (Tokyo: Iwanami Shoten, 1996), 26–27.

3. Quoted in Tomohiro Yara, "Withdrawal of US Marines Blocked by Japan in the 1970s," trans. Gavan McCormack, *The Asia-Pacific Journal* 11, no. 47: 4 (November 22, 2013), http://apjjf.org/2013/11/47/Yara-Tomohiro /4037/article.html.

4. Yara, "Withdrawal of US Marines."

5. Ibid.

6. Victor Argy and Leslie Stein, eds., *The Japanese Economy* (London: Macmillan Press, 1997), 11.

7. Shimabukuro Jun, *"Okinawa shinkō taisei"o tō: kowasareta jichi to sono saisei ni mukete* (Kyoto: Hōritsubunkasha, 2014), 5. Different from the military-industrial complex in the United States, postwar Japan fed its appetite for capitalist growth with state-driven construction in public works. In 1993, Japan outspent the United States on such construction by a ratio of 2.6 to1, or in proportion to relative land area, 32 to1. And just as Eisenhower warned how political contributions and lobbying from defense contractors would skew public policy, Japan's unique construction state also deeply affects the workings of its political machinery. Gavan McCormack, *The Emptiness of Japanese Affluence* (Armonk, N.Y.: M.E. Sharpe, 2001), 33.

8. Shimabukuro observes that postwar Japan operates in a circular system between the center of government in Tokyo and peripheral municipalities through a "politics of interest returns" (*rieki kangen seiji*). Jockeying between the center and periphery occurs in three ways. First, officials from the peripheries routinely pay their respects to Tokyo, and aging bureaucrats (*amakudari*) from Tokyo are sent off to spend their golden years in service of the peripheries so as to make room for new blood in the capitol. Second, the seniority system allows second or third-generation Diet members from long-standing conservative blocs to nominate candidates to represent

political parties that yield high returns for their local constituents. The third is a combination of the two. Shimabukuro, *"Okinawa shinkō taisei" o tō*, 28.

9. Ibid., 272.

10. For a first-hand account of this incident, see David Vine, *Base Nation: How U.S. Military Bases Abroad Harm American and the World* (New York: Henry Holt and Company, 2015), 256–259.

11. Shimoji Yoshio, "Don't Cry for Okinawa's Economy," *The Japan Times* 31, 2013.

12. Tomochi Masaki, "Zenkichi tekkyo oyobi zenhojokin teppaigo no Ryukyu (Okinawa) keizai ni kansuru ichi kōsatsu," *Ryukyu Dokuritsugaku Kenkyū* 3 (2006): 23.

13. Tatsuro Yoda, "Japan's Host Nation Support Program for the U.S.-Japan Security Alliance: Past and Prospects," *Asian Survey* 46.6 (2006): 939.

14. Yoda, "Japan's Host Nation Support Program," 937.

15. Ibid., 942.

16. For more on current discussions on autonomy in its various forms, see Arakaki Tsuyoshi, *Okinawa no jikoketteiken: sono rekishiteki konkyo to kinmirai no tenbō* (Tokyo: Kōbunken, 2015). For more on these debates from the immediate post-reversion period, see Ryan M. Yokota, "Reversion-Era Proposals for Okinawan Regional Autonomy," in *Rethinking Postwar Okinawa: Beyond American Occupation*, ed. Pedro Iocabelli and Hiroko Matsuda (Lanham, Md.: Lexington Books, 2017), 59–79.

For more on Ryukyu independence, see Matsushima Yasukatsu, *Ryukyu dokuritsuron: Ryukyu minzoku no manifesuto* (Tokyo: Bajiriko, 2014). Matsushima, together with Oyakawa Shinako, Tōbaru Kazuhiko, Teruya Midori, and Tomochi Masaki, has founded the Association of Comprehensive Studies for Independence of the Lew Chewans (ACSIL), thereby launching the contemporary independence movement.

17. "Jichiken kyōka 35% nozomu 'genkōdōri' hansū waru: Ryukyu shinpō kenmin ishiki chōsa," *Ryukyu shinpō*, January 1, 2017.

18. Foucault, *Security, Territory, Population: Lectures at the Collège de France, 1977–1978*, 64–65.

19. Matsushima Chōgi, "Okinawa kaihō to *Uchinānchu*: 'Henkan funsuika' 'kyōtei funsui' ka," *Jōkyō* (December 1971): 90.

20. Matsushima, "Okinawa kaihō to *Uchinānchu*," 90–91.

21. Ibid., 91.

22. Ibid., 90.

23. Michel Foucault, *The Birth of Biopolitics: Lectures at the Collège de France, 1978–1979*, ed. Michel Senellart, trans. Graham Burchell (New York: Palgrave Macmillan, 2008), 55.

24. It is worth noting here Kant's writings on globalization and miscegenation are identical in design as derivative of the teleological judgment presented in the latter half of the *Critique of the Power of Judgment*. Different from the *Critique of Pure Reason* concerned with the supremacy of human reason, the problematic of this third critique is centered on how to secure the internal unity of human reason over the infinite expanse of Mother Nature. Kant's answers with a philosophy of enclosure that regulates the boundary-crossing movement of circulation and mixing. For him, not only must this movement occur, but it must occur in a way in which the unity of the state or self is reinforced as a result. Hence, it is no coincidence that in this context he lodges a discussion of miscegenation and attempts to theorize a form of racial mixing that produces the universality of a white male subject as it exists in a constellation of other races. See Immanuel Kant, "Of the Different Races of Human Beings," in *Anthropology, History, and Education*, ed. Robert B. Louden and Günter Zöller, trans. Mary Gregor et al. (Cambridge: Cambridge University Press, 2011), 82–97. Also, for a discussion on how the Kantian "transcendental self" is inimical to "self-morphing matter," specifically as it relates to the experience of pregnancy and racial mixing, see Christine Battersby, *The Phenomenal Woman: Feminist Metaphysics and the Patterns of Identity* (New York: Routledge, 1998).

25. Tosaka Jun, "The Principle of Everydayness and Historical Time," trans. Robert Stolz, in *Tosaka Jun: A Critical Reader*, ed. Ken C. Kawashima, Fabian Schäfer, and Robert Stolz (Ithaca, N.Y.: Cornell East Asia Series, 2013), 15.

26. Matsushima Chōgi and Tanigawa Ken'ichi, "Okinawa=kokka o koeru mugen senritsu," *Jōkyō* 3 (1971), 213.

27. Tosaka, "Principle of Everydayness," 14–15.

28. Matsushima and Tanigawa, "Okinawa=kokka o koeru mugen senritsu," 223.

29. Here, Tosaka is perhaps most closely aligned to Benjamin in his critique of idealism. In a similar spatial metaphor that he presents in his translation essay, Benjamin writes:

Just as a tangent touches a circle lightly and at but one point, with this touch rather than with the point setting the law according to which it is to continue on its straight path to infinity, a translation touches the original lightly and only at the infinitely small point of the sense, thereupon pursuing its own course according to the laws of fidelity in the freedom of linguistic flux.

In this passage, the tangent does not touch the circle in order to suture it internally according to a "law" that fixes its meaning infinitely throughout time, but it touches upon the circle so as to unleash the "freedom of linguistic flux," or language in motion. This is why Benjamin prioritized syntax over grammar in his theory of translation. Walter Benjamin, "The Task of a Translator," in *Illuminations: Essays and Reflections*, ed. Hannah Arendt, trans. Harry Zohn (New York: Shocken Books, 1985), 80.

Benjamin goes on to develop a fuller critique of Kantian idealism in his *Trauerspiel* with a modified version of Platonic idealism. Benjamin's "idea" is still transcendental in the sense that it lies beyond human access, but unlike Kant's idealism (where this limitation serves as an enabling possibility for the limitless creation of knowledge in a human-centered world), it points to the *failure* of representation itself. This failure is what I have be referring to as allegory. Precisely because of the inaccessibility of the idea, humans are driven all the more passionately into its representation through different arrangements of phenomena. He writes, "The representation of an idea can under no circumstances be considered successful unless the whole range of possible extremes it contains has been virtually explored." Walter Benjamin, *The Origin of German Tragic Drama*, trans. John Osborne (London: Verso, 1998), 47. Here, "successful" is "virtual," and therefore never actualizable because it is humanly impossible to exhaust the infinite number of ways of representing the idea through phenomena. As humans, we do not live forever, and it is therefore our destiny to *fail* at representation. However, for Benjamin, this *failure* is a veiled gift from God because it is only by being reminded of it that we can be liberated from the cruel belief that we will someday gain access to the truth. For as Benjamin sees it, it is the cruelty of this promise—always seeking to defer the imperfection of the here and now to the perfection of the future of infinite time—that keeps humans imprisoned in a self-imposed phantasmagoria.

Relating this to the visual image of a mosaic, he writes: "The value of fragments of thought is all the greater the less direct their relationship to the underlying idea, and the brilliance of the representation depends as much on this value as the brilliance of the mosaic does on the quality of the glass paste." Benjamin, *Origin of German Tragic Drama*, 29. The "fragments" here are pieces of a mosaic or phenomena in the representation of an idea. The purpose of the fragment is to draw attention to each individual piece *in terms of its failure to provide a unified representation of the idea.* Mosaics invite the viewer to move from piece to piece by drawing attention to the constant failure of achieving a smooth unification of the whole. The eye cannot sit still because the fragment disrupts the experience of totality. We are invited to go from piece to piece without rest. Although we most certainly attempt to look at the mosaic as a whole, the experience of the mosaic itself would simply not be the same without the motion of jumping from piece to piece. In other words, the mosaic invites motion, much like the idea in its capacity as a monad that puts together phenomena in "their endless dance of (re)juxtaposition." James R. Martel, *Textual Conspiracies: Walter Benjamin, Idolatry, and Political Theory* (Ann Arbor: The University of Michigan Press, 2013), 46. It is only through motion that things can *matter*.

30. Shimabukuro Jun, *"Okinawa shinkō taisei"o tō*, 21. Italics are mine.
31. Noiri Naomi, "Amerajian wa chanpurū no kōsei yōso ni natteiruka?," in *Okinawa/Hawai: kontakuto/zōn toshite no tōsho*, ed. Ikue Kina, Ishihara Masahide, and Yamashiro Shin (Tokyo: Sairyūsha, 2010), 335.
32. Tonegawa Yutaka, *Kiyan Marī no seishun* (Tokyo: Chikuma Shobō, 1988).
33. Suzuki Teruko, *Deteoide kijimunā* (Narashino: Yū Kosumosu, 1990).
34. Noiri, Seiyā, Terumoto, and Yonamine, *Amerajian sukūru*, 98–99.
35. Tomiyama Malia, "Amerajian o ikiru," *Akemodoro*, no. 19 (2000): 11–26.
36. Fija Byron and Patrick Heinrich, "'Wanne Uchinānchu—I Am Okinawan.' Japan, the U.S., and Okinawa's Endangered Languages," *The Asia-Pacific Journal* 5, no. 11 (November 3, 2007), http://apjjf.org/-Patrick-Heinrich/2586/article.html.
37. Mitzi Uehara Carter, "Routing, Repeating, and Hacking Mixed Race in Okinawa," in *Hapa Japan: Identities and Representations*, ed. Duncan R. Williams (Los Angeles: USC Press, 2017), 133–146.
38. "Eigo ya shitsumon osame kutsū: Amerikakei Uchinānchu shinpo," *Ryukyu shinpō*, December 7, 2014.
39. Tanaka Midori J., *Harukanaru maboroshi no chichiyo* (Tokyo: Kōyūsha, 1982), 69–70. "Amirikā" is the pronunciation for "American" in Okinawan.
40. Tanaka, *Harukanaru maboroshi no chichiyo*, 69.
41. Ibid., 73.
42. Ibid., 73.
43. Maeshiro Morisada, Makino Hirotaka, and Takara Kurayoshi, *Okinawa no jiko kenshō: teiden "jōnen" kara "ronri" e* (Naha: Hirugisha, 1998), 33.
44. Maeshiro Morisada, Ōshiro Tsuneo, and Takara Kurayoshi, *Okinawa inishiatibu: Okinawa hatsu/chiteki senryaku* (Naha: Hirugisha, 2000), 52–53.
45. Takara Kurayoshi, *Ryukyu ōkoku* (Tokyo: Iwanami Shoten, 2009), 6–7.
46. Friedrich Nietzsche, *On the Genealogy of Morals; Ecce Homo*, trans. Walter Kaufmann and R. J. Hollingdale, ed. Walter Kaufmann (New York: Vintage Books, 1989), 45.
47. Tanaka, *Harukanaru maboroshi no chichiyo*, 176.
48. Ibid., 231, 243.
49. Ibid., 238.

50. Ibid., 182.
51. Benjamin, *Origin of German Tragic Drama*, 233.
52. *Josei Jishin*
53. Tanaka, *Harukanaru maboroshi no chichiyo*, 249.
54. Ibid., 256.
55. This reminds me of a similar account given by Mitzi Uehara Carter of her mother's response to an ethnographic interview on Okinawa and U.S. military bases in which she stated, "I mostly just tell him what he wanna hear." This informs Uehara Carter's approach to a critical ethnography in militarized spaces. Uehara Carter, "Nappy Roots and Tangled Tales: Critical Ethnography in a Militarised Okinawa," in *Under Occupation: Resistance and Struggle in a Militarised Asia-Pacific*, ed. Daniel Broudy, Peter Simpson, and Makoto Arakaki (Newcastle upon Tyne: Cambridge Scholars Publication, 2013), 8. Her piece is important because it shows how the dance between unofficial and official modes of speech circulate throughout the Okinawan diaspora and racialized communities trans-Pacifically.
56. Benjamin, *Origin of German Tragic Drama*, 66.
57. Ibid., 65.

CONCLUSION

1. "Henoko 'chiji shiji' 83%, shinkichi kensetsu 76% hantai, honshi kinkyū yoron chōsa" *Okinawa taimusu*, April 7, 2015.
2. Chinen Seishin, "The Human Pavilion," trans. Robert Tierney, in *Islands of Protest: Japanese Literature from Okinawa*, ed. Davinder L. Bhowmik and Steve Rabson (Honolulu: University of Hawaiʻi Press, 2016).
3. As Samuel Weber writes in reference to Benjamin's *The Origin of German Tragic Drama*, "what is dislocated is not just the unity of *a* character, but the unity of *character as such*." Weber, "Taking Exception to Decision: Walter Benjamin and Carl Schmitt," *Diacritics* 22, nos. 3/4 (1993): 15.
4. Ariko Ikehara, "Third Space as Decolonial Con/Text: Okinawa's American Champurū," *Journal of Transnational Asian Studies* 1, 1: 1 (Fall 2016), http://transnationalasia.rice.edu/Content.aspx?id=105
5. Ikehara, "Okinawa's American Champurū."
6. Ibid.
7. Ariko Ikehara, "Champurū Text: Decolonial Okinawan Writing," in *Rethinking Postwar Okinawa: Beyond American Occupation*, ed. Pedro Iocabelli and Hiroko Matsuda (Lanham, Md.: Lexington Books, 2017), 141–142.
8. Ifa Fuyū, *Okinawa rekishi monogatari: Nihon no shukuzu* (Tokyo: Heibonsha, 1998), 194.
9. Ifa, *Okinawa rekishi monogatari*, 194.

SELECTED BIBLIOGRAPHY

NEWSPAPERS IN JAPANESE

Akahata (Tokyo, 1952)
Asahi shinbun (Tokyo, 1953, 1956)
Dassōhei tsushin (Tokyo, 1969)
Minzoku no jiyū to dokuritsu no tameni (unknown, 1954–1955)
Okinawa taimusu (1948–1950, 2012)
Ryukyu shinpō (Naha, 2014, 2016–2017)
Uruma shinpō (Ishikawa, 1947, Naha, 1949)

NEWSPAPERS IN ENGLISH

Japan Times (Tokyo, 2013)
Washington Post (Washington, D.C., 1952)

ARCHIVES

OPA   Okinawa Prefectural Archives, Haebaru, Okinawa

SOURCES IN JAPANESE

Ahagon Shōkō. *Beigun to nōmin*. Tokyo: Iwanami Shoten, 1980.

———. *Ningen no sundeiru shima: shashin kiroku*. Unknown: Erio Shashin
Shuppan, 1988.

Aono Suekichi. *"Puroretaria riarizumu no jissen ni tsuite."* In *Undō kaika no
jidai: senki sōkan kara bunka renmei kessei made*. Ed. Noma Hiroshi. Tokyo:
San'ichi Shobō, 1955.

Aono Suekichi. "Shizen seichō to mokuteki ishiki" *Hirabayashi Hatsunosuke,
Aono Suekichi, Kurahara Korehito, Nakano Shigeharu shū*. Ed. Aono Suekichi,
et al. Tokyo: Chikuma Shobō, 1957.

Arakaki Tsuyoshi. *Okinawa no jikoketteiken: sono rekishiteki konkyo to kinmirai
no tenbō*. Tokyo: Kōbunken, 2015.

Arasaki Moriteru, ed. *Dokyumento Okinawa tōsō*. Tokyo: Aki Shobō, 1969.

———. *Sengo Okinawashi*. Tokyo: Nihon Hyōronsha, 1976.

———. *Okinawa gendaishi*. Tokyo: Iwanami Shoten, 1996.

chinin ushii. *ushii ga yuku: shokuminchi shugi o tanken shi watakushi o sagasu
tabi*. Naha: Okinawa Taimususha, 2010.

———. *Shiranfūnā no bōryoku: chinin ushii seiji hatsugenshū.* Tokyo: Miraisha, 2013.

Duus Masayo. *Haisha no okurimono: kokusaku ianfu o meguru senryōka hishi.* Tokyo: Kōdansha, 1979.

Fujime Yuki. *Sei no rekishigaku: kōshō seido, dataizai taisei kara baishun bōshihō, yūsei hogohō taisei e.* Tokyo: Fuji Shuppan, 1997.

Fujino Yutaka. *Sei no kokka kanri: baibaishun no kingendaishi.* Tokyo: Fuji Shuppan, 2001.

Gabe Masaaki. *Okinawa henkan to wa nan datta no ka: Nichi-Bei sengo kōshōshi no naka de.* Tokyo: Nihon Hōsō Shuppankyōkai, 2000.

Gekkan Okinawa Sha, ed. *Laws and Regulations During the U.S. Administration of Okinawa, 1945–1972.* Vol. 1. Naha, Ikemiya Shokai & Co., 1983.

Gushiken Sōsei, ed. *Okinawa no shakai fukushi 25 nen: Okisha kyōsōritsu 20 shūnen kinenshi.* Naha: Okinawa Shakai Fukushi Kyōgikai, 1971.

Hayashi Hirofumi. *Beigun kichi no rekishi: sekai nettowāku no keisei to tenkai.* Tokyo: Yoshikawa Kōbunkan, 2012.

Higashionna Kanjun. "Konketsuji." In *Higashionna Kanjun zenshū.* Vol. 5. Tokyo: Daiichi Shobō, 1978.

Hiroyama Yōichi. "Koza Jūjiro ni okeru kuro no machi to shiro no machi." In *Koza Bunka Box* 3. Ed. Okinawashi Sōmubu Sōmuka Shishi. Okinawa: Okinawa Shiyakusho, 2007.

Hokama Yoneko. "Kichi/guntai/baishun: baishun mondai ni shoten o atete." *Okinawa keiken* 1, no. 2 (1971): 41–45.

———. "Kikikaki: Okinawa no baishun mondai to Nihon fukki." In *Zenkyōtō kara ribu e: jūgoshi nōto sengohen,* ed. Onnatachi no Ima o Tōkai. Tokyo: Inpakuto Shuppankai.

———. "Kutsujoku to eikō karano shuppatsu." In *Okinawa, onnatachi no sengo: shōdo kara no shuppatsu.* Ed. Miyazato Etsu. Naha: Hirugisha, 1986.

Hong Yunshin. *Okinawa senjō no kioku to "ianjo."* Tokyo: Inpakuto Shuppankai, 2016.

Ichikawa Fusae, ed. *Nihon fujin mondai shiryō shūsei: jinken.* Vol. 1. Tokyo: Domesu Shuppan, 1976.

Ifa Fuyū. *Okinawa rekishi monogatari: Nihon no shukuzu.* Tokyo: Heibonsha, 1998.

Ikemiyagi Shūi. *Okinawa ni ikite.* Tokyo: Saimaru Shuppankai, 1970.

———. *Okinawa no Amerikajin: Okinawa jānarisuto no kiroku "Okinawa ni ikite" dai sanbu.* Tokyo: Saimaru Shuppankai, 1971.

Inafuku Seiki. *Okinawa no igaku: igaku, hoken tōkei shiryō hen.* Naha: Kōbundō, 1979.

———. *Okinawa no shippeishi.* Tokyo: Daiichi Shobō, 1995.

Ishida Ikuo. *Okinawa/dochaku to kaihō.* Tokyo: Gōdō Shuppan, 1969.

Iwata Hiroshi. *Gekikasuru sekai kiki to gendai kakumei: Marukusushugi no konnichiteki kadai.* Tokyo: Ryōjisha, 1969.

Kabira Nario. *Okinawa: kūhaku no ichinen, 1945–1946.* Tokyo: Yoshikawa Kōbunkan, 2011.

Nihon Kokkai Gijiroku. *Kanpō gōgai: dai 13 kai Kokkai Sangiin, dai 24 gō kaigiroku, dai 24 gō.* March 25, 1952, no. 24.

———. *Kanpō gōgai: dai 19 kai Kokkai Shūgiin kaigiroku, dai 7 gō.* January 29, 1954, no. 7.

Kanō Mikiyo. "'Konketsuji' mondai to tan'itsuminzoku shinwa no seisei." In *Senryō to sei: seisaku jittai hyōshō.* Ed. Keisen Jogakuen Daigaku Heiwa Bunka Kenkyūjo. Tokyo: Inpakuto Shuppankai, 2007.

Kanzaki Kiyoshi. *Baishun: Ketteiban/Kanzaki repōto.* Tokyo: Gendaishi Shuppankai, 1974.

———. "Gaishōron." In *Kichi Nihon.* Ed. Inomata Kōzō, Kimura Kihachirō, and Shimizu Ikutarō. Tokyo: Wakōsha, 1953.

———. *Musume o uru machi: Kanzaki repōto.* Tokyo: Shinkō Shuppansha, 1952

Katō Masahiro. "Bijinesu sentā kōsō to 'Yaejima.'" In *Koza Bunka Box.* Vol. 8. Ed. Okinawashi Sōmubu Sōmuka Shihi. Okinawa: Okinawa Shiyakusho, 2012.

Kawata Yō. "Kokkyō/kokka/daisanji Ryukyu shobun." *Jōkyō* 4 (1971): 64–91.

———. "Shinsayoku undō to Okinawa tōsō: Zengunrō daisanha no 'ryūzan' to 4.28 tōsō." *Jōkyō* (June 1970): 5–25.

Kayō Yoshiharu. "Shinbun kiji o chūshin ni miru tokuingai e no ofu rimittsu hatsurei (1951–52 nen)." In *Koza Bunka Box.* Vol. 3. Ed. Okinawashi Sōmubu Sōmuka Shishi. Okinawa: Okinawa Shiyakusho, 2007.

Kikuchi Natsuno. *Posutokoroniarizumu to jendā.* Tokyo: Seikyūsha, 2010.

Kinjō Kiyoko. *Hō joseigaku no susume: josei kara no hōritsu e no toikake.* Tokyo: Yūhikaku, 1992.

Kojima Tsunehisa. *Nihon shihonshugi ronsōshi.* Tokyo: Ariesu Shobō, 1976.

Kojō Yoshiko. "Nichibei anpo taisei to doru bōei seisaku: bōeihi futan yōkyū no rekishi kōzu." *Kokusai seiji* 115 (1997): 94–109.

Kokoro ni Todoke Onnatachi no Koe Nettowāku. "Kichi no tarai mawashi wa yameteyo!" *Kēshi kaji* 26 (March 2000): 29–37.

Kokuba Kōtarō. "Okinawa no Nihon fukki undo to kakushin seitō: minzoku ishiki keisei no mondai ni yosete." *Shisō* 2, no. 452 (1962): 79–92.

———. "Okinawa to Amerika teikokushugi: keizai seisaku o chūshin ni." *Keizai hyōron* 1 (1962): 110–129.

———. "Sekai Okinawa/1950 nendai no Beigun gunsei ni kō suru." *Sekai* 9 (2005): 98–104.

Kokuba Kōtarō, and Mori Yoshio. *Sengo shoki Okinawa kaihō undo shiryōshū.* Vol. 3. Tokyo: Fuji Shuppan, 2005.

Kurahara Korehito. "Geijutsuteki hōhō ni tsuite no kansō (kōhen)." In *Kurahara Korehito hyōronshū.* Vol. 2. Tokyo: Shin Nihon Shuppansha, 1980.

Maedomari Hiromori. *Hontō wa kenpō yori taisetsuna "Nichi-Bei chii kyōtei nyūmon."* Osaka: Sōgenha, 2013.

Maehara Hozumi. *Kenshō Okinawa no rōdō undō: Okinawa sengoshi no nagare no naka de.* Naha: Okinawaken Rōdōsha Gakushū Kyōkai, 2000.

Maeshiro Morisada, Makino Hirotaka, and Takara Kurayoshi. *Okinawa no jiko kenshō: teiden "jōnen" kara "ronri" e.* Naha: Hirugisha, 1998.

Maeshiro Morisada, Ōshiro Tsuneo, and Takara Kurayoshi. *Okinawa inishiatibu: Okinawa hatsu/chiteki senryaku.* Naha: Hirugisha, 2000.

Makino Hirotaka. *Saikō: Okinawa keizai.* Naha: Okinawa Taimususha, 1997.

Matsushima Chōgi. "Naze Kaunaānchu ka." *Kōzō* (June 1971).

———. "Okinawa kaihō to *Uchinānchu*: 'Henkan funsuika' 'kyōtei funsui' ka." *Jōkyō* (December 1971): 90–98.

Matsushima Chōgi, and Tanikawa Ken'ichi. "Okinawa=kokka o koeru mugen senritsu." *Jōkyō* (March 1971).

Matsushima Yasukatsu. *Ryukyu dokuritsuron: Ryukyu minzoku no manifesuto.* Tokyo: Bajiriko, 2014.

Miyada Hiroshi. "Okinawa keizai no tokuisei wa dōshite tsukurareta ka." In *Okinawa "jiritsu" e no michi o motomete: kichi keizai jichi no shiten kara.* Ed. Masaaki Gabe, Miyazato Seigen, Arasaki Moriteru, and Ōshiro Hajime. Tokyo: Kōbunken, 2009.

Miyagi Harumi. "Okinawa no Amerika gunkichi to seibōryoku: Amerika-gun jōriku kara kōwajōyaku hakkō mae no seihanzai no jittai o tōshite." In *Okinawa no senryō to Nihon no fukkō: shouminchishugi wa ikani keizoku shika ka.* Ed. Nakano Tshio, Namihira Tsuneo, Yakabi Osamu, and Yi Hyodŏk. Tokyo: Seikyūsha, 2006.

Miyahara Seiichi, Shimizu Ikutarō, and Ueda Shōzaburō, eds. *Kichi no ko: kono jijitsu o dō kangaetara yoika.* Tokyo: Kōbunsha, 1953.

Miyazato Etsu, ed. *Okinawa, onnatachi no sengo: shōdo kara no shuppatsu.* Naha: Hirugisha, 1986.

Miyazato Seigen. *Amerika no Okinawa tōchi.* Tokyo: Iwanami Shoten, 1966.

———. *Sengo Okinawa no seiji to hō: 1945–72 nen.* Tokyo: Tokyo Daigaku Shuppankai, 1975.

Mori Yoshio. *Tsuchi no naka no kakumei: Okinawa sengoshi ni okeru sonzai no kaihō.* Tokyo: Gendai Kikakushitsu, 2010.

Mori Yoshio, and Toriyama Atsushi, eds. *"Shimagurumi tōsō" wa dō junbi sareta ka: Okinawa ga mezasu "amayū" e no michi.* Tokyo: Fuji Shuppan, 2013.

Mori Yoshio, Tobe Hideaki, and Tomiyama Ichirō, eds. *Amayū e: Okinawa sengoshi no jiritsu ni mukete.* Tokyo: Hōsei Daigaku Shuppankyoku, 2017.

Nagasaki Hiroshi. *Hanran no 60 nendai: Anpo tōsō to Zenkyōtō undō.* Tokyo: Ronsōsha, 2010.

Nagumo Kazuo. *Beigun kichi to rōdō undō: senryōka no Okinawa.* Kyoto: Kamogawa Shuppan, 1996.

Nakandakari Asami. "Arakaki Mitoko 'mibōjin'ron: 1950 nen Okinawa no shinbun ni okeru 'sensō mibōjin' hyōshō o meguru kōsō." *Ryukyu Ajia shakai bunka kenkyū* 14 (October 2011): 41–77.

Nakano Yoshio, ed. *Sengo shiryō Okinawa.* Tokyo: Nihon Hyōronsha, 1969.

Nakaya Kōkichi. *Namae yo tatte aruke: Okinawa sengo sedai no kiseki Nakaya Kōkichi ikōshū.* Tokyo: San'ichi Shobō, 1972.

Nihon Dokyumentarisuto Yunion. "Shinario 'Motoshinkakarannū': '69–'71 Okinawa chōpen kiroku eiga—Okinawa erosu gaiden." *Eiga hihyō* 2 (October 1971): 58–77.

Nihon Kokkai Gijiroku. *Dai 13 kai Kokkai Sangiin, dai 24 gō kaigoruku dai 24 gō, Maarch 3, 1952, no. 24.*

———. *Kanpō gōgai: dai 13 kai Kokkai Sangiin, dai 24 gō kaigiroku, dai 24 gō.* March 25, 1952, no. 24.

———. *Kanpō gōgai: dai 19 kai Kokkai Shūgiin kaigiroku, dai 7 gō.* January 29, 1954, no. 7.

Noiri Naomi. "Amerajian wa chanpurū no kōsei yōso ni natteiruka?" In *Okinawa/Hawai: kontakuto zōn toshite no tōsho.* Ed. Ikue Kina, Ishihara Masahide, and Yamashiro Shin. Tokyo: Sairyūsha, 2010.

Noiri Naomi, Seiyā Midori, Terumoto Hirotaka, and Yonamine Masae. *Amerajian sukūru: Kyōsei no chihei o Okinawa kara.* Tokyo: Fukinotō Shobō, 2001.

Nunokawa Tetsurō. "Dokyumentarī e no shuttatsu: 'Motoshinkakarannūtachi' ga kaishi suru mono." *Eiga hihyō* 2 (October 1971): 50–57.

Oguma Eiji. *1968.* Vol. 1. Tokyo: Shin'yōsha, 2009.

———. *A Genealogy of 'Japanese' Self-Images.* Trans. David Askew. Melbourne: Trans Pacific Press, 2002.

———. *Shimizu Ikutarō: aru sengo chishikijin no kiseki.* Tokyo: Ochanomizu Shobō, 2003.

Okinawa Jinmintōshi Henshū Kankō Iinkai, ed. *Okinawa jinmintō no rekishi.* Naha: Okinawa Jinmintōshi Henshū Kankō Iinkai, 1985.

Okinawa Kokusai Daigaku Bungakubu Shakaigakka Ishihara Zemināru ed. *Sengo Koza ni okeru minshū seikatsu to ongaku bunka.* Ginowan: Ryokurindō Shoten, 1994.

Okinawaken Bunka Shinkōkai Kōbunshokan Kanribu Shiryōhenshūshitsu, ed. *Military Government Activities Reports* (Naha: Okinawaken Kyōiku Iinkai, 2000), 58.

Okinawaken Hansen Seinen Iinkai, ed. *Zengunrō hansenha*. Tokyo: San'ichi Shobō, 1970.

Okinawaken Josei Dantai Renraku Kyōgikai, ed. *Heiwa/byōdō/hatten o tomoshitsuzukete shiryōhen*. Okinawa: Ryukyu Shuppansha, 2003.

Okinawaken Kankyō Hokenbu Yobōka. *Okinawa sengo no hokenjo no ayumi: hokenjo 30 shūnen kinenshi*. Unknown: Okinawaken Kankyō Hokenbu Yobōka, 1981.

Okinawaken Sokoku Fukki Tōsōshi Hensan Iinkai, ed. *Okinawaken sokoku fukki tōsōshi*; Naha: Okinawa Jiji Shuppan, 1982.

Okinawashi Heiwa Bunka Shinkōkai, ed. *Koza hito/machi/koto: shashin ga toraeta 1970 nen zengo anata ga rekishi no mokugekisha*. Okinawa: Naha Shuppansha, 1997.

Okinawashi Kikakubu Heiwa Bunka Shinkōka, ed. *Beikoku ga mita Koza bōdō: Beikoku kōbunsho Ei-Wa taiyaku*. Okinawa: Yui Shuppan, 1999.

Okinawashi Urasoeshi, Ginowanshi, Gushikawashi, Ishikawashi oyobi Nakagamigun Rōjin Fukushi Sentā Un'ei Kyōgikai, eds. *Chūbu chiku shakai fukushi no kiseki: sōron*. Vol. 1. Okinawa: Okinawashi, Urasoeshi, Ginowanshi, Gushikawashi, Ishikawashi oyobi Nakagamigun Rōjin Fukushi Sentā Un'ei Kyōgikai, 1986.

Ōmori Minoru. *Sengo hishi 6: kinjirareta seiji*. Tokyo: Kōdansha, 1976.

Onga Takashi. "Koza no jidai o kangaeru: taifū ni yotte tsukurareta machi." In *Koza Bunka Box*. Vol.1. Ed. Okinawashi Sōmubu Sōmuka Shishi. Okinawa: Okinawa Shiyakusho, 1998.

Ōshiro Yasutaka. "Kokusaiji ni kansuru mondai to taiou no jidai kubun shian." *Okinawa chiiki fukushi kenkyū: Nihon shakai fukushi gakkai dai 49 kai zenkoku taikai kaisai kinen gō*. October 20, 2001.

Ōta Masahide. "Nokosareta mondai." *Ushio* (June 1972).

Ōyama Chōjō. *Okinawa dokuritsu sengen: Yamato wa kaerubeki "sokoku" dewa nakatta*. Tokyo: Gendai Shorin, 1997.

Ozawa Nobuo. "Panpan." In *Onna no sengoshi: Shōwa 20 nendai*. Vol. 1. Ed. Asahi Jānaru. Tokyo: Asahi Shinbunsha, 1984.

Ryukyu Ginkō Chōsabu, ed. *Sengo Okinawa keizaishi*. Naha: Ryukyu Ginkō, 1984.

Sakiyama Tami. *Kotoba no umareru basho*. Tokyo: Sunagoya Shobō, 2004.

Sekitani Michiō. "NichiBei anpō no ima: anzen hoshō ni kansuru denwa chōsa kara." *Hōsō Kenkyū to Chōsa*. March 2011. https://www.nhk.or.jp/bunken/summary/research/report/2011_03/110302.pdf.

Senaga Kamejirō. *Minzoku no higeki: Okinawa kenmin no teikō.* Tokyo: Shin Nihon Shuppansha, 1971.

———. *Okinawa kara no hōkoku.* Tokyo: Iwanami Shoten, 1959.

Shima Masu. *Shima Masu no ganbari jinsei: kichi no machi no fukushi ni ikite.* Okinawa: Shima Masu Sensei Kaisōroku Henshū Iinkai, 1986.

Shimabukuro Hiroshi. "Okinawa saidai no sangyō 'sekkusu keizai' no jittai." *Ushio* (June 1972).

Shimabukuro Jun. *"Okinawa shinkō taisei"o tō: kowasareta jichi to sono saisei ni mukete.* Kyoto: Hōritsubunkasha, 2014.

Shimizu Ikutarō. *Waga jinsei no danpen.* Tokyo: Bungei Shunjū, 1975.

Shiroma Seizen. "Shiroma Seizen." In *Watakushi no sengoshi.* Vol. 6. Naha: Okinawa Taimususha, 1982.

Statistics of Japan. "Heisei 27 nen kokusei chōsa: jinkō sokuhō shūkei kekka." February 26, 2016. http://www.stat.go.jp/data/kokusei/2015 /kekka/pdf/gaiyou.pdf.

Sugaya Naoko. "Okinawa no baishun mondai: fukki ni ka getsu mae." *Fujin mondai kondankai kaihō* 16 (June 1972): 7–13.

Suzuki Teruko. *Deteoide kijimunā.* Narashino: Yū Kosumosu, 1990.

Suzuki Yūko. "Karayukisan—'jūgunianfu'—senryōgun 'ianfu.'" In *Iwanami kōza kindai Nihon to shokuminchi: bōchosuru teikoku no jinryū.* Ed. Asada Kyōji, Mitani Taichirō, and Ōe Shinobu. Vol. 5. Tokyo: Iwanami Shoten, 1992.

Taira Yoshitoshi. *Sengo Okinawa to Beigun kichi: "juyō" to "kyozetsu" no hazama de, 1945–1972 nen.* Tokyo: Hōsei Daigaku Shuppankyoku, 2012.

Takamine Tomokazu. *Shirarezaru Okinawa no Beihei: Beigun kichi 15 nen no shuzai memo kara.* Tokyo: Kōbunken, 1984.

Takara Kurayoshi. *Ryukyu ōkoku.* Tokyo: Iwanami Shoten, 2009.

Takazato Suzuyo. "Kyōsei jūgun 'ianfu.'" In *Naha/onna no ashiato: Naha joseishi (kindaihen).* Ed. Nahashi Sōmubu Joseishitsu. Tokyo: Domesu Shuppan, 1998.

Takazato Suzuyo. *Okinawa no onnatachi: josei no jinken to kichi, guntai.* Tokyo: Akashi Shoten, 1996.

Takeda Makoto. *Okinawa kaikyū tōsō: Zengunrō sutoraiki (1972) to Beigun Kisenbaru enshū jitsuryoku soshi tōsō (1974–77).* Nagoya: Gendai Bunka Kenkyūsha, 2001.

Takemasa Ando. *Japan's New Left Movements: Legacies for Civil Society.* London: Routledge, 2014.

Takenaka Katsuo. *Gaishō: jittai to sono shuki.* Tokyo: Yūkōsha, 1949.

Takushi Etsuko. *Okinawa umi o wattata Amerikahei hanayometachi.* Tokyo: Kōbunken, 2000.

Tanaka Midori J. *Harukanaru maboroshi no chichiyo.* Tokyo: Kōyūsha, 1982.

Tasato Yūtetsu. *Ronshū: Okinawa no shūraku kenkyū.* Naha: Riuchūsha, 1983.

Teruya Zensuke. "Kōshū eisei gyōsei: yūsenteki jōkenka de dassoku."
    Okinawa genkōhōshi 3, no. 3 (March 1979), 2425.
Toba Kōji. *1950 nendai: "kiroku" no jidai.* Tokyo: Kawade Shobō Shinsha, 2010.
Tomiyama, Ichirō. *Bōryoku no yokan: Ifa Fuyū ni okeru kiki no mondai.* Tokyo:
    Iwanami Shoten, 2002.
———. *Kindai Nihon shakai to "Okinawajin": "Nihonjin" ni naru to iu koto.*
    Tokyo: Nihon Keizai Hyōronsha, 1990.
———. *Ryūchaku no shisō: "Okinawa mondai" no keifugaku.* Tokyo: Inpakuto
    Shuppankai, 2013.
———. *Senjō no kioku.* Tokyo: Nihon Keizai Hyōronsha, 1995.
Tomiyama Malia. "Amerajian o ikiru." *Akemodoro,* no. 19 (2000): 10–26.
———. "Beigun kichi." Facebook, July 19, 2013. https://www.facebook.com
    /photo.php?fbid=481134368644277&set=a.117687014989016.24618
    .100002431539882&type=3&theater.
———. "Yūki," *Buraku kaihō* 477 (November 2000): 10–11.
Tomochi Masaki. "Zenkichi tekkyo oyobi zenhojokin teppaigo no Ryukyu
    (Okinawa) keizai ni kansuru ichi kōsatsu." *Ryukyu Dokuritsugaku Kenkyū* 3
    (2006): *Comprehensive Studies for the Independence of the Lew Chewans* 3
    (2006): 5–31.
Tonegawa Yutaka. *Kiyan Marī no seishin.* Tokyo: Chikuma Shobō, 1988.
Toriyama Atsushi. *Okinawa: kichi shakai no kigen to sōkoku.* Tokyo: Keisō
    Shobō, 2013.
Tosaka Jun. "Fukko genshō no bunseki." In *Tosaka Jun zenshū.* Vol. 2.
    Tokyo: Keisō shobō, 1966.
Ueunten Wesley. "Ikari no umi kara no funki: Amerika gunsenryōka no
    Okinawa ni okeru Koza sōdo." Trans. Makoto Arakaki. In *Gendai
    Okinawa no rekishi keiken: kibō, aruiwa mikessei ni tsuite.* Ed. Mori Yoshio
    and Tomiyama Ichirō. Tokyo: Seikyusha, 2010.
Uno Kōzō. "Shihonshugi no sōshikika to minshushugi." In *Uno Kōzō
    chosakushū.* Vol. 8. Tokyo: Iwanami Shoten, 1974.
———. "Tōgyō yori mitaru kōiki keizai no kenkyū joron/ketsugo." In *Uno
    Kōzō chosakushū.* Vol. 8. Tokyo: Iwanami Shoten, 1974.
Yamazaki Takashi. "USCAR bunshō kara mita A sain seido to baishun/
    seibyō kisei: 1970 nen zengo no Beigun fūki torishimari iinkai gijiroku
    no kentō kara." *Okinawa kōbun shokan kenkyū kiyō* 10 (March 2008):
    39–51.
———. "USCAR bunsho kara mita A sain seido to ofu rimittsu." In *Koza
    Bunka Box.* Vol. 4. Ed. Okinawashi Sōmubu Sōmuka Shishi. Okinawa:
    Okinawa Shiyakusho, 2009.
Yamazato Akira. *Gyakuryū ni kōshite: Okinawa gakusei undōshi.* Tokyo:
    Okinawa Mondai Kenkyūkai, 1967.

Yonakuni Noboru. *Sengo Okinawa no shakai hendō to kindaika: Beigun shihai to taishū undō no dainamizumu.* Naha: Okinawa Taimususha, 2001.

Yara Tomohiro. *Gokai darake no Okinawa/Beigun kichi.* Tokyo: Junpōsha, 2012.

———. *Sajō no dōmei: Beigun saihen ga akasu uso.* Naha: Okinawa Taimususha, 2009.

SOURCES IN ENGLISH

Angst, Linda I. "Loudmouth Feminists and Unchaste Prostitutes: 'Bad Girls' Misbehaving in Postwar Okinawa." *U.S.-Japan Women's Journal* 36 (2009): 117–141.

Argy, Victor, and Leslie Stein, eds. *The Japanese Economy.* London: Macmillan Press, 1997.

Battersby, Christine. *The Phenomenal Woman: Feminist Metaphysics and the Patterns of Identity.* New York: Routledge, 1998.

Benjamin, Walter. "Critique of Violence." In *Reflections: Essays, Aphorisms, Autobiographical Writings.* Ed. Peter Demetz. Trans. Edmund Jephcott. New York: Schocken Books, 1978.

———. *The Origin of German Tragic Drama.* Trans. John Osborne. London: Verso, 1998.

———. "The Task of a Translator." In *Illuminations: Essays and Reflections.* Ed. Hannah Arendt. Trans. Harry Zohn. New York: Shocken Books, 1985.

———. *The Writer of Modern Life: Essays on Charles Baudelaire.* Ed. Michael W. Jennings. Trans. Howard Eiland et al. Cambridge: The Belknap Press of Harvard University Press, 2006.

Bowen-Struyk, Heather, and Norma Field, eds. *For Dignity, Justice, and Revolution: An Anthology of Japanese Proletarian Literature.* Chicago: University of Chicago Press, 2016.

Bowers, William T., William M. Hammond, and George L. MacGarrigle. *Black Soldier, White Army: The 24th Infantry Regiment in Korea.* Washington: Center of Military History, U.S. Army, 1996.

Buck-Morss, Susan. *The Dialectics of Seeing: Walter Benjamin and the Arcades Project.* Cambridge: MIT Press, 1991.

Chandler, Nahum D. *X: The Problem of the Negro as a Problem for Thought.* New York: Fordham University Press, 2014.

Chinen Seishin, "The Human Pavilion." Trans. Robert Tierney. In *Islands of Protest: Japanese Literature from Okinawa.* Ed. Davinder L. Bhowmik and Steve Rabson. Honolulu: University of Hawai'i Press, 2016.

Ching, Leo T. S. *Becoming "Japanese": Colonial Taiwan and the Politics of Identity Formation.* Berkeley and Los Angeles: University of California Press, 2001.

Cho, Grace M., and Hosu Kim. "The Kinship of Violence." *Journal of Korean Adoption Studies* 1, no. 3 (2012): 11, 12.

Crissey, Etsuko T., *Okinawa's G.I. Brides: Their Lives in America*. Trans. Steve Rabson. Honolulu: University of Hawai'i Press, 2017.

Cumings, Bruce. "The Origins and Development of the Northeast Asian Political Economy: Industrial Sectors, Product Cycles, and Political Consequences." *International Organization* 38, no. 1 (Winter 1984): 1–40.

De Man, Paul. *Blindness and Insight: Essays in the Rhetoric of Contemporary Criticism*. Trans. Wlad Godzich. Minneapolis: University of Minnesota Press, 2006.

Department of Defense. *Active Duty Military Personnel by Service Rank/Grade: December 2016*. https://www.dmdc.osd.mil/appj/dwp/dwp_reports.jsp.

———. *Base Structure Report: Fiscal Year 2015 Baseline*. http://www.acq.osd .mil/eie/Downloads/BSI/Base%20Structure%20Report%20FY15.pdf.

———. *Military and Civilian Personnel by Service/Agency by State/Country: December 2016*. https://www.dmdc.osd.mil/appj/dwp/dwp_reports.jsp.

Derrida, Jacques. "Force of Law: The 'Mystical Foundation of Authority.'" In *Deconstruction and the Possibility of Justice*. Ed. David Carlson, Drucilla Cornell, and Michel Rosenfeld. New York: Routledge, 1992.

Director-General for Statistics and Information Policy, Ministry of Health, Labour, and Welfare, Ed. *Vital Statistics of Japan 2015*. Vol. 1. Tokyo: Kōseishō Daijin Kambō Tōkei Jōhōbu, 2015.

Dower, John W. *Embracing Defeat: Japan in the Wake of World War II*. New York: W. W. Norton, 1999.

Endo, Katsuhiko. "A Secret History: Tosaka Jun and the Kyoto Schools." In *Confronting Capital and Empire: Rethinking Kyoto School Philosophy*. Ed. Viren Murthy, Fabian Schäfer, and Max Ward. Leiden: Brill, 2017.

———. "A Unique Tradition of Materialism in Japan: Osugi Sakae, Tosaka Jun, and Uno Kozo." *Positions: East Asian Cultures Critique* 20, no. 4 (Fall 2012): 1009–1039.

———. "The Multitude and the Holy Family: Empire, Fascism, and the War Machine." In *Tosaka Jun: A Critical Reader*. Ed. Ken C. Kawashima, Fabian Schäfer, and Robert Stolz. Ithaca, N.Y.: Cornell East Asia Series, 2013.

———. "The Science of Capital: The Uses and Abuses of Social Sciences in Interwar Japan." Ph.D. diss., New York University, 2004.

Fanon, Frantz. *Black Skin, White Masks*. Trans. Charles Lam Markmann. New York: Grove Press, 1967.

Field, Norma. *In the Realm of a Dying Emperor: Japan at a Century's End*. New York: Vintage Books, 1991.

Fija, Byron, and Patrick Heinrich. "'Wanne Uchinānchu—I Am Okinawan.'
    Japan, the U.S., and Okinawa's Endangered Languages." *The Asia-Pacific
    Journal* 5, no. 11 (November 3, 2007). http://apjjf.org/-Patrick-Heinrich
    /2586/article.html.
Fisch, Arnold G., Jr. *Military Government in the Ryukyu Islands, 1945–1950.*
    Washington: Center of Military History, U.S. Army, 1988.
Foreign Relations of the United States, 1948. Vol. VI. The Far East and
    Australasia. Washington: United States Government Printing Office, 1974.
Foucault, Michel. "Intellectuals and Power." In *Language, Counter-Memory,
    Practice: Selected Essays and Interviews.* Ed. Donald F. Bouchard. Trans.
    Donald F. Bouchard and Sherry Simon. Ithaca, N.Y.: Cornell University
    Press, 1977.
———. *Security, Territory, Population: Lectures at the Collège de France,
    1977–1978.* Ed. Michel Senellart. Trans. Graham Burchell. New York:
    Palgrave Macmillan, 2007.
———. *The Birth of Biopolitics: Lectures at the Collège de France, 1978–1979.*
    Ed. Michel Senellart. Trans. Graham Burchell. New York: Palgrave
    Macmillan, 2008.
Fujitani, Takashi. *Race for Empire: Koreans as Japanese and Japanese as
    Americans During World War II.* Berkeley and Los Angeles: University of
    California Press, 2011.
Gibney, Frank. "Okinawa: Forgotten Island," *Time* 54, no. 22:26.
Haver, William. *The Body of This Death: Historicity and Sociality in the Time of
    AIDS.* Stanford: Stanford University Press, 1996.
Higa, Mikio. *Politics and Parties in Postwar Okinawa.* Vancouver: Publications
    Centre, University of British Columbia, 1963.
Hong, Yunshin. *"Comfort Stations" as Remembered by Okinawans During
    World War II.* Trans. Robert Ricketts. Leiden: Brill, forthcoming.
Ikehara, Ariko. "A Third as Decolonial Con/Text: Okinawa's American
    Champurū." *Journal of Transnational Asian Studies* 1, no. 1:1 (Decem-
    ber 2016). http://transnationalasia.rice.edu/Content.aspx?id=105.
———. "Champurū Text: Decolonial Okinawan Writing." In *Rethinking
    Postwar Okinawa: Beyond American Occupation.* Ed. Pedro Iocabelli and
    Hiroko Matsuda. Lanham, Md.: Lexington Books, 2017.
Johnson, Chalmers A. *MITI and the Japanese Miracle: The Growth of Indus-
    trial Policy, 1925–1975.* Stanford: Stanford University Press, 2012.
Kant, Immanuel. "Of the Different Races of Human Beings." In *Anthropol-
    ogy, History, and Education.* Ed. Robert B. Louden and Günter Zöller.
    Trans. Mary Gregor et al. Cambridge: Cambridge University Press, 2011.
Karlsson, Mats. "Kurahara Korehito's Road to Proletarian Realism." *Japan
    Review* 20 (2008): 231–273.

Kawashima, Ken C. "Notes Toward a Critical Analysis of Chronic Recession and Ideology: Tosaka Jun on the Police Function." In *Tosaka Jun: A Critical Reader*. Ed. Ken C. Kawashima, Fabian Schäfer, and Robert Stolz. Ithaca, N.Y.: Cornell East Asia Series, 2013.

———. *The Proletarian Gamble: Korean Workers in Interwar Japan*. Durham, N.C.: Duke University Press, 2009.

Kinjo, Masaki. "Internal Revolution: The Postwar Okinawan Literature of Kiyota Masanobu and Medoruma Shun." Ph.D. diss., Cornell University, 2017.

Koepnick, Lutz P. "Allegory and Power: Walter Benjamin and the Politics of Representation." *Soundings: An Interdisciplinary Journal* 79, no. 2 (Spring/Summer 1996): 59–78.

Koshiro, Yukiko. *Trans-Pacific Racisms and the U.S. Occupation of Japan*. New York: Columbia University Press, 1999.

Kovner, Sarah. *Occupying Power: Sex Workers and Servicemen in Postwar Japan*. Stanford: Stanford University Press, 2012.

Kramm, Robert. *Sanitized Sex: Regulating Prostitution, Venereal Disease, and Intimacy in Occupied Japan, 1945–1952*. Berkeley and Los Angeles: University of California Press, 2017.

Pascoe, Peggy. *What Comes Naturally: Miscegenation Law and the Making of Race in America*. New York: Oxford University Press, 2009.

Laclau, Ernesto. *On Populist Reason*. London: Verso, 2005.

Lattimore, Eleanor. "Pacific Ocean or American Lake?" *Far Eastern Survey* 14, no. 22 (1945): 313–316.

Legg, Stephen. *Prostitution and the Ends of Empire: Scale, Governmentalities, and Interwar India*. Durham, N.C.: Duke University Press, 2014.

Lie, John. "The State as Pimp: Prostitution and the Patriarchal State in Japan in the 1940s." *The Sociological Quarterly* 38, no. 2 (Spring 1997): 251–263.

Lukács, Georg. "Class Consciousness." In *History and Class Consciousness: Studies in Marxist Dialectics*. Trans. Rodney Livingstone. Cambridge: MIT Press, 1979.

———. "Legality and Illegality." In *History and Class Consciousness: Studies in Marxist Dialectics*. Trans. Rodney Livingstone. Cambridge: MIT Press, 1979.

———. "Reportage or Portrayal?" In *Essays on Realism*. Ed. Rodney Livingstone. Trans. David Fernbach. Cambridge: MIT Press, 1981.

Martel, James R. *Textual Conspiracies: Walter Benjamin, Idolatry, and Political Theory*. Ann Arbor: University of Michigan Press, 2013.

———. *The One and Only Law: Walter Benjamin and the Second Commandment*. Ann Arbor: University of Michigan Press, 2014.

Marx, Karl. *Capital*. Vol. 1. Trans. Ben Fowkes. London: Penguin Classics, 1990.

Matsumura, Wendy. *The Limits of Okinawa: Japanese Capitalism, Living Labor, and Theorizations of Community*. Durham, N.C.: Duke University Press, 2015.

McCormack, Gavan. "Introduction." In *Multicultural Japan: Palaeolithic to Postmodern*. Ed. Donald Denoon et al. Cambridge: Cambridge University Press, 1996.

———. "Japan's Client State (Zokkoku) Problem." *The Asia-Pacific Journal* 11, no. 25:2 (June 23, 2013). http://apjjf.org/2013/11/25/Gavan -McCormack/3961/article.html.

———. *The Emptiness of Japanese Affluence*. Armonk, N.Y.: M.E. Sharpe, 2001.

McCormack, Gavan, and Satoko Oka Norimatsu. *Resistant Islands: Okinawa Confronts Japan and the United States*. Lanham, Md.: Rowman and Littlefield Publishers, Inc., 2012.

Morris, M. D. *Okinawa: A Tiger by the Tail*. New York: Hawthorn Books, 1968.

Nelson, Christopher. *Dancing with the Dead: Memory, Performance, and Everyday Life in Postwar Okinawa*. Durham, N.C.: Duke University Press, 2008.

Nelson, Kim Park. *Invisible Asians: Korean American Adoptees, Asian American Experiences, and Racial Exceptionalism*. New Brunswick, N.J.: Rutgers University Press, 2016.

Nietzsche Friedrich. *On the Genealogy of Morals: Ecce Homo*. Ed. Walter Kaufmann Trans. Walter Kaufmann and R. J. Hollingdale. New York: Vintage Books, 1989.

Nomura Kōya. "Undying Colonialism: A Case Study of the Japanese Colonizer." Trans. Annmaria Shimabuku. *CR: The New Centennial Review* 12, no. 1 (2012): 93–116.

Okada, Yasuhiro. "Race, Masculinity, and Military Occupation: African American Soldiers' Encounters with the Japanese at Camp Gifu, 1947–1951." *The Journal of African American History* 96, no. 2 (Spring 2011): 179–203.

Okamura, Hyoue. "The Language of 'Racial Mixture': How Ainoko Became Haafu, and the Haafu-gao Makeup Fad." *Asia Pacific Perspectives* 14 (Spring 2017). https://www.usfca.edu/center-asia-pacific/perspectives /v14n2/okamura.

Onishi, Yuichiro. *Transpacific Antiracism: Afro-Asian Solidarity in Twentieth-Century Black America, Japan, and Okinawa*. New York: New York University Press, 2013.

Saito, Mitsuo. *The Japanese Economy*. Singapore: World Scientific Publishing, 2000.

Sakai, Naoki. "Two Negations: The Fear of Being Excluded and the Logic of Self-Esteem." In *Contemporary Japanese Thought*. Ed. Richard F. Calichman. New York: Columbia University Press, 2005.

Sakai, Naoki, and Hyon Joo Yoo, eds. *The Trans-Pacific Imagination: Rethinking Boundary, Culture, and Society*. Singapore: World Scientific Publishing, 2012.

Sandars, Christopher T. *America's Overseas Garrisons: The Leasehold Empire.* New York: Oxford University Press, 2000.

Sanders, Holly V. "Prostitution in Postwar Japan: Debt and Labor." Ph.D. diss., Princeton University, 2005.

Sarantakes, Nicholas E. *Keystone: The American Occupation of Okinawa and U.S.-Japanese Relations.* College Station: Texas A & M University, 2001.

Sartre, Jean-Paul. *Black Orpheus.* Trans. S. W. Allen. Paris: Présence Africaine, 1976.

———. *Critique of Dialectical Reason.* Vol. 1. Trans. Alan Sheridan-Smith. London: Verso, 2004.

———. *What Is Literature?* Trans. Bernard Frechtman. London: Methuen and Co. Ltd., 1950.

Sasaki-Uemura, Wesley M. *Organizing the Spontaneous: Citizen Protest in Postwar Japan.* Honolulu: University of Hawai'i Press, 2001.

Schäfer, Fabian. *Public Opinion, Propaganda, Ideology: Theories on the Press and Its Social Function in Interwar Japan, 1918–1937.* Leiden: Brill, 2012.

Schmitt, Carl. *Dictatorship: From the Origin of the Modern Concept of Sovereignty to Proletarian Class Struggle.* Cambridge: Polity Press, 2014.

———. *Political Theology: Four Chapters on the Concept of Sovereignty.* Trans. George Schwab. Cambridge: MIT Press, 1985.

———. *The Concept of the Political.* Trans. George Schwab. Chicago: University of Chicago Press, 1996.

———. *The* Nomos *of the Earth in the International Law of the* Jus Publicum Europaeum. Trans. G. L. Ulmen. New York: Telos Press, 2003.

Schonberger, Howard B. *Aftermath of War: Americans and the Remaking of Japan, 1945–1952.* Kent, Ohio: Kent State University Press, 1989.

Shimabuku, Annmaria. "Petitioning Subjects: Miscegenation in Okinawa from 1945 to 1952 and the Crisis of Sovereignty." *Inter-Asia Cultural Studies* 11, no. 3 (2010): 355–374.

———. "Schmitt and Foucault on the Question of Sovereignty under Military Occupation." *Política Común* 5 (2014). http://dx.doi.org/10.3998/pc.12322227.0005.007.

———. "Who Should Bear the Burden of U.S. Bases? Governor Nakaima's Plea for a 'Relocation Site Outside of Okinawa Prefecture, but within Japan.'" *The Asia-Pacific Journal* 9, no. 45:1 (November 16, 2011). http://www.japanfocus.org/-Annmaria-Shimabuku/3641.

Shinjou, Ikuo. "The Political Formation of the Homoerotics and the Cold War: The Battle of Gazes at and from Okinawa." In *The Trans-Pacific Imagination: Rethinking Boundary, Culture, and Society.* Ed. Naoki Sakai and Hyon Joo Yoo. Singapore: World Scientific Publishing, 2012.

Spivak, Gayatri C. "Can the Subaltern Speak?" In *Marxism and the Interpretation of Culture*. Ed. Lawrence Grossberg and Cary Nelson. Urbana: University of Illinois Press, 1988.

Takazato, Suzuyo. "The Past and Future of Unai, Sisters in Okinawa." *AMPO Japan-Asia Quarterly Review* 25, no. 4 (1995): 74–79.

Takemae, Eiji. *Inside GHQ: The Allied Occupation of Japan and Its Legacy*. Trans. Robert Ricketts and Sebastian Swann. New York: Continuum, 2002.

Takeuchi, Michiko. "'Pan-Pan Girls' Performing and Resisting Neocolonialism(s) in the Pacific Theater: U.S. Military Prostitution in Occupied Japan, 1945–1952." In *Over There: Living with the U.S. Military Empire from World War Two to the Present*. Ed. Maria Höhn and Seungsook Moon. Durham, N.C.: Duke University Press, 2010.

Tosaka, Jun. "The Fate of Japanism: From Fascism to Emperorism." Trans. John Person. In *Tosaka Jun: A Critical Reader*. Ed. Ken C. Kawashima, Fabian Schäfer, and Robert Stolz. Ithaca, N.Y.: Cornell East Asia Series, 2013.

———. "The Police Function." Trans. Ken C. Kawashima. In *Tosaka Jun: A Critical Reader*. Ed. Ken C. Kawashima, Fabian Schäfer, and Robert Stolz. Ithaca, N.Y.: Cornell East Asia Series, 2013.

———. "The Principle of Everydayness and Historical Time." Trans. Robert Stolz. In *Tosaka Jun: A Critical Reader*. Ed. Ken C. Kawashima, Fabian Schäfer, and Robert Stolz. Ithaca, N.Y.: Cornell University Press, 2013.

Uehara Carter, Mitzi. "Mixed-Race Okinawans and Their Obscure In-Betweeness." *Journal of Intercultural Studies* 35, no. 6:646–661. http://dx.doi.org/10.1080/07256868.2014.963531.

———. "Nappy Roots and Tangled Tales: Critical Ethnography in a Militarised Okinawa." In *Under Occupation: Resistance and Struggle in a Militarised Asia-Pacific*. Ed. Daniel Broudy, Peter Simpson, and Makoto Arakaki. Newcastle upon Tyne: Cambridge Scholars Publication, 2013.

———. "Routing, Repeating, and Hacking Mixed Race in Okinawa." In *Hapa Japan: Identities and Representations*. Ed. Duncan R. Williams. Los Angeles: USC Press, 2017.

Vine, David. *Base Nation: How U.S. Military Bases Abroad Harm America and the World*. New York: Henry Holt and Company, 2015.

Walker, Gavin. *The Sublime Perversion of Capital: Marxist Theory and the Politics of History in Modern Japan*. Durham, N.C.: Duke University Press, 2016.

Weber, Samuel. "Taking Exception to Decision: Walter Benjamin and Carl Schmitt." *Diacritics* 22, nos. 3/4 (1993): 5–18.

Weltfish, Gene. "American Racisms: Japan's Secret Weapon." *Far Eastern Survey* 14, no. 17 (1945): 233–237.

Yara, Tomohiro. "Withdrawal of US Marines Blocked by Japan in the 1970s." Trans. Gavan McCormack. *The Asia-Pacific Journal* 11, no. 47:4 (November 22, 2013). http://apjjf.org/2013/11/47/Yara-Tomohiro/4037/article.html.

Yoda, Tatsuro. "Japan's Host Nation Support Program for the U.S.-Japan Security Alliance: Past and Prospects." *Asian Survey* 46.6 (2006): 937–961.

Yokota, Ryan M. "Reversion-Era Proposals for Okinawan Regional Autonomy." In *Rethinking Postwar Okinawa: Beyond American Occupation*. Ed. Pedro Iocabelli and Hiroko Matsuda. Lanham, Md.: Lexington Books, 2017.

Yoneyama, Lisa. *Cold War Ruins: Transpacific Critique of American Justice and Japanese War Crimes*. Durham, N.C.: Duke University Press, 2016.